KNOWLEDGE:
ITS CREATION, DISTRIBUTION, AND
ECONOMIC SIGNIFICANCE

VOLUME II

THE BRANCHES
OF LEARNING

KNOWLEDGE:
ITS CREATION, DISTRIBUTION, AND
ECONOMIC SIGNIFICANCE

VOLUME II

THE BRANCHES OF LEARNING

BY FRITZ MACHLUP

PRINCETON UNIVERSITY PRESS

CONTENTS

ANALYTICAL TABLE
OF CONTENTS

PREFACE

IN VOLUME I of *Knowledge: Its Creation, Distribution, and Economic Significance* (Princeton University Press, 1980) I attempted to give a rough outline of the planned eight-volume series. I warned the reader then that the outline was tentative and likely to change, but I did not expect that I would alter my plans so early as with Volume II. With the sympathetic understanding of the editorial board of the Princeton University Press, I decided to limit the material first intended for the second volume to the first two parts originally assigned to it—"The Branches of Learning" and "The Departments of Erudition." I had completed much of the manuscript for these two parts in 1978 and was anxious to get them into print. They make a self-contained book.

At this juncture I may with some confidence "predict" that Volume III will contain the two economic parts originally planned for inclusion in the second volume: "The Economics of Knowledge and Information" and "Knowledge as Human Capital." Organized in some twenty chapters, the manuscript for these parts is now complete and ought to be published without undue delay, especially because the literature on these topics is growing at a rapid rate. "The Economics of Knowledge and Human Capital" is the tentative title for Volume III.

I am still working on "The Disciplines of Information," largely a descriptive and methodological survey of recently developed, and still developing, fields of study dealing with information, intelligence, and communication. As a result of this "cell division," the whole work is likely to become a series of ten volumes.

The research for the volume on "Education," now probably Volume V, is in an advanced stage of development. Some of the research projects on various aspects of education are still in progress, but hundreds of folders of working papers are ready to be written up in more than forty chapters.

At the end of Volume I, a table recorded the number of lines retained from various pages of my earlier book, *The Production and Distribution of Knowledge in the United States* (Princeton University Press, 1962). No such table appears in this Volume II, for the simple reason that it contains not a single line from the earlier book. Nothing in the present volume has been prepublished anywhere. Readers who want to know what they may expect to find in this volume may look for a preview in the brief Chapter 1, "Introduction."

My acknowledgments of financial support are complicated by the fact that no fewer than nine agencies and foundations have been sponsoring my research: the National Science Foundation, the National Endowment for the Humanities, the Ford Foundation, the John and Mary Markle Foundation, the Alfred P. Sloan Foundation, the Exxon Education Foundation, the Spencer Foundation, the Earhart Foundation, and the National Institute of Education. The largest part of the funds was awarded for the research on education and for the statistical work on some of the later volumes. The research on the materials used for the present volume was financed chiefly by the Ford Foundation and the Earhart Foundation.

As I mentioned in the preface to Volume I, more than sixty research assistants have been involved in the work on the forthcoming volumes. Only two, however, can be credited with significant assistance in the research for Volume II: Jessica Kennedy, who helped me on several chapters on "The Branches of Learning," and Mary Taylor Huber, who did much of the research on academies and universities for "The Departments of Erudition" and also on some of the philosophers discussed in Part One. The editorial care for the volume was again entrusted to Peggy Riccardi; fortunate is the author who can work with such a sensitive and perceptive editor.

Princeton University and   FRITZ MACHLUP
New York University

VOLUME II

The Branches
of Learning

CHAPTER 1

INTRODUCTION

IN THE INTRODUCTION to Volume I of this work I called it an interdisciplinary and transdisciplinary undertaking. I did not specify all the disciplines that would be called upon in carrying out the project. After a good deal of further reading and thinking about the unity and division of the sciences, I feel better prepared to indicate which of the established disciplines will be involved in the work according to my present plans.

The Disciplines Involved in This Work

That economics is one of the relevant disciplines is clear; indeed, "economic significance" is part of the title of the series of volumes. I shall, however, defer talking about the roles assigned to economics, leaving it till the end of this *tour d'horizon*. This is the polite thing to do for an author whose professional home is economics.

Philosophy, the "science of the sciences," should come first in the order of introductions at an interdisciplinary party. Philosophy, as a matter of fact, was given pride of place in Volume I. The first two parts of that volume involved epistemology, analytic philosophy, and a few morsels of history of the philosophy of science. More such morsels will be found in the present volume. Volumes III and IV will include long discussions of methodology. The volume on Education (probably Volume V) will contain chapters explicitly concerned with the philosophy of education in general, and with social philosophy and ethics in particular. Political philosophy will be involved in the discussions of academic freedom and, again, in the volume on Research and New Knowledge, Cognitive and Artistic. That the parts devoted to discussions of artistic creation and communication will draw upon aesthetics should be understood.

Psychology will have a prominent role to play in several of the planned volumes. In the survey of the Sciences of Information, cognitive psychology will be one in the cluster of disciplines to be examined. In the part on Knowledge as Human Capital, the psychologists' controversy about genetic and acquired abilities—heredity versus environment (nature versus nurture)—will be discussed. In the volume on Education learning theory will be involved both explicitly and implicitly. And in the volume on The Media of Com-

munication psychological research on the effects of TV-watching on
reading ability and reading habits, on youth violence and criminality,
and on intellectual and emotional development will be reviewed.

Sociology will be implicit throughout the work. My earlier book,
The Production and Distribution of Knowledge in the United States,
published in 1962, has been credited with laying "the foundations
for a theory of growth of knowledge as part of the sociology of knowledge."[1] Much of what will be learned in the volumes to come will
have implications for the sociology of knowledge, and much of what
will be examined must draw on various areas of sociology. As I see
it, the notions of social knowledge, or a social stock of knowledge,
and its social usefulness and valuation, are sociological concepts
before they are economic concepts. Moreover, the social priorities
in evaluating and promoting the creation and distribution of knowledge, in general and of particular kinds, are issues of sociology as
much as they are issues of economics.

At several junctures in this work anthropology will be called upon
in various ways. There will be a brief section on the anthropology
of education; but anthropological research will be of the essence in
such inquiries as how young people spend their time as students
enrolled in different types of colleges, majoring in different fields,
and living in different social environments. An inquiry into bilingual
education will in significant aspects rely on techniques of anthropological interpretation.

Political science will be the point of reference in a section on the
politics of education and will inform discussions of various problems
of education, such as the question of the length of compulsory schooling, the financing of schools by federal, state, and local governments,
the tax treatment of expenses for nonpublic schooling, and general
issues of school reform. Political principles will likewise be involved
in evaluating questions of government support for research in the
natural sciences, the social sciences, engineering, and in the humanities; of government support for the performing arts, for literature, music, the visual arts. In the volume on The Media of Communication politics will underlie discussions of industrial organization
and regulation of the print media and, even more manifestly, the
electronic media. Political science, jointly with economics, will provide the tools for the analysis of patent monopolies and copyrights.
The discussion of governmental information services will include
implications of the growth of government and the overgrowth of

---

[1] Moshe Sarell, Book Review, *American Sociological Review*, vol. 28 (October 1963),
p. 841.

bureaucracy. Perhaps the most important participation of political science will be in evidence in the last volume of the planned series, when some fashionable theories of the distribution of political power in the knowledgeable society will be examined.

I have previously mentioned the cluster of disciplines that I called "the sciences of information." They include information science, library science, computer science, informatics, mathematical theory of communication, systems theory and systems analysis, operations research, cognitive psychology, artificial intelligence, robotics, cybernetics, decision sciences, semiotics, and cognitive science. My task will be to analyze the topology of these fields of study, their contents and techniques, and their methodological interrelationships. At the time I am writing these lines, I cannot yet say whether some of these disciplines are overlapping, cognate, or complementary. I shall have to examine mutually inconsistent claims to the effect that one of the fields includes, or is included in, another. This methodological investigation is interdisciplinary in a sense different from that used earlier in this introduction: previously the various disciplines were expected to be of help in studying various problems and issues, now the disciplines themselves are the objects of analysis. They are the problems to be examined.

There are, however, a few more disciplines to be drawn upon in the elucidation of problems of knowledge, especially in the category now commonly designated as the humanities. These disciplines will be indispensable in the discussion of artistic creation and communication. I shall have to consult studies of the classics, literary criticism, musicology, art criticism, and architecture when I write about the production of literary works such as novels, novellas, and plays, about composition and performance of musical works, about dance and ballet, paintings, drawings, sculptures, and architectural designs and structures. To confine illustrations to the last-mentioned subject, architectural design is undoubtedly production of knowledge, but the preparation of blueprints and builders' instructions must not be treated as equivalent to the artistic creation by an original, inventive and imaginative architect. I have recently read some fascinating treatises on the combination of engineering and sculpturing that can produce an architectural structure—a cathedral, music hall, office building, great library, or spectacular bridge—that "speaks to us," at least to the more perceptive among us. Adding up the figures that may represent the annual cost of "architectural information" would be a dull job indeed if the results were not associated with an appropriate qualitative interpretation of the knowledge produced.

I have mentioned the classics as one of the auxiliary disciplines in my work; perhaps I should add some words of explanation. No knowledge of classical languages is needed for a report on the number of students enrolled in courses in Latin or Greek, or on the total cost of teaching these languages. On two occasions, however, my (modest) knowledge of Latin was of help: when I had to consult the Latin version of Bacon's *Advancement of Learning* in order to check Bacon's meaning of some words or sentences, and when I had to prepare an accurate statement of the classification of disciplines proposed in Johann Heinrich Alsted's *Encyclopaedia*, published in Latin.

History is the discipline most extensively involved in this series of volumes. For every branch of knowledge production, from education and research to artistic creation and communication, to the media of communication, the information services, and the information machines, historical sketches will be provided. Volume III will offer a history of economic doctrines relating to information and knowledge. Volume I contained exercises in historical semantics regarding the meanings of scientific and humanistic knowledge. The heaviest concentration of historical research is embodied in the present book, Volume II. Its first part presents intellectual history, its second part institutional history. Later on in this introduction I shall have more to say about my historical endeavors.

In at least six volumes of this work statistics will play a leading role. The statistics employed will not be of any complex mathematical type, using correlation and regression analyses. Primitive time series will do the required job; some of the data will be culled from primary and secondary sources, though other data will have to be developed by estimation on the basis of appropriate indicators. The detective work needed in some instances to obtain the relevant figures for the annual cost of activities instrumental in knowledge acquisition or in rendering information services may call for ingenuity, but not for mathematical sophistication. The only references to regression analysis will occur in connection with attempts by analysts of the formation of human capital to separate the effects of schooling from those of other factors contributing to the improvement of human productive capacity.

Now, having finished the round of disciplines participating in this ambitious undertaking, I may return to economics. Among the tasks assigned to economic analysis will be an examination of the production of knowledge as an economic activity—both creating new knowledge and disseminating existing knowledge, including current, timely information of merely transitory relevance or usefulness. To ascertain how much of the nation's total economic resources is being devoted to various kinds of knowledge production and information in different sectors of the economy, public and private, represents quantitative analysis of interest to many—to some in the capacity of developers of public policy, to some as concerned taxpayers, to some as producers of knowledge or providers or users of information, and to some merely as curious observers of the economic scene. However, to ascertain the cost of knowledge production is only a part of the economic problem at issue; the benefits derived have to be valuated in some fashion before one can judge whether they were worth the costs incurred. Alas, the valuation of benefits is often a highly delicate, perhaps insoluble problem; but even if rigorous answers are not attainable in instances where market prices fail to give acceptable clues, the problem has to be scrutinized and reasonable approximations have to be arrived at. Besides the benefits and costs of knowledge and information services, many other aspects of incomplete and vague information, of misperception and of misinformation, of different speeds of diffusion, and of lags in the revision of expectations have to be investigated, especially with regard to the working of the market mechanism and the function of market prices as guides in the allocative processes of the economy. The economics of information and knowledge has become an important specialty in the discipline, with a literature that is growing by leaps and bounds. More about all this in Volume III; none of it in this Volume II.

Economists Invited, Together with All Others

The present volume will not be on economics; this need not mean that it is out of bounds, or off limits, for economists. Good economists, ordinarily, are educated people, that is, they have acquired intellectual knowledge in areas other than economics.[2] They will perhaps welcome a book that takes them across disciplinary frontiers. In expressing my trust in the intellectual curiosity of economists, I do not mean to say that most of my readers are economists. Indeed, I am counting on a multidisciplinary readership of my volumes reporting on multidisciplinary research.

I admit that not all of my excursions into so many different fields

---

[2] ". . . an economist who is only an economist . . . is a pretty poor fish." Lionel Robbins, *An Essay on the Nature and Significance of Economic Science* (London: Macmillan & Co., 2nd ed., 1935), p. ix. — ". . . nobody can be a great economist who is only an economist—and I am even tempted to add that the economist who is only an economist is likely to become a nuisance if not a positive danger." Friedrich A. Hayek, "The Dilemma of Specialization," in Leonard D. White, ed., *The State of the Social Sciences* (Chicago: University of Chicago Press, 1956), p. 463. The gradation from "pretty poor fish" to "nuisance" and to "positive danger" suggests degrees of risk or injury similar to those used in medical or criminal evaluations.

are "really necessary." I may repeat from my introduction to Volume I what I said after defending several of my expansionist moves as being dictated by developments in economics and other disciplines:

> None of this explains why I deal in Volume II with the history of ideas about the branches of learning. The answer is simply that it fascinates me, and I think that others may be interested too. Moreover, the intellectual history is closely connected with the institutional history of higher learning—academies, libraries, and universities—and can explain some of the systems of classification and departmentalization at present. Useless knowledge? Perhaps. But knowing for fun is a respectable human activity; and having fun need not be judged useless.[3]

Useful and Useless Knowledge

To raise the question what knowledge is useful or useless invites a quibble—one, I am afraid, that I cannot properly dodge. For if we call "useful" any knowledge that gives some knowers some pleasure to learn or to have, then almost all knowledge is useful. On the other hand, if we call "useful" only those bits of knowledge that help the knower carry out his job and earn a living, then only small fractions of what people know may be called useful. The question cannot be approached before we decide what is meant: useful to whom and for what?

If the knower's own judgment is taken as the criterion, his subjective evaluation of his subjective knowledge will count. In the scheme that I adopted and explained in Volume I, I distinguished five types of knowledge:

> (1) Practical knowledge: useful in the knower's work, his decisions, and actions; can be subdivided, according to his activities, into
> a) Professional knowledge
> b) Business knowledge
> c) Workman's knowledge
> d) Political knowledge

---

[3] Fritz Machlup, *Knowledge: Its Creation, Distribution, and Economic Significance*, vol. I, *Knowledge and Knowledge Production* (Princeton: Princeton University Press, 1980), p. 23.

e) Household knowledge

f) Other practical knowledge

(2) Intellectual knowledge: satisfying his intellectual curiosity, regarded as part of liberal education, humanistic and scientific learning, general culture; acquired, as a rule, in active concentration with an appreciation of the existence of open problems and cultural values.

(3) Small-talk and pastime knowledge: satisfying the non-intellectual curiosity or his desire for light entertainment and emotional stimulation, including local gossip, news of crimes and accidents, light novels, stories, jokes, games, etc.; acquired, as a rule, in passive relaxation from "serious" pursuits; apt to dull his sensitiveness.

(4) Spiritual knowledge: related to his religious knowledge of God and of the ways to the salvation of the soul.

(5) Unwanted knowledge: outside his interests, usually accidentally acquired, aimlessly retained.[4]

The word "useful" appears only in the description of the first type, practical knowledge; three other types, however, intellectual, pastime, and spiritual knowledge, are deemed to satisfy some personal needs. If "useful" knowledge is meant to exclude some types of knowledge besides clearly "unwanted" knowledge, it seems most reasonable to make useful equivalent to practical knowledge.

This materialistic interpretation of usefulness has implications that may accord with the preconceptions of some people but offend the preconceptions of others. For example, the same bundle of knowledge will be practical, professional knowledge for some—the practitioners or teachers professing the field—but intellectual knowledge for others. Not being a professor of music or physics, I derive purely intellectual satisfaction from whatever I know of music or physics. Similarly, if my friends in the departments of music or physics know anything about economics, it will be their intellectual knowledge; for them only the knowledge of the field they practice or profess is practical. On these grounds I have sometimes distinguished between training and education: the former, instrumental in the acquisition of practical knowledge; the latter, promoting the acquisition of intellectual knowledge. These distinctions, all based on personal attitudes and subjective considerations, are, however, not what scholars, legislators, and public functionaries have in mind when they support the promotion of "useful" knowledge to the exclusion of something they deem "useless."

When Benjamin Franklin in 1743 founded the American Philosophical Society "for the promotion of useful knowledge," he gave us a pretty good idea of what he meant by "useful" knowledge. He wrote in his "Proposal" that the "hints" and "observations" received from "men of speculation" might, "if well-examined, pursued and improved, . . . produce Discoveries to the Advantage of some or all of the British Plantations, or to the Benefit of Mankind in general."[5] He proposed that the core of the membership should be a group consisting of "a Physician, a Botanist, a Mathematician, a Chemist, a Mechanician, a Geographer, and a general Natural Philosopher." Although he did not enumerate the areas of knowledge that would fail the test of usefulness, Franklin referred to the Royal Society of London as his model, and the stated objectives of the Royal Society were explicit about "not meddling with Divinity, Metaphysics, Moralls, Politicks, Grammar, Rhetorick or Logick."[6] Historical studies are not mentioned either among the eligible or among excluded areas of scholarship, but I suspect that the ban on moral philosophy—"social and cultural sciences," in present-day terminology—would extend to historical research.

The American Philosophical Society rescinded in 1815 its restriction on the scope of useful knowledge and created a committee on "history, moral science, and general literature." This show of academic liberality did not persuade the "practical majority" of the American people. Even to this day we find members of legislative and other official bodies adhering to a narrow concept of useful knowledge. Some would restrict the allocation of public funds to the support of applied research and deny appropriations for basic research, that is, research without practical objectives with respect to products or processes. More clearly stated, knowledge not immediately applicable, not likely to induce improvements in products or increases in productivity except perhaps in a distant future, is not considered useful. The criterion of usefulness, in this interpretation, is seen in contributions to material national objectives, not in the satisfaction of intellectual curiosity.

In this restricted sense of useful knowledge, research in intellectual history will probably have to be tagged as useless. It is true that

[5] Benjamin Franklin, "Proposal for Promoting Useful Knowledge among the British Plantations in America," May 14, 1743. Reprinted in American Philosophical Society, *Year Book 1976*, pp. 11-12 (or any other year).

[6] Charles R. Weld, *A History of the Royal Society, with Memoirs of the Presidents* (London: J. W. Parker, 1848), vol. 1, p. 146.

studies in the history of ideas will rarely, if ever, result in any advances of technology, in improvements of productive capacity, or in increases of national product, gross or net. Intellectual knowledge is not practical knowledge, neither from the social nor the private point of view. But I want to stress that a high ratio of intellectual to practical knowledge is the mark and the measure of a person's or a nation's cultural development.

The Idea of Classifying the Branches of Learning

The present volume offers intellectual knowledge *par excellence*. That the topic should arouse the intellectual curiosity of virtually all who are interested in "knowledge" is not an excessively fanciful idea. Indeed, in a series of volumes on knowledge including "intellectual knowledge," one should expect to be told how some of the great creators of knowledge and many of the institutions cultivating higher learning have divided and classified their universe. Part One, "The Branches of Learning," will survey the classifications proposed by philosphers and encyclopaedists. Part Two, "The Departments of Erudition," will review the arrangements of subjects adopted by academic institutions: academies of sciences, academic libraries, and universities.

The grouping of subjects or subject areas in branches of learning was called in Latin *partitiones scientiarum* (Francis Bacon). To regard each academic discipline as a science is in accordance with an old tradition, still observed in non-English-speaking countries but abandoned in English academic practice in the middle of the nineteenth century.

The original meaning of the Latin word *scientia* was very much broader: besides science, or higher learning, it referred to all kinds of knowledge and all ways of knowing, including awareness (of everyday matters), insight, and skill (how-to knowledge). In learned discourse, however, "science" had a restricted meaning: for almost 2,000 years it denoted "absolutely certain" knowledge, excluding empirical knowledge. In the seventeenth century, the meaning of "science" was expanded to include any well-ordered body of coherent knowledge. Only in the nineteenth century was the meaning of the term in English restricted to experimental or natural sciences; and in the twentieth century new restrictions were proposed, recognizing only mathematical and nomological disciplines. Readers interested in these developments may find it helpful to read the sections "Scientific Knowledge" and "Humanistic Knowledge" in

Volume I of this work.[7] In my survey of the branches of learning I shall not use any restrictive definitions of "science," but shall use this word in the same all-inclusive sense in which it was used by the philosophers and encyclopaedists who did the classifying.[8]

I cannot vouch for the comprehensiveness of my survey of philosophical or encyclopaedic classifications of disciplines. Indeed, I know of a good many omissions. Over ninety classifications were described in the only work that attempted a similar survey, Robert Flint's *History of Classification of the Sciences*.[9] I shall discuss no more than thirty classifications. I was more selective in that I omitted classifications that were mere reproductions of earlier lists of disciplines and those that were presented without reasoned argument or historical reference. On these grounds I omitted, for example, the classification used by Giambattista Vico (1668-1744), eminent Italian philosopher and historian. He simply took it for granted that his scheme of dividing the sciences was reasonable for his purposes. In his book *New Science* (1725) he was concerned with philosophy of history and prehistorical cultural development.[10] Vico's contribution

[7] Machlup, *Knowledge*, vol. I, pp. 62-70 and 70-90.

[8] Many people, learned philosophers as well as naive laymen, are fond of the idea of awarding the title "science" for meritorious behavior, like a medal or decoration voted by a jury. The French writer Michel Foucault has a particularly complicated test for "scientificity." Michel Foucault, *The Archaeology of Knowledge*, translated from the French by A. M. Sheridan Smith (New York: Pantheon Books, 1972). He flunks "pseudo-sciences (like psychopathology), sciences at the prehistoric stage (like Natural History), or sciences entirely penetrated with ideology (like political economy)"—despite their "positivity," "coherence," and "demonstrativity" (p. 178). He demands compliance "with the experimental or formal criteria of scientificity" (p. 182). He sets up a sequence of tests any system of statements has to pass before it can be awarded the intermediate titles of "knowledge," "discipline," and the penultimate title "science." First comes the "threshold of positivity," then the "threshold of epistemologization"; the crossing of the "threshold of scientificity" does not lead to the highest degree in this order, for there is still the "threshold of formalization" (pp. 186-187). There is much to say for Foucault's requirements of qualifying, comprehensive, and final examinations if one wishes to judge differences in the methodological character of coherent systems of knowledge; what I find objectionable is to make these tests obligatory for semantic decisions. To decide whether psychopathology, botany, or economics should or should not be taught at the university is a pragmatic question; to decide whether these subjects are "really sciences" is of no pragmatic and little intellectual relevance.

[9] Robert Flint, *Philosophy as Scientia Scientiarum and A History of Classifications of the Sciences* (New York: Scribner's, 1904).

[10] *The New Science of Giambattista Vico*. Translated from the 3rd edition (1744) by Thomas Goddard Bergin and Max Harold Fisch (Ithaca, New York: Cornell University Press, 1948), p. 100. The 1744 edition of *La Scienza Nuova* was carefully edited by Fausto Nicolini (Bari: Gius. Laterza, 1928). The 1st edition was published in Naples in 1725.

was his elaboration of methodological principles that recognized and developed the differences between explanations of natural and cultural phenomena. In these respects Vico was centuries ahead of his time. But his classification of the sciences was merely incidental to his historical and philosophical discourse, and rather unimportant at that.

Although I went far afield and included, for example, Arab philosophers and historians, I have not searched the sources on Chinese philosophy and history of science, except for a superficial browsing in Needham's *Science and Civilization in China*.[11] I shall report on the existence of a Chinese encyclopaedia of really monumental scale, but I have no report on any systematic classification of the sciences proposed and discussed in Chinese literature. I must also admit my failure to consult sources on Indian science. I did not aim at anything like complete coverage; my objective was to compare principles and criteria of classification.

Part Two of this volume, "The Departments of Erudition," pursues the same objective but on different routes, namely, through institutional histories of academies of sciences, research libraries, and colleges and universities. The divisions of academies into classes and sections, the divisions of library catalogues into subject groups and subjects, and the divisions of universities into faculties, schools, departments, and programs reflect classifications of disciplines for purposes of organization and administration.

My survey of academies includes nine European countries and the United States. As to the period covered, it begins with the oldest of the still existing academies, the dei Lincei in Rome, founded in 1603; and it ends with the youngest American "specialized" academies established in the 1960s and even later. The description of library catalogues goes back to the libraries of Alexandria, organized around 260 B.C., and to the first known consistently classified bibliography prepared by Conrad Gesner in 1548: it includes also the cataloguing systems of the last hundred years, from Melvil Dewey in 1876, to Cutter, Brown, Bliss, and others, and to the system of the Library of Congress in Washington. The longest chapter, "Universities: Faculties and Departments," presents a history of universities, from the ninth century to the present, with the focus on the divisions of academic learning.

There is no scarcity of histories of universities, either histories of cosmopolitan or national scope, or histories of particular institutions,

---

[11] Joseph Needham, *Science and Civilization in China*, 5 vols. to date (Cambridge: At the University Press, 1954-1976).

but there is probably no history that has been written with the eye focused on the theme chosen for this volume: the organization of the universities into three or four faculties and later into more specialized divisions; the distribution of teaching and studying among major studies and curricula; the fragmentation of higher learning into increasingly narrow specialties; the reintegration of specialized fields into multidisciplinary programs; and the attempts of bringing the departmental systems into harmony with the philosophers' schemes of classifying the branches of learning. Some of the discussions in this chapter may serve as background for the forthcoming volume on Education, for, inevitably, some problems of higher education reflect the developments in the fission and fusion of academic disciplines.

I do not claim to have made any new discoveries, nor can I honestly advertise that this book will be of great pragmatic usefulness to anybody. If I may advertise anything about this volume, I may say that it offers a large dose of deliciously useless knowledge, so avidly wanted by those (sometimes impractical) people who, inspired by a collector's fervor, have elected to collect "education" in the humanist's sense, that is, to accumulate that sophisticated store of learning which, since it does not add to our professional or vocational skills, makes us educated persons.

PART ONE

The Branches of Learning

This part will be devoted to intellectual history: the history of the classification of the sciences—*partitiones scientiarum*—or of the "disciplines," as the branches of learning are called in modern English usage. This history of more or less systematic arrangements, or taxonomic ordering, of systematic knowledge will be presented in six chapters.

Chapter 2 The Taxonomy of the Branches
　　　　　　 of Learning
Chapter 3 Classical and Medieval Synopses
　　　　　　 of Doctrines
Chapter 4 The Tree of Knowledge
Chapter 5 The Circle of Learning
Chapter 6 The Mapping of the Sciences
Chapter 7 Unified Science and
　　　　　　 the Propaedia

THE TAXONOMY OF
THE BRANCHES OF LEARNING

BECAUSE many educators and philosophers are concerned exclusively with intellectual knowledge, they often disregard all other types of knowledge, which to most people—the common man or woman, the practical people, the masses—bulk much larger. With the focus on higher learning, the philosophers who set out to classify *knowledge* have come up with arrangements of the branches of *learning*, or intellectual knowledge. Some of these taxonomists were quite deliberate in so limiting their universe of discourse. This is surely true of Francis Bacon, who propagated the metaphor of *the tree of knowledge* in his book *On the Advancement of Learning* (in Latin, *De augmentis scientiarum*). I am honoring his ambitious undertaking by naming this volume and this part of my work "The Branches of Learning."

The Changing Universe of Learning

Why did many philosophers undertake the formidable task of attempting to order the universe of learning? They evidently believed that a comprehensive taxonomy would facilitate man's understanding of that universe. That universe, however, has not remained unchanged over the decades and centuries: it expanded as new discoveries were made, as new explanations of old phenomena were invented, and as old fields of inquiry were split apart to be developed into new specialties; it also dropped contents found to be unwanted ballast; and many of its parts that seem to have indefinite tenure have, over time, considerably changed in their appearance. Thus it should not surprise us that a succession of philosophers have come up with a sequence of revised or new classifications. Nor should it surprise us that the principles of classification have been modified, except the one principle that a classification should join "like" items and separate "unlike" ones. Yet, the judgment of what constitutes relevant likeness and relevant unlikeness has also changed over time.

Among the fascinating features in the development of the classification of learning is the hardiness of certain notions which we now consider rather unhelpful, but which survived for surprisingly long periods before they were abandoned. Other notions, however, which were rejected and cast aside for some time, were later reintroduced, with or without recognition of their earlier reign. In selecting the successive classifiers for inclusion in this survey I was, to a large extent, guided by the continuity in the development of taxonomic and methodological thought over the almost two thousand years between Aristotle and Francis Bacon, and the almost four hundred years since Bacon.

Classifying, Cataloguing, and Tabulating

Another guiding principle of selection was the classifier's intention not only to cover the universe of learning but to present a complete enumeration of all its members. A classification scheme may be intended to provide various classes into which all existing (or potentially existing) species *could* be sorted, but are not actually sorted, by the system builder. Alternatively, a classification scheme may be presented with all existing species named and *actually* enumerated as members of the class (or genus) to which they are assigned by the system builder.

It is strange that many, perhaps most, discussions of classification fail to make this distinction. To distinguish various boxes into which all species can be fitted is one thing; to sort all known species and put them into these boxes is another. Perhaps, to emphasize the difference, one should speak of the first as classifying and of the latter as cataloguing; but one cannot seriously hope that such imposed meanings would be observed, for the verb "classifying" has been used for both activities, for distinguishing the classes and for sorting the things into the classes.[1]

These activities can be broken down in a variety of ways. We may, for example, divide the area into three parts: one, as the field of those who devise the system of classification, a second, as the field of those who sort the individual items into the boxes designed, and a third, as the field of those who take an inventory or make a listing of the contents of the boxes. One may prefer, however, a simple dichotomy between box makers and box users, and a subdivision of the latter into those who fill the boxes and those who help searchers for particular

[1] Ranganathan, a widely respected, prolific writer on library classification, was one of the specialists who proposed different terms for the two different activities: the *classificationist* is "one who designs a scheme of classification and provides a set of guiding postulates and principles" for its use, whereas the *classifier* is "one who classifies a universe in accordance with a preferred scheme for classification. . . ." Shiyali Ramamrita Ranganathan, *Prolegomena to Library Classification* (New York: Asia Publishing House, 3rd ed., 1967), p. 79.

items in the boxes. Still another distinction can be made differentiating those who design the labels for the boxes, those who design the labels for the items assigned to the boxes, and those who enumerate the labeled items for easy search and retrieval by others.

Philosophers, Encyclopaedists, Bibliographers, and Librarians

All the above alternative distinctions should have made it clear that classifications are made for different purposes and by different types of people. There are the *philosophers*, whose only purpose is to facilitate orderly thinking, systematic analysis of the universe; their chief concern is an overview of things (chiefly abstract) and an understanding of their interrelationships. There are the *encyclopaedists*, who want to present their work in a systematic but not alphabetic order; they are concerned with orderly presentation of their material, with outlining and organizing the universe in a methodical way so that the reader might comprehend where all the things should be placed, and where he should look for them if he wants to gain deeper insights. There are the *bibliographers*, whose task is to help readers and researchers become aware of all, or of the most important, publications in their special fields; complete listings secure the cumulative character of knowledge formation, promote the generation of new or amended knowledge, and can avoid loss of knowledge previously created, duplication of research previously completed, and repetition of error previously corrected. Finally, there are the *librarians*, concerned with orderly listing of published titles in all fields of knowledge, orderly stacking of volumes, and orderly cataloguing, to help the user of books and journals find what he wants to read or consult.

Emphasizing these divisions of interests and labor, I propose to distinguish the philosophers, the encyclopaedists, the bibliographers, and the librarians, but to bear in mind that there are among them those who can rightfully claim to be in two or even in all categories. Focusing first on the philosophers, we may say that virtually all of them, and especially philosophers of science, have proposed classifications of sciences in the first sense of making general distinctions, but only a relative few have presented exhaustive enumerations or tabulations naming all the known sciences or branches of learning they would admit into what they regarded as the appropriate classes.

At least one study is available that undertakes to bring together all classification systems for subjects or fields of learning. Ernest Cushing Richardson in his book on *Classification* presented an "Appendix containing an Essay towards a Bibliographical History of Systems of Classification."[2] In its third edition his list included 163 entries under the heading "Theoretical Systems" and 177 entries under "Practical Systems." Most of these 340 systems are only listed (with brief bibliographic references), but some are described with outlines of up to one page in length. Richardson was primarily a librarian and secondarily a bibliographer; he is best known as the originator, in 1912, of the classification system for the library of Princeton University. He followed the principle that "the practical always prevails over the theoretical,"[3] but he realized that what is practical for the general reader may not be practical for the specialist.[4]

Robert Flint, a Scottish philosopher and the author of *History of Classification of the Sciences*, should also be mentioned here.[5] Flint, understandably, emphasizes the logical and philosophical aspects of classification over those that are practical from the librarian's point of view. He describes and discusses ninety-two systems of classification proposed by philosophers and encyclopaedists and cites many additional ones, considered less worthy of detailed attention.

Selecting the Sample for This Survey

In a sketch of a history of an idea the principles of statistical sampling are not applicable. My selections for inclusion in the sample, as all selections for doctrinal history, are highly arbitrary, determined largely by the accidents of my knowledge of the literature and my searches for precursors, followers, and critics of some authors and works regarded as those most influential, pivotal, and paradigmatic for the history of the classification of learning.

My plan is to divide the survey into five chapters. In Chapter 3, "Classical and Medieval Synopses of Doctrines," I shall give the briefest possible vignettes of Aristotle, Porphyry, Augustine, Grosseteste, Albertus, Aquinas, Roger Bacon, Llull, and Khaldûn.

[2] Ernest Cushing Richardson, *Classification: Theoretical and Practical* (1st ed., New York: Scribner's, 1901; 2nd ed., 1912; 3rd ed., New York: H. W. Wilson, 1930; reprinted, Hamden, Conn.: Shoe String Press, 1964), pp. 43-151.

[3] Ibid., p. ix.

[4] In appraising an alphabetical list of subject headings, Richardson calls it "the most popular and most unscientific of systems, the joy of the general reader, the despair of the specialist, an invaluable system as supplement or index to the system of logical classification, a futile and embarrassing system when the object is exhaustive research and this is the exclusive classification [available]." Ibid., p. 151.

[5] Robert Flint, *Philosophy as Scientia Scientiarum and A History of Classifications of the Sciences* (New York: Scribner's, 1904). I discovered this work through a reference in Richardson's book, but unfortunately only after I had completed the entire Part One. I am inserting these passages one year after I finished my manuscript. The final products are sufficiently different to justify publication.

Chapter 4, titled "The Tree of Knowledge," will be almost entirely devoted to the presentation of the Baconian system, with only a brief notice of Hobbes's tabulation of the sciences and a comment on Descartes. There will follow Chapter 5, on "The Circle of Learning," offering, after a brief historical introduction on encyclopaedias, reports on Alsted's great *Encyclopaedia*, on Leibniz's projects, on Chambers' *Cyclopaedia*, and on the French *Encyclopédie*, organized and largely written by Diderot and d'Alembert. Chapter 6, called "The Mapping of the Sciences," will, after a brief reference to Kant, review the taxonomic works of eight philosophers of the nineteenth century: Hegel, Bentham, Ampère, Comte, Cournot, Spencer, Pearson, and Peirce. Chapter 7, "Unified Science and the Propaedia," will deal with two collective encyclopaedic projects of the twentieth century: the plans for an *Encyclopaedia of Unified Science*, with references chiefly to the writings of Carnap and Neurath; and the organization of the *Propaedia*, one of the three major parts of the fifteenth edition of the *Encyclopaedia Britannica*.

This sketch of the history of an idea stretches from 350 B.C. to A.D., 1974 covering—besides several authors who are merely cited—twenty-nine philosophers or encyclopaedists (from Aristotle to Adler), whose work is discussed in subsections of various lengths.[6]

The selection does not reflect an evaluation of the authors' general influence or their importance as thinkers or system builders. If a great philosopher is not included in this survey or if his most important contributions to higher learning are not mentioned, this is consistent with the objective of the present undertaking: its focus is exclusively on schemes for the classification of the branches of learning.

---

[6] The reader interested in a more comprehensive history is referred to the work by Robert Flint, cited in the preceding footnote. It contains discussions of the following writers: Plato, Aristotle, Varro, Capella, Cassiodorus, Isidore of Seville, The Venerable Bede, Alcuin, Hugo of St. Victor, St. Bonaventura, Vincent of Beauvais, Albertus Magnus, Thomas Aquinas, Roger Bacon, Dante, Poliziano, Nizolio, Campanella, Descartes, Francis Bacon, Alsted, Comenius, Weigel, Hobbes, Locke, Leibniz, Vico, Wolff, Kant, Sulzer, Krug, Ephraim Chambers, d'Alembert, Diderot, Fichte, Schelling, Hegel, de Tracy, Bentham, Coleridge, Jannelli, Romagnosi, Longo, Ventura, Ferrarese, de Pamphilis, Arnott, Comte, Ampère, Proudhon, Duval-Jouve, Rosmini, Gioberti, Whewell, Lubbock, Lindsay, Ramsay, Schopenhauer, Dove, Cournot, W. D. Wilson, Sir William Hamilton, Renouvier, Peccenini, di Giovanni, Spencer, Zeller, Bain, Cantoni, Valdarnini, Peyretti, Labanca, Conti, Erdmann, Corleo, Bourdeau, Shields, Stanley, Daniel G. Thompson, de Roberty, Wundt, Masaryk, Naville, de la Grasserie, Pearson, Janet, Goblot, Stadler, Trivero, Durand, Haddon, and Geddes.

CHAPTER 3

CLASSICAL AND MEDIEVAL SYNOPSES
OF DOCTRINES

BEGINNING with Aristotle and ending with the Arab historian Ibn Khaldûn, the first period surveyed spans approximately 1,750 years. Only two of the authors selected belong to antiquity, the other six belong to the Middle Ages. Four of these were alive in 1250.

I shall confine myself to the briefest descriptions of the sorting schemes they proposed or suggested.

Aristotle's Distinctions

Aristotle (384-322 B.C.) made all sorts of distinctions relevant to scientific knowledge in general or to individual sciences in particular, and many of these distinctions have proved influential over more than 2,000 years, some continuing still to be influential in our days. Thus, he distinguished between knowledge *a priori* and knowledge *a posteriori*; between the process of discovering and learning, on the one hand, and that of proving and demonstrating, on the other; and he distinguished between theoretical and practical knowledge, with productive knowledge as a third class. Within physics, he proposed to separate knowledge of (four types of) causes, (three kinds of) substances, (four categories of) changes, and (three kinds of) motions; within biology he stressed the taxonomic character of natural history (botany and zoology); within the class of practical knowledge he assigned greatest importance to ethics. He tried to elucidate the differences between physics, mathematics, and theology, all of which he regarded as "the three theoretical philosophies."[1] He distinguished between "universal mathematics," which applies "alike to all [things]," and "geometry and astronomy," which "deal with a certain particular kind of thing." Probably his most enduring distinction was that between the speculative modes of thinking (leading to ratiocinative knowledge) in the theoretical science of physics, and the inductive generalizations from natural observation in the empirical science of biology.

There has been much discussion among the interpreters of Aris-

[1] John Alexander Smith and William David Ross, eds., *The Works of Aristotle*, vol. VIII, *Metaphysics* (Oxford: Clarendon Press, 1908), bk. VI, chap. 1, p. 1026ª.

totle's works about where in his scheme of things logic and rhetoric would find their most appropriate places. Logic may be seen merely as an introduction to philosophy or it may be placed among the practical sciences, perhaps even among the productive sciences (producing arguments). Similarly, rhetoric may be regarded as an auxiliary to politics, but it can be seen as a practical science (influencing conduct) or a productive one (producing orations). Economics may be, together with rhetoric, a science auxiliary to politics, or a separate discipline among the practical sciences.

We shall see later how closely the tabulators of sciences have stuck to most of these notions. Yet, despite all this classificatory work, Aristotle was not among those who presented a comprehensive system of all the sciences known at his time.

Much would have to be said about the lasting and pervasive influence of Aristotle and other thinkers of the Hellenistic period. Historians of philosophy may find it incredible that barely a page is given to "Aristotle's Distinctions" unless they remember the narrow objective we have set for this survey and realize that the distinctions to be enumerated are only those relating to a classification of the disciplines.[2]

Porphyry's Ladder

Among the commentators and exegesists of Aristotle's works I should mention Porphyry (A.D. 232-302), usually described as a Neoplatonist and "Antichristianist." He is best known for a simple metaphor, designed to aid in the understanding of the interrelations of genera and species: the tree as a symbol of branching and twigging.[3] Porphyry's explanations do not go beyond Aristotle's but the symbol of the branching tree may have been first used by Porphyry; it certainly was not taken from Aristotle.[4]

---

[2] A little more about the influence of Hellenistic learning upon scholarship and intellectual life in the millenia that have followed may be found in Part Two of this volume, especially in the discussion of the library of Alexandria.

[3] Porphyry suggested the "tree" in a passage in his Eisagoge, his Greek commentaries on Aristotle. It became known chiefly through references in the works of Boethius (480-525), Peter Abelard (1079-1142), and William of Sherwood (ca. 1205-ca. 1267), all of whom wrote (in Latin) of "Porphyry's Tree." See Anicius Manlius Torquatus Severinus Boethius, "In Isagogen Porphyrii Commenta" in Corpus Scriptorum Ecclesiasticorum Latinorum, vol. 48, pp. 135-169, English translation in Richard McKeon, trans. and ed., Selections from Medieval Philosophers, vol. I (New York: Scribner's, 1929), pp. 70-99; these Selections contain also "Peter Abailard, The Glosses . . . on Porphory," pp. 208-258. For Sherwood's references see Norman Kretzmann, trans. and ed., William of Sherwood's Introduction to Logic (Minneapolis: University of Minnesota Press, 1966), pp. 53-54.

[4] I. M. Bocheński, Formale Logik (Freiburg and Munich: Karl Alber, 1956), p. 155.

The essence of the idea is a sequence of dichotomous divisions starting from the category "substance" and ending with individual species of "men" like Socrates or Plato. Substance divides into corporeal and incorporeal substance; the former, body, divides into animate and inanimate body; the former, animate body, divides into sensitive and insensitive animate bodies; the former, animal, divides into rational and nonrational animals; the former, rational animal, divides into mortal and immortal; the former, man, divides into individuals like Socrates or Plato. "Substance is the most general, because there is no higher genus; . . . man is the most specific, because there is no lower species [of rational mortal animal]. Those in between are subalterns, and are genera with respect to those below, species with respect to those above."[5]

An arrangement in a hierarchical system of ordering, descending from the highest category down to individual species, is not well pictured by a tree. A tree grows from the roots up to the top. Perhaps it is for this reason that some philosophers changed the Porphyrian tree into the Porphyrian ladder—which one may climb up or down. But this is not of the essence; what matters in Porphyry's arrangement is the principle of successive bifurcations or "binary opposition" (of the "yes or no" type) at each level.[6] This principle has served philosophers and encyclopaedists in the classification of the branches of learning (see Chambers or Bentham) or in any other classification; and it has become almost indispensable in modern computer science.

Saint Augustine's Liberal Disciplines

Aurelius Augustinus (354-430), the influential Christian church father and saint, born in Numidia (present-day Algeria), was fond of tabulating the sciences of his time. He did this with slight variations in several of his works (de Ordine; Retractationes; Confessiones). His lists are generally regarded as traditional, though he has been credited with giving wider currency to the designation (employed by Cicero) disciplinae liberales, later called the liberal arts.[7]

Augustine's lists have five to eight entries, as he omitted at least one—not always the same—from each enumeration. The full slate

[5] Kretzmann, trans. and ed., William of Sherwood, p. 54.

[6] Encyclopaedia Britannica, 15th ed. (Chicago, 1974), Macropaedia, vol. 1, p. 916.

[7] Henri Irénée Marrou, Saint Augustin et la fin de la culture antique (Paris: Boccard, 1938), p. 188. — Other sources attribute the designation of the "liberal" arts or disciplines to Varro (116-27 B.C.), a friend of Cicero and an early "encyclopaedist." The most vocal proponents of the seven liberal arts, besides Augustine, were Capella in his Satyricon (before A.D. 439), and Cassiodorus in his De artibus et disciplinis liberalium litterarum (before 550). Cassiodorus called the trivium the "scientiae sermonicinales" and the quadrivium, the "scientiae reales."

comprises Grammar, Dialectics, Rhetoric, Arithmetic, Music, Geometry, Astrology (or Astronomy), and Philosophy. Leaving philosophy aside as the all-embracing universe of knowledge and wisdom, one quickly recognizes the other seven as the curriculum of the lower and higher studies, the trivium—grammar, rhetoric, and logic—and the quadrivium—arithmetic, geometry, astronomy, and music.

Grosseteste's Compendium

Robert Grosseteste (ca. 1175-1253), Bishop of Lincoln, author of the *Compendium Scientiarum*, was called "one of the great encyclopaedic thinkers of the world," and one who, in "view of the limited opportunities then afforded for the acquisition and diffusion of learning, and the difficulty of procuring the materials of study, must be ranked among the foremost who have sought to reduce diversity to unity, and to survey the whole extent of what is knowable, with the aid of observation and experiment, and in the light of all-embracing principles."[8]

In his *Compendium* Grosseteste furnished a classification of all the departments of scientific knowledge recognized at his time. He arranged them into twenty classes; in modern nomenclature, they were (1) the divisions of philosophy, (2) a compendium of natural philosophy, (3) mathematics, (4) metaphysics, (5) grammar, (6) rhetoric, (7) logic, (8) the art of medicine, (9) arithmetic, (10) music, (11) geometry, (12) astronomy, (13) optics, (14) astrology, (15) mechanics,[9] (16) mathematical sciences in general, (17) politics, (18) economics, (19) ethics, and (20) a discourse on the unity and simplicity of knowledge.

Grosseteste's influence was manifest in the writings of Albertus Magnus, Thomas Aquinas and, most significantly, Roger Bacon.

Albertus Magnus's Compilations

Albertus Magnus (1193/1206-1280), Dominican friar, is best known as the teacher of Thomas Aquinas and as an exhaustive "compiler and glossator" of Aristotle's work. Admirers called him "doctor universalis," disparagers, "the Ape of Aristotle." Yet it has been said that

[8] Francis Seymour Stevenson, *Robert Grosseteste: Bishop of Lincoln* (London: Macmillan & Co., 1899), pp. 49-50.

[9] Stevenson gives "astronomy" as both class 12 and class 15 but mentions that in another arrangement Grosseteste had included "mechanics" and "poetry." Having no access to the (supposedly lost) manuscript, I took the liberty of replacing the second of the twice-entered astronomy with mechanics. For "poetry" I have no other space but this footnote.

"by regarding theology and philosophy as two different pursuits he initiated a new approach" to the teachings of the church.[10]

Albertus's perspective regarding the classification of the sciences can most conveniently be sketched by his own declaration of intention, at the beginning of his *Physica*, "to make the essential branches of philosophy intelligible." He specifies them as natural philosophy, or physics; metaphysics, with theology; and mathematics. In the context he mentions "moral science," *scientia moralis*.[11]

Thomas Aquinas's Reconstructions

Thomas Aquinas (1227-1274), Dominican disciple of Albertus Magnus, and the most respected scholastic—Aquinas to worldly philosophers, Saint Thomas to religious writers—was intensely interested in the ordering of the sciences. Philosophers of science have often disagreed on whether, and on which issues, Aquinas was an unreconstructed Aristotelian, a modified or refined Aristotelian, or an outright "original" Thomist. The majority of his interpreters have been inclined to trace most of his classificatory and methodological pronouncements to Aristotle's work.[12]

In distinguishing between revelation and reason as two separate sources of knowledge (or truth), one under the name of theology, the other under the name of philosophy, Aquinas followed earlier church fathers, especially his teacher Albertus. He is unquestionably an Aristotelian in his distinctions between material objects and formal objects of science, and a slightly modified Aristotelian in distinguishing four orders of science: Natural Philosophy, Rational Philosophy, Moral Philosophy, and Practical Sciences (or Mechanical Arts). These orders correspond to four habits of science regarding the role of the intellect. In Natural Philosophy the intellect does not

[10] *Chambers's Encyclopaedia* (Oxford: Pergamon, 1967), vol. I, p. 230. The chief works of Albertus are the *Liber de Causis*, the *Theologica Aristotelis*, and the *Parva Naturalia*. All of these are included in *B. Alberti Magni Opera Omnia*, edited by Auguste Borgnet (Paris: Louis Vivès, 1890).

[11] *Opera Omnia*, vol. 3 *Liber Primus Physicorum*, p. 2. — The article on "Albertus Magnus, Saint" in the latest edition of the *Encyclopaedia Britannica*, gives a misleading enumeration of the sciences Albertus proposed to distinguish: "Albertus undertook—as he states at the beginning of his *Physica*—'to make . . . intelligible to the Latins' all the branches of natural science, logic, rhetoric, mathematics, astronomy, ethics, economics, politics, metaphysics." The Latin text does not, in the pages in question, speak of economics or politics. Perhaps the author of the article felt justified in reading these into Albert's reference to moral science.

[12] The works by Saint Thomas Aquinas most relevant to our subject are *Summa Theologica* (8 vols.) and "Commentary on the Sentences of Petrus Lombardus," all contained in his *Opera Omnia*, published in 25 vols. (Parma: Fraccadori, 1852-1872).

create, but only observes, what exists in nature; in Rational Philosophy the intellect "produces" through mental acts related to the concepts of things; in Moral Philosophy the intellect generates acts of will; and in Practical Philosophy, or the Practical Arts, the intellect generates activities that produce things or changes in the external world.[13]

This quadripartition of the world of science accommodated many but not all the disciplines that Aquinas examined in his writings. Natural Philosophy was supposed to include Metaphysics as well as Psychology, but it was not immediately clear whether Mathematics would also be assigned to it. By adopting the traditional Aristotelian division of Theoretical Philosophy into Natural Philosophy, Mathematics, and Metaphysics, Aquinas ensured a good place for Mathematics and also furnished a rationale for this favored treatment. Natural Philosophy, according to this view, is concerned with things that are bound to matter both in their being (existence) and in their knowability, with "things that exist only in matter and that have definitions in which sensible matter is an indispensable part." Although the objects of Mathematics may be "bound in their existence to matter . . . , their definitions do not include sensible matter."[14] Metaphysics, the third division of Theoretical Philosophy, includes objects that "can be without matter in their existence." It is subdivided into Ontology, Epistemology, Value Theory, and Theology, its "most important part."

Whereas speculative science (Theoretical Philosophy) seeks truth, practical science (Practical Philosophy) aims "at some production." The Science of Morals is its most important part; some Aristotelians divided it into Monastics, Economics, and Politics, but Aquinas did not adopt this scheme. Among the practical sciences, Aquinas enumerated "the mechanical arts, such as medicine, shipbuilding, strategy."[15]

In contrast to philosophers of science of later times (16th to 19th century), Aquinas did not include history among the sciences. Following Saint Augustine, he held that "we can have no scientific knowledge of human events because they are individual and contingent."[16]

[13] Hans Meyer, The Philosophy of St. Thomas Aquinas (St. Louis and London: A. Herder, 1944), p. 361.
[14] Ibid., p. 363.
[15] Ibid., p. 365
[16] Ibid., p. 366.

Roger Bacon's Interconnections

Roger Bacon (1214-1292/94) was a student of Grosseteste's at Oxford and later associated with Albertus Magnus and Thomas Aquinas at Paris. This was after the ban on the study of Aristotle (1209) had been mitigated and there was no longer any difficulty studying Aristotle or his Arabian commentators.[17] Bacon's "central thought," as laid down in his *Opus Majus* and its two appendices, the *Opus Minus* and the *Opus Tertium*, was the unity of science: "All the sciences are connected; they lend each other material aid as parts of one great whole, each doing its own work, not for itself alone, but for the other parts. . . ."[18]

Roger Bacon's classifications can perhaps, with some license, be derived from the outlines of his works, one from the *Opus Majus*, another from the *Scriptum Principale* (of which we have only fragments). The former has seven parts: I. The Four General Causes of Human Ignorance and Error (Undue regard to Authority, Custom, Popular Prejudice, and False Conceit), II. The Close Affinity between Philosophy and Theology, III. The Utility of the Study of Foreign Languages, IV. The Utility of Mathematical Science (Its Method and Objects—Its Uses in Astronomy, Optics, Theology, Chronology, Astrology, and the Correction of the Calendar—Geographical Treatise), V. Perspective or Optics (General Principles of Vision, Physical and Mental—Direct Vision—Reflection and Refraction), VI. Experimental Science (A General Means of Investigation and Verification—Its Three Prerogatives), and VII. Moral Philosophy (The Final and Supreme Science—Man's Relation to God—Civic and Personal Morality—Comparative Study of Religions—Superiority of the Christian Faith).[19]

The *Scriptum Principale* was planned by Bacon to have four volumes: I. Comparative Grammar and Logic (Corresponding to the trivium, that is, grammar, rhetoric, and logic; finished parts: *Compendium Studii Philosophiae* and *Grammatica Graeca*), II. Mathematics: (1) Preliminary Principles (*Communia Mathematicae*), (2) Special Branches, (corresponding to the quadrivium, that is, geometry, arithmetic, astronomy, and music), III. Natural Science: (1) General Principles (*Communia Naturalium*), (2) Perspective or Optics, (3) Astronomy, including Geography and Astrology, (4) Barology (the science of weights), (5) Speculative Alchemy, (6) Agriculture, (7) Medicine,

---

[17] John Henry Bridges, *The Life and Work of Roger Bacon*, edited by H. Gordon Jones (London: Williams & Norgate, 1914), p. 150.

[18] Ibid., p. 139.

[19] Ibid., p. 151, note C.

(8) Experimental Science, IV. Metaphysics and Morals (probably corresponding to Part VII of the *Opus Majus*, see above).[20]

The most original thought in Roger Bacon's system is, by general consensus, contained in the eighth division of "Natural Science," that is, "Experimental Science." The combination of mathematical with experimental method is recognized as the distinguishing feature of Roger Bacon's philosophy of science.

Llull's Trees

I now turn to "one of the most astonishing, strangest figures of the Middle Ages," the Catalan philosopher and mystic Ramon Llull (1234-1315), whom French writers have called Raymond Lulle.[21] In his *Ars Generalis* Llull endeavored to lead the sciences from diversity to unity and to establish a *scientia universalis* with universal principles embracing the special principles of all sciences. Five hundred years later, this idea was fervently propagated by Leibniz and, still later, in 1935, it was put forward by the "Unity of Science" movement launched by Carnap and others (see below, Chapters 5 and 7).

Another idea of Llull's was the tree of science (or "knowledge": *arbor scientiae*), the metaphorical depiction of the branches of learning often attributed to Francis Bacon. Bacon was familiar with Llull's work, criticized it in several respects, but did not give him credit for the tree of knowledge (see below, Chapter 4). Whereas Bacon later employed the metaphor to symbolize the branches of one huge tree, or at best, three trees, Llull sometimes spoke of as many as sixteen trees, each with trunk and branches, boughs and twigs, and also leaves, flowers, and fruits. The classification for which these metaphorical devices were used is, however, rather primitive, reflecting the state of contemplative thought of the time: a mixture of religious, mystic, and rationalistic excogitation. Thus, we find an elementary tree (concerned with cosmogony), a vegetal tree, a sensuous tree, an imaginal tree (concerned with the mental impressions of elementary, vegetal, and sensuous things), a human tree (soul and body), a moral tree, an imperial tree (politics), an apostolic tree (church hierarchy),

[20] Ibid., p. 152, note D.

[21] Jean-Claude Frère, *Raymond Lulle* (Paris: Culture, Art, Loisirs, 1972), p. 13. — Llull's major works are *Ars Major* and *Ars Generalis*, included in *Opera Omnia*, edited by Ivo Salzinger (Mainz, 1721-1742), 10 vols. in Latin; also in *Raimundi Lulli opera latina*, edited by Friedrich Stegmüller (Freiburg and Palma de Mallorca, 1960). A Spanish collection, edited by G. Rosselo, appeared as *Obras rimadas* (Palma de Mallorca, 1859). Recent editions of encyclopaedias no longer include Llull. For calling my attention to this interesting philosophic classifier of sciences, I am indebted to Dr. Kennerly Merritt Woody, the erudite bibliographer for history and religion at the Princeton University Library.

a celestial tree, an angelic tree, an eternal tree (beatitude and damnation), a maternal tree (devoted to Our Lady), a tree of Jesus Christ, and a divine tree. Besides these fourteen, there were two extra trees: the tree of examples and the tree of questions.[22]

The existence of "experimental" sciences was recognized by Llull in other works, in which he gives somewhat less mystical accounts of astronomy, physics, chemistry, and medicine.

Ibn Khaldûn's Enumeration

The exhaustive (and exhausting) enumeration of the branches of learning by Francis Bacon, published in 1605 (and to be examined in the next chapter), may have been the most influential work of its kind, but it was surely not the first. For example, a number of Arabic books with taxonomies of the sciences had appeared as many as six centuries earlier. Historians of Arab philosophy report on a "Catalogue of Sciences" (in Latin De Scientiis) by Muhammad al-Farabi (died 950). It enumerates 1. the linguistic sciences, 2. logic (containing the eight books of Aristotle's Organon), 3. mathematics (comprising arithmetic, geometry, optics, astronomy, music, statics, and mechanics), 4. physics (with the Aristotelian subdivisions), 5. metaphysics, 6. politics, 7. jurisprudence, and 8. theology.[23]

Another philosopher, Ibn Sînâ (Abu Ali, in Latin Avicenna, 980-1037) extended al-Farabi's classification, though he confined it to the "rational" sciences, which he divided into "speculative sciences" (seeking after truth) and "practical sciences" (aiming at well-being). Among the former were physics (comprising eight basic sciences derived from Aristotle and seven derivative sciences, to wit, medicine, astrology, physiognomy, dream interpretation, talismans, charms, and alchemy), mathematics (including music), and metaphysics (with five subdivisions taken over Aristotle and two derivatives, "prophetic inspiration" and eschatology). The inclusion of dream interpretation and charms among physics, and of prophetic inspiration among other "rational" sciences is interesting to note, as is also the fact that medicine and alchemy are classified as speculative, not as practical, sciences. Practical sciences comprised personal morality, domestic morality, and politics, with prophetology as an appendage.[24]

One of the later works by an Arab historian and social scientist

---

[22] Frère, Lulle, pp. 69-72.

[23] Georges C. Anawati, "Science," in Peter M. Holt, Ann K. S. Lambton, and Bernard Lewis, eds., The Cambridge History of Islam (Cambridge: At the University Press, 1970), p. 743.

[24] Ibid., pp. 743-744.

has become available in an English translation: the *Muqaddimah* [Introduction, or Prolegomena] *to History* by Ibn Khaldûn (1332-1406). The oldest of the preserved manuscripts of this work is dated 1394. It was intended as a part of a history but in fact became an independent work.[25] Its sixth chapter is given to a discussion of "The Various Kinds of Sciences."[26]

According to Ibn Khaldûn, the "sciences that exist in contemporary civilization" are of two kinds: the traditional sciences "based on the authority of the given religious law," and the philosophical sciences, which are "natural to man and to which he is guided by his own ability to think."[27] The traditional religious sciences are derived exclusively from the Qur'an (Koran) and the Sunnah, for, as Ibn Khaldûn says, "the [Islamic] religious law has forbidden the study of all [other] revealed scriptures."[28]

Ibn Khaldûn enumerated the following traditional religious sciences: 1. the science of the interpretation of the Qur'an; 2. the science of the reading of the Qur'an; 3. the science of Prophetic traditions;[29] 4. the science of the principles of jurisprudence, subdivided into the science of controversial questions and the science of dialectics;[30] 5. the science of jurisprudence, including the laws of inheritance;[31] 6. the science of speculative theology, including studies of the degrees of faith, anthropomorphism, and schools of theologians and philosophers;[32] 7. the science of Sufism (Mohammedan ascetic mysticism);[33] 8. the science of dream interpretation.[34]

[25] Ibn Khaldûn, *The Muqaddimah: An Introduction to History*, translated from the Arabic by Franz Rosenthal in three volumes (Princeton: Princeton University Press, 2nd ed., 1967 [1st ed., Pantheon Books for the Bollingen Foundation, 1958]). Ibn Khaldûn's *Muqaddimah* was said to represent "the most comprehensive synthesis in the Human Sciences ever achieved by the Arabs. . . ." Charles Issawi, *An Arab Philosophy of History* (London: John Murray, 1950), p. 1. Arnold Toynbee wrote that Ibn Khaldûn in his *Muqaddimah* "conceived and formulated a philosophy of history which is undoubtedly the greatest work of its kind that has ever yet been created by any mind in any time or place." Arnold J. Toynbee, *A Study of History*, vol. III (London: Oxford University Press, 1934), p. 322. — Needless to say, in the present survey we are not concerned with the philosophy of history or human sciences but only with the classification of the disciplines.

[26] Ibn Khaldûn, *Muqaddimah*, vol. II, pp. 411-463 and vol. III, pp. 3-480.

[27] Ibid., vol. II, p. 436.

[28] Ibid., p. 438.

[29] Ibid., pp. 447-463.

[30] Ibid., vol. III, pp. 23-34.

[31] Ibid., pp. 3-23. In reversing the order of entries 4 and 5 I follow the arrangement by Anawati, p. 745.

[32] Ibid., pp. 34-75.

[33] Ibid., pp. 76-103. Anawati refers to this discipline as "mysticism."

[34] Ibid., pp. 103-110.

The intellectual sciences—"not restricted to any particular religious group"—"comprise four different sciences": 1. logic; 2. physics; 3. metaphysics; and 4. the mathematical sciences.[35] The science of logic is subdivided according to the eight books of Aristotle's *Organon*, that is, into categories, hermeneutics, analytics, apodeictica, topics, sophistry, rhetoric, and poetics.[36] The science of physics is subdivided, each part related also to a craft: medicine and agriculture are the major branches. Ibn Khaldûn mentions four other disciplines without stating whether they are part of physics or metaphysics: the sciences of sorcery (magic) and talismans,[37] the science of "letter magic,"[38] and the science of alchemy (which Ibn Khaldûn proceeds to "refute").[39] Metaphysics is treated as a separate science but discussed in its relations to theology and philosophy in general, which Ibn Khaldûn also refutes and condemns as "corrupting the students."[40]

The mathematical sciences are divided into geometrical sciences, numerical sciences, music, and astronomy. The geometrical sciences deal with quantities and measurements in lines, planes, and solids, including spherical figures and conical sections, surveying of land, and optics.[41] Among the numerical sciences Ibn Khaldûn enumerates arithmetic, calculation (regarded as a craft), algebra, business arithmetic, and the partition of inheritances (a craft, not to be confused with the laws of inheritance included in the traditional religious sciences).[42] Music is treated as a mathematical science because "it is the knowledge of the proportions of sounds and modes and their numerical measurements."[43] The fourth mathematical science is astronomy.[44] Among its subdivisions is "the science of astronomical tables" (which is also an important craft), and astrology (which Ibn Khaldûn refutes and regards as harmful "to human civilization").[45]

---

[35] Ibid., p. 111. — In a different arrangement, he speaks of seven "basic philosophical sciences" by characterizing arithmetic, geometry, astronomy, and music as basic sciences, in lieu of the more comprehensive group of mathematical sciences (p. 112).

[36] Ibid., pp. 137-147.

[37] Ibid., pp. 156-227. — Anawati groups these disciplines and also "prestidigitation" as parts of physics.

[38] Ibid., pp. 171-227.

[39] Ibid., pp. 227-246.

[40] Ibid., pp. 152-155 and 246-259.

[41] Ibid., pp. 111-112 and 129-133.

[42] Ibid., pp. 118-129.

[43] Ibid., p. 112.

[44] Ibid., pp. 112 and 133-137.

[45] Ibid., p. 262.

Although some secondary sources stop at this point in Ibn Khaldûn's enumeration of the sciences, he has actually a few more on which to report.[46] They are the "sciences concerned with the Arabic language," subdivided into grammar, the science of lexicography, the sciences of syntax and style and of literary criticism, and the science of literature.[47] The inclusion of these disciplines (nowadays regarded as humanities) among the sciences is a matter of course for those accustomed to the cosmopolitan, comprehensive meaning of science. Noteworthy in Ibn Khaldûn's discussion is his attempt to separate sciences from crafts, with the explicit recognition that some fields, such as medicine, are both science and craft, or knowing and doing. Writers, publishers, and poets may take pleasure in noting that the "craft of book production" is given a separate section,[48] and the "craft of poetry" is treated extensively in six sections.[49] Some publishers, however, may take exception to Ibn Khaldûn's judgment that "the great number of scholarly works available is an obstacle on the path to attaining scholarship."[50]

[46] For example, Anawati, "Science," pp. 745-746.
[47] Ibn Khaldûn, *Muqaddimah*, vol. III, pp. 319-341.
[48] Ibid., vol. II, pp. 391-394.
[49] Ibid., vol. III, pp. 313-480.
[50] Ibid., p. 288.

CHAPTER 4

THE TREE OF KNOWLEDGE

MOST PEOPLE KNOW of the tree of knowledge from the first book of the Old Testament. But that was a different tree and a different knowledge, not what Francis Bacon (1561-1626) meant to suggest when he wrote about the tree of knowledge; nor what either Porphyry or Llull meant.[1] Porphyry, in the third century, had used the metaphor of the tree for his scheme of classifying concepts into bifurcating branches; and Llull, in the thirteenth century, had used the same device when he proposed no fewer than sixteen trees for classifying various systems of thought; but it was Francis Bacon who used the metaphor for a detailed and closely argued classification of all higher

[1] Is there any symbolic relationship between Bacon's tree of knowledge and the biblical tree of knowledge? I am inclined to deny it for several reasons. (1) Bacon's tree was supposed to aid in presenting a scheme of classification—divisions and subdivisions—by reference to the limbs and branches (or "arms and boughs") of the tree; in contrast, it is through its fruits—which Adam and Eve were forbidden to eat—that the biblical tree played its role. (2) Whereas the branches of Bacon's tree supported exercises in taxonomy, Adam had demonstrated his skill in taxonomy—by naming "every beast of the field and every fowl of the air"—long before he tasted the fruit of the tree of knowledge in the Garden of Eden (Genesis, 2:19, 20). (3) The knowledge classified with the help of Bacon's tree is different in character from that of the biblical tree of the "knowledge of good and evil" (Genesis, 2:17, 3:5). (4) One of the main effects of eating the fruit of the tree of knowledge in Eden is "that your eyes shall be opened," that man and woman recognized "that they were naked" and became ashamed of each other (Genesis, 3:5, 3:7). The Hebrew word for knowledge has carnal knowledge as one of its major meanings and the verb "to know" (ya dah) means "to have sexual intercourse," or "to know by direct contact." See The Interpreter's Dictionary of the Bible, vol. 3, p. 43, and vol. 4, p. 696. None of these associations is alluded to in Bacon's tree of knowledge. (5) The Bible scholar Martin Buber rejected interpretations of the "tree of knowledge of good and evil" as instrumental in "acquisition of sexual desire," "acquisition of moral consciousness," and "cognition in general" (which would be suggested by taking "good and evil" to denote "all kinds of things"); instead, he interpreted "knowledge of good and evil" to mean "cognizance of opposites." Martin Buber, "The Tree of Knowledge," in Nahum N. Glatzer, ed., On The Bible: Eighteen Studies by Martin Buber (New York: Schocken Books, 1968), pp. 14-21. None of these meanings would be referred to by the classification of disciplines pictured by Bacon's tree. (6) The renditions of the biblical "knowledge" in various languages offer little help. The Hebrew daat was translated into Greek as gnosis, into Latin as scientia, into French as connaissance, and into German as Erkenntnis. The latter two would surely not be consistent with the "Learning" classified on Bacon's tree.

learning. The exposition of Bacon's system will take up most of this chapter. Only a brief section at the end will report on Thomas Hobbes's tabulation of the sciences, and a briefer section still will discuss Descartes' philosophic principles.

Bacon's Divisions of the Sciences

Bacon's classification of learning—his *partitiones scientiarum*—became the model for almost all later taxonomic and encyclopaedic efforts regarding intellectual knowledge. It merits a careful description, though not with all details; to reproduce his tree of knowledge with all its boughs and twigs would tax most readers' patience excessively and would surely be more confusing than helpful. Bacon's taxonomic zeal led him to enumerate, explicate, and illustrate the "divisions of the sciences" at great length. In the version contained in the collected *Works* the exposition extended over 345 pages (which, however, included many digressions on a variety of subjects). The essay was organized in nine books, each subdivided into several chapters, each dealing with another division and numerous subdivisions of one of the many branches of the tree.[2]

Bacon presented the image of the tree of knowledge in a brief passage (in Book III) setting forth that "the divisions of knowledge are . . . like the branches of a tree that meet in one stem (which stem grows for some distance entire and continuous before it divides itself into arms and boughs)"; and that "before we enter into the branches," we "constitute one universal science. . . . This science I distinguish by the name of *Philosophia Prima*."[3] It deals largely with "Transcendentals or Adventitious Conditions of Essences."[4] Bacon's remarks about the tree of knowledge—or, in literal translation, the tree of doctrines—are preceded by Books I and II of the treatise, which

---

[2] Bacon published his work first in English under the title *Of the Proficience and Advancement of Learning, Divine and Human* (London: Henri Tomes, 1605), 119 pp. arranged in two books. A revised and enlarged Latin edition was published under the title "De dignitate et augmentis scientiarum" in the first volume of Bacon's *Opera* (London: John Haviland, 1623), 493 pp. The original Book II of the first English edition was subdivided into Books II and IX of the Latin. There were later editions both in English (London; 1629, 1633, etc.) and in Latin (Amsterdam, 1662). An English collection of *The Works of Francis Bacon*, edited by James Spedding, Robert Leslie Ellis, and Douglas Denon Heath (London: Longman & Co. with 14 other publishers, 1860) contains in Volumes IV and V a retranslation of Books II to IX from the Latin text of *de augmentis* under the title "Of the Dignity and Advancement of Learning" (345 pages). My page references to Bacon's work will be to this edition.

[3] Bacon, vol. IV, p. 337.

[4] Ibid., p. 340.

deal with even more general distinctions.[5] In Chapter I of Book II, Bacon presented "The Division of All Human Learning into History, Poësy, and Philosophy."[6] These three divisions of learning are related to "the Three Intellectual Faculties,—Memory, Imagination, and Reason."[7]

History, Poësy, and Philosophy

The two main branches of History are Natural History and Civil History, each with many subdivisions. In general, divisions may be by subject matter or by use. Natural History has two uses, narrative— "for the sake of the knowledge of things themselves that are committed to the history"—and inductive—"the stuff and material of a solid and lawful Induction, . . . the nursing-mother of philosophy."[8] Civil History is first divided into Ecclesiastical History, Civil History proper, and Literary History. Civil History proper may be divided in two different ways: Memorials ("history unfinished"), Antiquities ("history defaced"), and Perfect History; or, alternatively, into History Pure and Mixed. Further subdivisions are distinguished on the basis of other principles in a rather complex fashion. For example, Perfect History may be of three kinds—Chronicles, Lives, and Relations; and Chronicles themselves may be distinguished as either Universal or Particular, or as Annals or Journals.[9]

Poësy, "the second principal part of Learning," is divided into Narrative, Dramatic (or, in another version, "Representative"), and Parabolical. Poësy is regarded as "feigned history"—narrative, "a

[5] One may object to the use of a tree as an appropriate metaphor or symbol for the divisions and subdivisions of learning, because it falsely suggests that the branches and twigs have gradually "grown" out of the "stem" of a universal science. History of science has shown that the "branches" were often a systematic or logical aggregation of previously existing "twigs" and that the "stem" was the result of a subsequent desire to unify what had been separate areas of inquiry. Thus, the temporal order of the development is falsified and the notion of organic growth is contradicted. The suggestion of development in time, implied in all vertical representations—the tree growing up from the ground or the kinship diagrams showing the order of "descending generations" from the top down—is misleading. Horizontal representations may be less suggestive of temporal sequences, though it may be more cautious to show the divisions and subdivisions from the right to the left for readers who write from the left to the right, and use the opposite arrangement for readers of Arabic and Hebrew.

[6] Bacon, vol. IV, p. 292.

[7] Bacon's triad was probably derived from the "trinity of the human soul," discussed by St. Augustine: Memory, Reason and Will. In a quotation of St. Augustine in Peter Lombard's Four Books of Sentences, translated by Richard McKeon, the trinity is given as "memory, understanding, and will." McKeon, Selections from Medieval Philosophers, vol. I (New York: Scribner's 1929), p. 194.

[8] Bacon, vol. IV, p. 298.

[9] Ibid., pp. 300-314.

mere imitation of history"; dramatic, presenting past actions "as if they were present"; and parabolical, "typical history," serving for illustration, but also for "infoldment" (veil, concealment). Bacon thinks that Poësy, "being . . . a plant which comes from the lust of the earth without a formal seed, . . . has sprung up and spread abroad more than any other kind of learning."[10] Bacon's judgment regarding the wide spread of Poësy aside, what is important is that he includes Poësy within the category of "Learning," or intellectual knowledge.

It was especially in connection with Philosophy that Bacon proposed the metaphor of the tree of knowledge. "Universal Science" (*Philosophia Prima*) forms the stem of the tree. Science is divided into Sacred Theology and Philosophy. The latter has three main branches, one "concerning the Deity" (Natural Theology or Divine Philosophy), another "concerning Nature" (Natural Philosophy), the third "concerning Man" (Moral Philosophy). Thus "the object of philosophy is threefold—God, Nature, and Man."[11]

Divine Philosophy

Bacon's differentiation of Sacred Theology and Natural Theology relates to the sources from which the Knowledge of God derives: Inspiration (revelation) on the one hand, contemplation, on the other. Natural Theology ("also rightly called Divine Philosophy") "suffices to refute and convince Atheism, and to give information as to the law of nature; but not to establish religion."[12]

Only a brief chapter, a little over 2 pages long, is devoted to Divine Philosophy. This compares with four chapters, together 29 pages, devoted to Natural Philosophy and Mathematics; and eighteen chapters, with 235 pages, to Moral Philosophy. The subject of Sacred Theology, which grows beside Philosophy directly out of the trunk of the tree of knowledge (Universal Science, or Primary Philosophy), is treated separately in Book IX, covering 9 pages.[13]

Natural Philosophy

Natural Philosophy is "divided into the Inquisition of Causes and the Production of Effects: Speculative and Operative." The speculative branch of natural philosophy divides into Physics, which "inquires of the Efficient Cause and the Material," and Metaphysics, inquiring "of the Final Cause and the Form."[14] (These formulations

[10] Ibid., p. 318.
[11] Ibid., p. 337.
[12] Ibid., p. 341.
[13] Books VII, VIII, and IX are contained in Volume V of Bacon's *Works*.
[14] Bacon, vol. IV, pp. 343-344.

are clearly derived from Aristotle.) Physics branches off into three doctrines: of the Principles of Things, of the Fabric of Things, and of the Variety of Things, with the last divided into "Things Concrete" and "Things Abstract." Abstract Physics, in turn, divides into doctrines of the "Configurations of Matter" and of "Motions," simple or compound. It is "in the configurations of matter, in simple motions, in the sums or aggregates of motions, and in the measures of motions" that "the Physic of Abstracts is perfected."[15] Metaphysics deals not only with Final Causes but also with Forms ("dense, rare, hot, cold, heavy, light, tangible, pneumatic, volatile, fixed, and the like") in the abstract, the reflections ascending from the concrete instances of Natural History via the generalizations and speculations of Physics to arrive at the pure forms of Metaphysics.[16]

The operative branch of Natural Philosophy is divided into Mechanics and Magic. (Bacon points to the parallelism of this division with that of the speculative branch into Physics and Metaphysics.) Bacon takes pains to distinguish the kind of mechanics that should be assigned to Natural History from the one that forms a part of operative Natural Philosophy. And he attempts to "purify" the word "Magic," defining it as "the science which applies the knowledge of hidden forms to the production of wonderful operations."[17] References to Alchemy and Astrology will suffice to suggest the kinds of knowledge Bacon felt obliged to accommodate in his scheme.

Bacon calls Mathematics "the great Appendix of Natural Philosophy, both Speculative and Operative." He prefers to treat it as an "auxiliary science" but, if he "meant to set it down as a substantive and principal science," he would prefer "to place it as a branch of Metaphysics. For Quantity . . . must be reckoned with as one of the Essential Forms of Things."[18] As it is, "Mathematics and Logic, which ought to be but the handmaids of Physic, . . . presume on the strength of the certainty which they possess to exercise dominion over it."[19] Mathematics is either Pure (with "Quantity entirely severed from matter and from axioms of natural philosophy," as in Arithmetic and Geometry) or Mixed (considering "quantity in so far as it assists to explain, demonstrate, and actuate" some axioms and parts of natural philosophy). Bacon predicts that "as Physic advances farther and farther every day and develops new axioms, it will require fresh

[15] Ibid., p. 357.
[16] Ibid., p. 364, paraphrased.
[17] Ibid., pp. 366-367.
[18] Ibid., pp. 369-370.
[19] Ibid., p. 370.

assistance from Mathematic in many things, and so the parts of Mixed Mathematics will be more numerous."[20]

Moral Philosophy

The "doctrine concerning Man" has a twofold division in Bacon's scheme. There is, first, the division into "Philosophy of Humanity" and "Philosophy Civil," the former dealing with "man segregate," the latter with "man congregate" (that is, "man in society"), and, second, a "general doctrine concerning . . . the State of Man," which divides into "doctrine concerning the Person of Man," and "doctrine concerning the League [or connection] of Mind and Body."[21] I shall forego a listing of the further subdivisions of these divisions and confine myself to mentioning that the extensive ramification includes such things as Physiognomy and the Interpretation of Dreams. The first set of branches, however, is more interesting. Philosophy of Humanity is divided into doctrines concerning the Body of Man and concerning his Soul;[22] the former divide into Medicine, Cosmetic, Athletic, and "Voluptuary Art,"[23] the latter, the doctrines of the Soul (or the Mind), divide, after considerable complication, into Logic and Ethics, "the doctrine concerning the Intellect . . . and the doctrine concerning the Will of man." They "are, as it were, twins by birth."[24]

Logic has four branches: "the Arts of Discovering, of Judging, of Retaining, and of Transmitting." The Art of Discovery may be concerned with the discovery of Arts (subdivided into "Learned Experience" and "the New Organon") or with the discovery of Arguments (subdivided into "Promptuary" and "Topics," either "General" or "Particular").[25] The Art of Judging may be either by Induction or by Syllogism.[26] The Art of Retaining is divided into the doctrine concerning the Helps of Memory—writing, of course—and the doctrine concerning Memory itself,[27] which is subdivided into Prenotion and Emblem. Memory is enhanced by a "prenotion that what we are seeking must be something which agrees with order"[28] as, for ex-

---

[20] Ibid., p. 371.
[21] Ibid., pp. 372-374.
[22] Ibid., p. 372.
[23] Ibid., pp. 379, 395.
[24] Ibid., p. 405.
[25] Ibid., p. 421.
[26] Ibid., p. 428.
[27] That Memory is one of the three intellectual faculties—the one that supports History as distinct from Philosophy (or Science)—need not exclude a "doctrine concerning Memory" and "doctrines concerning Helps of Memory" from being parts of scientific knowledge, which is based on Reason, a different intellectual faculty.
[28] Bacon, vol. IV, p. 436.

ample, a word that rhymes with one in a previous verse. Emblem means reliance on "sensible images" rather than on "intellectual conceptions."[29] The "fourth division of Logic," the Art of Transmitting knowledge to others, divides into three doctrines: concerning the Organ of Discourse, the Method of Discourse, and the Illustration of Discourse.[30] Each of these three doctrines is subdivided, but some of the parts get intertwined and are hard to disentangle. The major part of the Organ of Discourse is Grammar, divided into two parts relating either to Speech or to Writing; but in addition to Words and Letters, there are Gestures; and there are Notations representing neither letters nor words, but things and notions, and which are understood by people who speak different languages. The distinction between Hieroglyphics, Real Characters, and Cyphers is of interest in this context, as is the distinction of Literary Grammar and Philosophic Grammar. The diversity of Method of Discourse is too great to name even some of those which Bacon presents.[31] The "doctrine concerning Illustration of Discourse" relates to the science of Rhetoric, or Oratory; and Bacon uses forty-five pages to illustrate it, chiefly with examples of Sophisms,[32] Antitheses,[33] and "Lesser Forms."

Ethics, or Moral Knowledge, is divided into the Platform of Good and the Culture of the Mind. The former divides into Simple and Comparative Good; the Simple Good into Individual Good and Good of Communion; the Individual Good into Active and Passive Good; the Passive Good into Conservative and Perfective Good. Going back three steps (or subdivisions) to the Good of Communion, we find it subdivided into General and Respective Duties—and we are prepared for applications in the area of politics. But before we proceed to the thick branch of Philosophy Civil, the second branch of the doctrine concerning Man, we ought to go back to the second branch of Ethics, the doctrine of the Culture of the Mind. Bacon divides it into the doctrine concerning the Characters of Mind, the Affections, and the Remedies, and appends to it a disquisition on the Congruity between the Good of the Mind and the Good of the Body.

Now to Philosophy Civil. It divides into three doctrines: Conversation, Negotiation, and Government. The two doctrines of Negotiations are that concerning Scattered Occasions and that concerning Advancement in Life. For the doctrine of Government Bacon discusses only two of its many subdivisions, the doctrines concerning

[29] Ibid., p. 437.
[30] Ibid., p. 438.
[31] Ibid., pp. 448-454.
[32] Ibid., pp. 459-472.
[33] Ibid., pp. 473-492.

the Extension of Bounds of Empire and that concerning Universal Justice (also called the Fountains of Law).

The Main Outline of Bacon's Classification

With our attention to the smaller branches, boughs, and twigs of the tree of knowledge, we may have lost a clear view of its larger outline, of its main branches. As a matter of fact, Bacon's scheme suggests three trees, not one: the three trees of history, poësy, and philosophy. They are growing on different soils, and their roots are the three supposedly separate intellectual faculties of Memory, Imagination, and Reason.

Let us have another look at the main outline of the system. History is either Natural History or Civil History. Poësy includes all representative arts. Philosophy, apart from Sacred Theology, has three main branches: Divine Philosophy (about God), Natural Philosophy (about Nature), and Moral Philosophy (about Man). Natural Philosophy is either Speculative or Operative; the speculative branch divides into Physics and Metaphysics, the operative branch into Mechanics and Magic.[34] Moral Philosophy has a branch dealing with "man segregate" and another dealing with "man in society." The first branch is concerned both with the human body, including Medicine and Athletics, and with the mind, including Logic and Ethics. The second branch, called Philosophy Civil, comprises what today would be regarded as social sciences.

The basic idea of separating the branches of learning, or, rather, the three trees, according to the intellectual faculty employed—memory, imagination, and reason—has not proved fortunate for the development of the philosophy of science. It gave it a wrong direction by separating what ought to be joined, and in fact is joined, in most or all intellectual activities. Remembered experience, inventive imagination, and pure ratiocination vigorously interact in the writing of history, in artistic composition, and in virtually all mental processes involved in the philosophies, sciences, and doctrines concerning god, nature, and man. Emphasis on the distinctiveness and sep-

[34] We should not turn up our noses at Bacon's inclusion of magic as a science, nor at his discussion of angels and evil spirits in his chapter on natural theology. Remember the time the treatise was written: 1605 and 1623. Recall that in our time, more than 350 years later, millions of people are intensely interested in knowing "under which star" they were born; and that in 1976 a young woman in Germany died after an exorcism was authorized by officials of the church and administered by a priest for the purpose of driving out the evil spirits by which she—an epileptic— had been possessed. Bacon, however, closed his discussion of the "knowledge" about angels and spirits with the courageous remark that he would "challenge no small part of it . . . as superstitious, fabulous, and fantastical" (p. 343).

arateness of the intellectual faculties employed has tended to continue an unwholesome segregation of the institutional faculties at the universities and to impede the understanding of the universe of learning. It is unhelpful to see natural history—say, the knowledge of species of plants, animals, and minerals, or the origins of stars and planets, the development of the earth, and so forth—as branches on a tree quite separate from natural science. It is equally unhelpful to see political history and political science, or economic history and economic science, as branches of different trees. To be sure, differences in methodology and in the objectives of inquiry may be important and should not be overlooked, but one may doubt that they constitute the most appropriate principles for the classification of the various branches of learning.

To say this is not to denounce Bacon. If anyone is to be reproached, it should be those who have adhered too closely to Bacon's model and have allowed it to endure and to dominate the classification systems of higher learning in subsequent centuries.[35]

Hobbes's Demonstrations of Consequences

Thomas Hobbes (1588-1679) presented in his Leviathan[36] a table classifying the sciences on principles quite different from those that had guided Bacon in building his system. Hobbes had for a few years been an amanuensis of Bacon's, helping on Latin translations. As he worked for Bacon in the very years in which the Advancement of

[35] Of the early followers of Bacon who accepted the three "separate" sources of human learning, I may mention Antonio Zara, Anatomia ingeniorum et scientiarum (1614), who distinguished 16 sciences of the imagination, 8 sciences of the intellect, and 12 sciences of memory. As we shall see later, Bacon's tripartition was accepted by Ephraim Chambers' Cyclopaedia in 1728; and by d'Alembert and Diderot in their great Encyclopédie in 1751. Interesting in this context is the view of Cournot: "To tell the truth, there is nothing that is really worthy of attention in Bacon's work besides the fundamental idea of the tripartite division [of human knowledge]." Antoine-Augustin Cournot, Essai sur les fondements de nos connaissances et sur les caractères de la critique philosophique (Paris: L. Hachette, 1851), vol. 2, p. 258. On the whole we may endorse the appreciation of Bacon's work that is expressed in Eiseley's tribute: "It is not possible to realize the full magnitude of Bacon's achievement without some knowledge of this age of the scientific twilight—an age when men first fumbled with the instruments of science yet, in the next breath, might consider the influence of stars upon their destinies or hearken to the spells of witchcraft. Loren Eiseley, Francis Bacon and the Modern Dilemma (Lincoln, Nebraska: University of Nebraska Press, 1962), p. 16.

[36] Thomas Hobbes of Malmesbury, Leviathan or the Matter, Forme, and Power of a Common-Wealth Ecclesiasticall and Civill (London: Andrew Crooke, 1651). Page references are to the Penguin edition (Harmondsworth: Penguin Books, 1968). The quaint spelling of many words corresponds to the original, faithfully reproduced in the Penguin edition.

Learning was translated into Latin, it would not be unreasonable to presume that Hobbes may have assisted in that task. The *Leviathan* was completed in 1651, that is, twenty-six years after the publication of Bacon's *De Augmentis Scientiarum*, surely enough time to move away from the Baconian classification.

Hobbes distinguished two kinds of knowledge: (1) "Knowledge of Fact," based on sense and memory, of things "past and irrevocable";[37] and (2) "Knowledge of the Consequence of one Affirmation to another," based on reason.[38] The "Register of Knowledge of Fact" is called History, which may be "Naturall History" if it deals with "such Facts . . . as have no Dependance on Man's Will," and "Civill History" if it concerns "the Voluntary Actions of men in Commonwealths."[39] The "Demonstrations of Consequences of one Affirmation to Another" are in the "Registers of Science," also called "Books of Philosophy,"[40] which are "of many sorts" and may be divided according to a schema that provides for a pattern of subdivisions yielding twenty-four sciences. Characteristically, history is *absolute* knowledge (as "required in a Witnesse") whereas science is *conditional* knowledge (as required for predictions).

Hobbes does not provide a tabulation of the divisions of *history*, though his book devotes plenty of text to them. The tabulation of the divisions of *science* is marked by an extreme fastidiousness in emphasizing that every branch of scientific knowledge is defined in terms of "consequences." For example, Mathematics deals with "Consequences from Quantity and Motion, determined by Figure [Geometry] and by Number [Arithmetic]"; Astrology, with "Consequences from the Influence of the Starres"; Ethics, with "Consequences from the Passions of Men"; Logic, with "Consequences from Speech," and so forth. The shortened definition of science, as reproduced in the table, reads "Knowledge of Consequences; which is called also Philosophy." The word "Consequences" appears twenty-nine times in the tabulation of the sciences.

The first division is between "Naturall Philosophy" and "Civill Philosophy." The latter divides into "Consequences from the Institution of Common-Wealth, to the Rights and Duties of the Body Politique, or Sovereign," and "Consequences from the same, to the Duty and Right of the Subjects." "Naturall Philosophy" divides into "Consequences from . . . Quantity and Motion" and "Physiques, or Consequences from Qualities." If we omit the consecutive dichoto-

---

[37] Ibid., p. 115.
[38] Ibid., p. 147.
[39] Ibid., p. 148.
[40] Ibid., p. 148.

mies or bifurcations and list immediately the ultimate species of science, we end up with *Philosophia Prima*, Geometry, Arithmetic, Astronomy, Geography, Engineering Science, Architectural Mechanics, and Navigational Science as members of the class of Consequences of Quantity and Motion; and with Meteorology, Sciography ("Consequences from the Light of Starres" and "the Motion of the Sunne"), Astrology, Mineralogy, Optics, Music, Ethics, Poetry, Rhetoric, Logic, and "The Science of Just and Unjust," as members of the class of "Consequences from Qualities."[41] Lost in the interstices between "Physiques" and the ultimate specialties are "Consequences from the Qualities of Animals in generall," from which Hobbes goes to the "Consequences from the Senses," excluding thereby several important biological specialties. The most flagrant omission, however, is Chemistry; the word, or any equivalent or proxy, is absent from the table, and the subject cannot easily be accommodated within any of the brackets provided in Hobbes's table.

Some of the most conspicuous deviations of Hobbes's scheme from that of Bacon should be noted: (1) Hobbes regards *Philosophia Prima* as the final offshoot of a bough from a branch of Natural Philosophy; Bacon regarded it as the stem, or trunk, of the tree from which all branches of science derive. (2) Hobbes accords no place in his scheme to Theology; Bacon saw Sacred Theology as one of the main branches of Universal Science, or *Philosophia Prima*, and Natural Theology, or Divine Philosophy, as one of the three branches of Philosophy (the other two being Natural Philosophy and Moral Philosophy). (3) Hobbes has no place for Metaphysics; Bacon showed it as a branch of Natural Philosophy, coordinate with Physics and concerned with final causes and abstract forms. (4) Hobbes considers Ethics and Logic as distant derivatives of the "Consequences from the Qualities of Men," which in the table are four subdivisions removed from Physics, one of the two branches of *Natural* Philosophy; Bacon regarded Ethics and Logic as subdivisions of the doctrines of the soul, or mind, which were parts of the Philosophy of Humanity, a branch of *Moral* Philosophy. (5) Hobbes gives Poetry a place among the natural sciences, for he regards it as one of the consequences of speech, and

---

[41] The enumeration reproduced in this paragraph includes twenty-one sciences, omitting three for which Hobbes supplied no names: (1) the science of the "Consequences of the Qualities from Liquid Bodies that fill the space between the Starres; such as are the Ayre, or substance aetheriall"; (2) the science of "Consequences from the Qualities of Vegetables"; and (3) the science of "Consequences from the rest of Senses" (other than "Vision" and "Sounds"). With regard to the second I suppose that all terms used for subdivisions of botany were reserved for natural history; and that Hobbes was groping for something like "biochemistry"—or perhaps "agronomy."

therefore as one in the sequence of subdivisions in a direct line of descent from Physics; Bacon saw Poetry (Poësy) grow on a different tree with roots of Imagination, entirely separate from Science. (6) Hobbes considers Music as a natural science, inasmuch as it is a consequence of sounds, derived from physics; Bacon had no place for Music, though one would have expected to find it as a division of "Poësy," springing from the fountain of Imagination, had he not described Poësy as "feigned history." (7) Hobbes does not recognize Imagination as a separate source of knowledge but regards it as a part of Memory—the two "are but one thing";[42] Bacon had treated Imagination, Memory, and Reason as three separate sources of knowledge.

Without trying to judge whether Hobbes's classification system is better or worse than Bacon's, or whether it was better in some respects and worse in others, I can state that most of the successors in the enterprise of classification sided with Bacon on most issues. This was especially true, as we shall see in the next chapter, in the case of the French encyclopaedists.

Descartes' Philosophic Principles

It would be excessively wasteful to attempt a survey of the literature that used the Baconian metaphor of the tree of knowledge as an aid in the classification of the sciences. One exception may be permitted in consideration of the eminence of the author: René Descartes (1596-1650). In the preface to the French translation of his *principii philosophiae* Descartes wrote that ". . . philosophy as a whole is like a tree whose roots are metaphysics, whose trunk is physics, and whose branches, which issue from this trunk, are all the other sciences."[43]

Descartes' concept of physics is unusually wide. It includes, besides "the true principles of material things" inquiries into "how the whole universe is composed, and then in particular what is the nature of this earth and of all the bodies which are most commonly found in connection with it, like air, water and fire, the loadstone and other minerals." Beyond these come the inquiries "into the na-

---

[42] Hobbes, *Leviathan*, p. 89.

[43] First edition 1644 in Latin. Translated into French (by Abbé Claude Picot) in 1647. A letter from Descartes to the translator is used as the preface to the French edition; this preface contains the passage in the text above quoted, from an English translation, *The Philosophical Works of Descartes*, translated by Elizabeth S. Haldane and G.R.T. Ross, vol. I (Cambridge: At the University Press, 1969), p. 211. — I am indebted to James R. Alt of the Princeton University Library for directing my attention to the relevant passages in Descartes.

ture of plants, animals, and above all of man. . . ." Descartes selects "three principal sciences" among "all the other sciences" branching from the tree: "medicine, mechanics, and morals." The "highest and most perfect moral science" presupposes a complete knowledge of the other sciences and "is the last degree of wisdom."[44]

[44] Ibid.

CHAPTER 5

The Circle of Learning

Much misinformation about the history of encyclopaedias can be obtained from the literature on the subject. Some authors report the existence of encyclopaedias in ancient Greece; others suggest that the first encyclopaedia was produced in 1694, only a little more than half a century before the first volume of the great French *Encyclopédie* was published.[1] The first of these errors is probably due to a linguistic confusion: the ancient Greeks indeed used the word "encyclopaedia"; their reference, however, was not to any written works but rather to the curriculum for general education of the young. The second error is simply due to poor scholarship, a failure to "look it up": all of our contemporary encyclopaedias contain articles on the history of encyclopaedias.

Encyclopaedias

Encyclopaedias in the sense of reference works—dictionaries, lexica—did not exist in ancient Greece; they came later.[2] M. Terentius Varro (116-27 B.C.) is often credited with having published one of the earliest reference works, *Libri novem disciplinarum* (the books of the nine disciplines), covering the seven liberal arts (grammar, dialectics, rhetoric, geometry, arithmetic, astronomy, and music) and two practical arts, medicine and architecture. Pliny's *Natural History*, written in the first century A.D., may be regarded as an encyclopaedic reference work. Arranged in 2,493 chapters, it covered the organization of knowledge, cosmography, astronomy, meteorology, geography, anthropology (including the invention of arts), physiology, zoology, botany, medical uses of plants and animals, metals, minerals, stones and gems (including the fine arts). This work appeared in as many as 43 editions in the subsequent 1,500 years.

Early in the fifth century an African scholar, Martianus Capella, published in Latin verse and prose a sort of encyclopaedia, called

[1] See, for example, the chronological table in Stephen J. Gendzier, ed., *Denis Diderot's Encyclopedia: Selections* (New York: Harper & Row, 1967), pp. xxiii-xxvii.

[2] Detailed accounts of the major encyclopaedic reference works published over the centuries can be found in most of the encyclopaedias now on our shelves. See, for example, the article "Encyclopaedia" in *Encyclopaedia Britannica*, 11th ed. (1910), vol. 9, pp. 369-382, and 14th ed. (1967), vol. 8, pp. 363-377.

the *Satyricon*. This work is also known as *The Marriage of Philology and Mercury*, Mercury being the bridegroom, Philology the bride, and the seven bridal attendants the seven liberal arts: Grammar, Dialectic, Rhetoric, Geometry, Arithmetic, Astronomy, and Music.

The idea of publishing comprehensive reference works was not confined to the Mediterranean countries and the western world. A work of colossal dimensions was compiled in China in the seventeenth century; the British Museum possesses a copy—bound in 700 volumes.

The first reference works with the word "Encyclopaedia" in the title were published in 1608 and 1630 by Johann Heinrich Alsted, a German Protestant theologian. His system of classifying the disciplines will be discussed in more detail later in this chapter.

An encyclopaedic project that failed to come to fruition should be mentioned at this point in our chronological account: the project of Comenius (Jan Amos Komensky, 1592-1670), the famous educational reformer and language teacher. He planned to produce a triad of works, "Pansophia," "Panhistoria," and "Pandogmatica." He actually published in 1630 a volume the title of which included the word "Pansophia,"[3] but the plan of the triad was not carried out.

Several French dictionaries were started soon thereafter, including one by the French Academy, published in 1694, and one by Pierre Bayle,[4] published in 1697. They competed with one another, not only by extending their coverage but also by including critical comments on the rival products. The first alphabetical encyclopaedia written in English was by John Harris, published in 1704 under the title *Lexicon technicum or an Universal Dictionary of the Arts and the Sciences*.[5] Famous German lexica appeared in 1704, 1721, and 1732, the last of these—by Johann Heinrich Zedler—over a period of eighteen years in sixty-four volumes with a total of 64,309 pages (not counting four supplementary volumes).

An English work, published in 1728, introduced a system of cross-references. It was Ephraim Chambers' *Cyclopaedia or Universal Dic-*

---

[3] Johann Amos Comenius, *Pansophiae prodromus* (1630). It was an educator's plea to overcome religious and secular conflict through scientific research and the "universalization of knowledge."

[4] Pierre Bayle, *Dictionnaire historique et critique* (Rotterdam, 1697), 2 vols. This "dictionary" had no references to terms or subjects, but only to persons, in alphabetical order. Later editions were translated into English and German.

[5] John Harris, *Lexicon Technicum: or, an Universal English Dictionary of Arts and Sciences Explaining not only the Terms of Art but also the Arts themselves* (London: Dan. Brown and seven other publishers, vol. I, 1704, vol. II, 1710). — The title is mistakenly rendered as *Lexicon technologicum* in Gendzier's tabulation, *Diderot's Encyclopedia*, p. xxiii.

tionary of Arts and Sciences, containing an Explication of the Terms and an Account of the Things Signified thereby in the several Arts, Liberal and Mechanical, and the several Sciences, Human and Divine.[6] In the preface Chambers provided an "analysis of the divisions of knowledge," forty-seven in number, inspired by, but rather different from, Bacon's classification of learning. More about this later in this section.

After some scandalous intrigues concerning a planned French edition of Chambers' *Cyclopaedia*, which never materialized although the manuscripts had been completed, a great French project was launched. In November 1750 a prospectus in eleven pages was distributed by four publishing houses of Paris, announcing the publication, beginning in 1751, of an *Encyclopédie ou Dictionnaire Raisonné des Sciences, des Arts et des Métiers*, in eight volumes of text and two volumes of plates, under the editorship of Denis Diderot jointly with Jean le Rond d'Alembert.[7] The work was completed in 1772 on a scale much larger than promised: seventeen volumes of text and eleven volumes of plates. (Its system of ordering the universe of learning will be explained later.) A few years later, Charles Joseph Panckoucke started work on a new, enlarged edition, for which he secured a royal privilege in 1780. The first volume of his *Encyclopédie Méthodique ou par ordre de matière* appeared in 1782. After he devised a classification of knowledge for this work, Panckoucke became more ambitious and projected a set divided into forty-four parts and fifty-one dictionaries. When the work was completed in 1832, fifty years after the publication of the first volume, it had grown to 166 volumes.

In 1771, the *Encyclopaedia Britannica*, published in weekly installments beginning in 1768, was completed in its first edition in three volumes. The second edition, completed in 1784, was bound in ten volumes; the third edition, completed in 1797, in eighteen volumes. But instead of continuing with the story of the *Britannica*—which in 1974, with its fifteenth edition, had expanded to thirty volumes—I shall return to the task set for this chapter: to report on the taxonomic systems developed by the encyclopaedists who un-

[6] Ephraim Chambers' *Cyclopaedia* must not be confused with *Chambers's Encyclopedia*, published in 10 volumes, between 1859 and 1868, by Robert and William Chambers, publishers, not related to Ephraim Chambers. The first edition of their work was based on a translation of the 10th edition of Brockhaus, the well-known German *Conversations-Lexicon*.

[7] The prospectus acknowledges on the title page the English dictionaries by Chambers, Harris, and de Dyche. The four publishers are Briasson, David, Le Breton, and Durand. The year is stated as 1751 and the "approval and privilege of the King" are noted.

dertook to divide the "circle of learning" into its major and minor sectors.[8]

Alsted's Encyclopaedias

Johann Heinrich Alsted (1588-1638) was, as I have mentioned, the first to publish reference works with the word "encyclopaedia" in the title. One of these works, in Latin, was published in 1608 and 1620 (presumably in two editions).[9] The second, a monumental Latin work of 2,543 pages in small print, published in 1630, will be described here.[10]

The encyclopaedia, bound in two thick volumes, is divided into seven "tomes" subdivided into thirty-five "books." It begins with forty-eight synoptical tables and ends with an index of one hundred nineteen pages. Thus there is no difficulty in presenting Alsted's classification system. One has only to reproduce the titles of the tomes and books to obtain a clear picture of his scheme of arranging the universe of scientific and other intellectual knowledge.

Tome I, "The Preconceptions [praecognita] of the Disciplines," includes Book 1 on "Hexilogy,"[11] the theory of the modes of thinking (habitūs intellectuales); Book 2 on "Technology," relating, not to what is now meant by the term, but to the order of the disciplines;

[8] This brief survey of encyclopaedic undertakings has been confined to general reference works, thereby excluding reference works on specific disciplines or subject groups. In more recent times, specialized reference works have been produced and given the name "Encyclopaedia of . . . ," inconsistent with the meaning of a complete cycle of learning. If scholars and publishers, however, have with good conscience appropriated the name "circle" for what is at best a sector or segment of a circle, we have no choice but to record the fact. Readers may want to know that the shelves of the reference rooms of our libraries contain hundreds of reference works with "encyclopaedia" in the title. We counted 76 works entitled "Encyclopaedia of . . . ." in the catalogue of one university library. To give an idea of the scope of these "encyclopaedic" reference works, I present a selection of the specialties treated: Encyclopedia of Aberrations, E. of Anthropology, E. of the Arts, E. of Astrology, E. of Bible Creatures, E. of Education, E. of Fairies, E. of Information Systems and Services, E. of Islam, E. of Librarianship, E. of Literature, E. of Mystery and Detection, E. of Occultism & Parapsychology, E. of Philosophy, E. of Physics, E. of Psychology, E. of Religion, E. of the Social Sciences, E. of Social Work, E. of Superstitions, E. of Theology, E. of Wines and Spirits, E. of World History.

[9] Johann Heinrich Alsted, Cursus philosophici encyclopaedia (Herborn, 1620). — The earlier publication year, 1608, is given in the article "Encyclopaedia" in the 11th edition of the Encyclopaedia Britannica.

[10] Johann Heinrich Alsted, Encyclopaedia septem tomis distincta (Herborn, 1630).

[11] The Oxford English Dictionary has an entry "Hexiology," defined as "that branch of science which treats of the development of and behaviour of a living creature as affected by its environment." This is surely not what Alsted meant by hexilogia.

Book 3 on "Archelogy," the principles of the disciplines; and Book 4 on "Didactics," the teaching and learning of the disciplines.

Tome II, "Philology," contains Book 5 on *Lexica*, the art of word meanings, a combination of dictionaries for Hebrew, Syriac, Arabic, Greek, and Latin words and classified glossaries of terms in arts and sciences; Book 6 on "Grammar" for Hebrew, Aramaic, Greek, Latin, and German; Book 7 on "Rhetoric"; Book 8 on "Logic"; Book 9 on "Oratory"; and Book 10 on "Poetry."

Tome III, "Theoretical Philosophy" consists of ten books: Book 11 on "Metaphysics," defined as the science of *entis in genere*; Book 12 on "Pneumatics" or the nature of spirits or noncorporeal beings; Book 13 on "Physics"; Book 14 on "Arithmetic"; Book 15 on "Geometry"; Book 16 on "Cosmography"; Book 17 on "Uranometry," including both astronomy and astrology; Book 18 on "Geography" with maps of the Old World and of Palestine of the Old and New Testaments; Book 19 on "Optics"; and Book 20 on "Music."

Tome IV, "Practical Philosophy," contains Book 21 on "Ethics"; Book 22 on "Economics," administering the family household; Book 23 on "Politics," administering the state; and Book 24 on "Scholastica," school administration.

Tome V, "The Three Superior Faculties," is on the three university faculties teaching the learned professions: Book 25 on "Theology"; Book 26 on "Jurisprudence"; and Book 27 on "Medicine."

Tome VI, "Mechanical Arts," includes Book 28 on "General Mechanics (*Mechanologia Generalis*) and Miscellaneous Special Mechanics"; Book 29 on "Physical Mechanics," such as agriculture, gardening, animal husbandry, baking, vine-growing, brewing, pharmacology, and metallurgy; and Book 30 on "Mathematical Mechanics" for instruments and activities of all sorts, including printing, optical mechanics, sundials, watch-making, drawing, painting, musical instruments, automata, navigation, toys and games, hunting and fishing.

Tome VII, "A Medley of Disciplines" (*farragines disciplinarum*), contains Book 31 on "Mnemonics," the art of cultivating one's memory; Book 32 on "History"; Book 33 on "Chronology"; Book 34 on "Architecture"; and Book 35 on "Miscellaneous Arts" (*liber quodlibeticus*), dealing with diverse matters such as *apodemica, critica, paroemiographia, aenigmatographia*, covering such things as magic, cabbala, alchemy, magnetism, the art of explaining paradoxes, the art of conversing, the art of using tobacco (*tobacologia*), and so forth.

I used restraint in giving only the titles of the thirty-five books, and in suppressing the definitions or explanations that Alsted added for each of the disciplines. Readers conversant with Latin would have found his simple and concise formulations delightful. An interesting feature of the classification is that Alsted was quite discriminating in characterizing the various disciplines as arts, sciences, doctrines, disquisitions, and useful knowledge (*prudentia*). "Disquisitions" is my own term intended as a rough equivalent for what Alsted probably meant when he said in his Book 1 that it is designed to "teach" (*liber praecipit de habitibus intellectualibus*); the other three books of Tome I are also disquisitions. The disciplines described and discussed in the five books on Philology are called arts (*artes*), and so are Jurisprudence, Medicine, the Mechanical Arts, and also Mnemonics. The designation "science" (*scientia*) is given to the ten disciplines discussed in Tome III, from Metaphysics via Physics and Arithmetic to Music, and also to Chronology and Architecture. The term "doctrine" was used only for one discipline, namely, Theology. (We may recall that "doctrine" was the designation that Francis Bacon was wont to use for the majority of disciplines.) Finally, the designation "prudence," or "useful knowledge," as I have chosen to translate *prudentia*, was used by Alsted for the four disciplines of Practical Philosophy, that is, Ethics, Home Economics, Politics, and School Administration. This sort of semantic discrimination makes good sense to me, but its adoption would probably give rise to much disagreement among philosophers and scientists of different persuasions, resulting in long arguments of little or no pragmatic value. (See Bentham, below, regarding the traditional distinction between arts and sciences.)

In appraising Alsted's encyclopaedia one should bear in mind that Alsted and Francis Bacon were contemporaries, and that Bacon's *Advancement of Learning* was published in 1605 and 1623 and Alsted's two encyclopaedias in 1608 and 1630. Without trying to suggest a comparative evaluation of their systems, I merely wonder about the difference in their influence upon later generations. Alsted's name is now hardly known, even among historians of science and philosophy.

Leibniz's Projects

After the detailed report in the previous chapter on the stems, branches, boughs, and twigs of learning exhibited in Bacon's taxonomic scheme, it may seem surprising that a relatively brief sketch should suffice to describe the encyclopaedic ambitions of Gottfried Wilhelm Leibniz (1646-1716). The simple explanation is that this great philomath and polyhistor never carried out his plans. Over more than fifty years of his life he entertained and cultivated the idea of producing an encyclopaedia that would be "the public treasury of learning but also a logical and didactic system of the sciences."[12]

Leibniz advanced his projects in the years between 1664 and his death in 1716 in a large number of finished and unfinished papers and in letters to friends, fellow scientists, and sovereigns. Often in rather general terms, but sometimes with detailed outlines, his proposals visualized the formation of a large team of the most eminent scientists (savants) of his day, each writing about his own field of specialization; occasionally, however, Leibniz would design a more modest project, which he might carry out as the sole author.[13] The various outlines he drafted over the years showed changes in emphasis that reflected the progress of his own learning from an early preoccupation with juridical and other moral sciences to a more prominent treatment of the mathematical and natural philosophies and, still later, to the primacy accorded to the development of a discipline of "General Science" that would yield methods of deriving the fundamental propositions of each of the various sciences.[14]

One of Leibniz's earlier plans (1671) was to correct and amplify the encyclopaedia produced by Johann Heinrich Alsted.[15] One of his later projects (1714) was to organize the preparation of a triple-set encyclopaedia: the large set would be a "Universal Atlas," containing practically everything that is of importance in every field of learning; the middle set would contain what one usually expects to find in an encyclopaedia, but it would be thoroughly systematic, demonstrative, and analytic, and it would include a synoptic table showing the order of, and interconnections among, the different sciences; the small set would be a sort of handbook confined to the essentials in all fields. In the preparation the authors should begin with the middle set; they would elaborate its contents to expand it to the large set,

---

[12] The quotations in this section are taken from a large variety of Leibniz's papers, fragments, and letters written between 1664 and 1716 and collected by Carl Immanuel Gerhardt, ed., Leibnizens mathematische Schriften (vols. 1 and 2, Berlin: A. Asher & Co.; vols. 3-7, Halle: H. W. Schmidt; 1849-1863), Onno Klopp, ed., Die Werke von Leibniz: Historisch-politische und staatswissenschaftliche Schriften (Hannover: Klindworth, 11 vols., 1864-1888), and others, as quoted in French or Latin by Louis Couturat, La Logique de Leibniz (Paris: Félix Alcan, 1901). The English renditions are mine. The quotation in the text above is taken from Couturat, p. 124.

[13] Couturat, Logique, p. 162.

[14] Ibid., pp. 162-163.

[15] Leibniz had the highest praise for Alsted's encyclopaedia, but he held that "the most necessary requirement for an encyclopaedia is to demonstrate accurately the elements of a true philosophy." (My translation.) Gothofredi Guillelmi Leibnitii Opera Omnia, edited by Louis Dutens (Geneva: de Tournes Brothers, 1768), vol. 5, p. 183.

and condense the contents to prepare the small one.[16] The idea of a triple-set encyclopaedia remained on the shelf for 260 years; it was carried out—without acknowledgement to Leibniz—when *Britannica 3* came out in 1974 as a *Macropaedia*, a *Micropaedia*, and a *Propaedia*.

It may be of sufficient interest to show here one of the several outlines drafted by Leibniz for a "theoretical" encyclopaedia (which was to be accompanied by a "practical" one). It was to be organized in sixteen parts: I. Rational Grammar; II. Logic; III. Mnemonics (the art of aiding the memory); IV. Topics (the art of inventing); V. Combinatorics; VI. Logistics (universal mathematics or the logic of quantities); VII. Arithmetic; VIII. Geometry; IX. Mechanics; X. Poeography (the science of the physical qualities of substance); XI. Homoeography (the science of classifying substances in diverse species); XII. Cosmography (which includes astronomy, physical geography, and meteorology); XIII. Idography (the science of organic bodies, the species of animals and plants); XIV. Moral Science (corresponding to psychology in the present sense, though not in the sense used by Leibniz himself, which was the rationalist and metaphysical science of the soul and of the spirit);[17] XV. Geopolitics (which includes human geography and history); and XVI. Natural Theology (the science of noncorporeal substances). This outline, in contrast to earlier ones, which had given more conspicuous places to metaphysics, jurisprudence, and politics, allocates eight classes, one half of the whole, to mathematics and physics.[18]

Most of Leibniz's projects had two ideas in common: (1) that, thanks to close collaboration of all competent savants in the joint undertaking, controversies among different schools of thought would be resolved, and (2) that, thanks to the development of a "rigorous and infallible method" of the "General Science" as a "perennial philosophy," the progress of the sciences could be speeded up.[19]

Leibniz's encyclopaedia never materialized. He attributed the fail-

---

[16] Couturat, *Logique*, p. 174.

[17] Leibniz was among the earliest to use the word *psychologia* [psychology], which, according to historians of science, had been introduced by Rudolf Goclenius in 1590. Aristotle had written *peri psychē* ("about the soul" or, in Latin, *de anima*). The name "psychology" for the old discipline attained wide currency only with the publication of two volumes by Christian Wolff, in Latin, on Empirical Psychology (1732) and Rational Psychology (1734). See Robert J. Richards, "Christian Wolff's Prolegomena to Empirical and Rational Psychology: Translation and Commentary," *Proceedings of the American Philosophical Society*, vol. 124, no. 3 (June 1980), p. 227.

[18] Couturat, *Logique*, pp. 128-129.

[19] Ibid., p. 150.

ure to the lack of support from the princes and sovereigns he had approached, the resistance by the various academies of science to whom he had appealed, the unwillingness of fellow scientists to collaborate in the great task, the scarcity of young, devoted people capable of assisting him in his work, and the many demands on his own time by historical and political research assignments that distracted him from the more important work on the encyclopaedia.[20]

Chambers' Bifurcations

In the preface to his *Cyclopaedia*, Ephraim Chambers (1680-1740) offered a "division of knowledge" in tabular form, covering only half a page.[21] Such conciseness would have been impossible had he attempted to reproduce Bacon's classification of the whole universe of learning or even only Bacon's tree of rational knowledge. Besides brevity, an allegiance to the principle of bifurcation characterizes Chambers' procedure. Every category of knowledge divides into two subcategories, most of which divide again into two subgroups; only in the ultimate, not further divisible subgroups—often denoted as the *Infimae species*—does Chambers list more than two fields as belonging to any semifinal group.

In Chambers' scheme, "knowledge" is either "natural and scientific" or "artificial and technical." The former is either "sensory" (like history) or "rational" (like physics, metaphysics, pure mathematics, ethics, theology). "Artificial and technical knowledge" is either "internal" (like logic) or "external," which in turn is either "real" (like "mixed mathematics" or "symbolical" (like grammar, rhetoric, poetry). Altogether, forty-seven fields of scientific or technical knowledge are included in the scheme. Among the reasons for our interest in Chambers' classification scheme is the realization that the French encyclopaedists were well acquainted with it—they mentioned Chambers' work on the title page of their *Encyclopédie*—but nevertheless retained or adopted much of the less helpful features of the old Baconian system.

Diderot's and d'Alembert's Systematic Table

In the first sentence of his article "Encyclopédie," published in the French *Encyclopédie*, Diderot (1713-1784) explained that the word "*encyclopédie*" "means the interconnection of all knowledge;

---

[20] Ibid., p. 175.

[21] Ephraim Chambers, *Cyclopaedia or Universal Dictionary of Arts and Sciences* (London: J. & J. Knapton, 1728), p. iii.

it is made up of the Greek preposition *en*, meaning in, and the nouns *kyklos*, circle, and *paideia*, knowledge."[22]

Although the reference to the circle need not rule out an interpretation as simply a bounded area into which all bits and pieces of learning, general or particular, can be thrown without system or order, the intended meaning of the metaphor was surely different. The circle was meant to suggest a well-ordered universe of learning; and such an order presupposed a reasonable system of classification of the subjects of knowledge.

Bacon's taxonomic scheme was 145 years old when Diderot announced the plans for the French *Encyclopédie*. Diderot stuck to Bacon's scheme and replicated it in a streamlined form in the *Prospectus* of 1750. D'Alembert (1717-1783) reproduced the tabulation (with slight changes) and discussed its main entries in his "Preliminary Discourse" in the first volume of the *Encyclopédie* in 1751. "As an encyclopaedia," wrote d'Alembert for the editors of the work, "it must present the order and interconnections of human knowledge; as a systematic dictionary of the sciences, arts, and crafts, it must contain for each science and each art, liberal or mechanical, its general principles . . . and also the most essential details that constitute its body and substance."[23] It is most helpful to have, both in Diderot's *Prospectus* and in d'Alembert's "Discourse," the schematic representation of the classification—"Système Figuré des Connoissances Humaines"—to guide the reader through the ramifications.[24]

Exactly as in Bacon's treatise, the three principal human faculties, Memory, Imagination, and Reason, are taken as the basis for the

[22] Denis Diderot, "Encyclopédie," in *Encyclopédie, etc.* (Paris: Briasson and three other publishers, vol. V, 1755), p. 685. — I translated the French *enchaînement* as "interconnection," and *connoissance* as "knowledge"; the Greek *paideia*, however, is derived from *païs*, "child," and thus refers to the education of the young; hence, it would be better rendered as "learning," rather than "knowledge."

[23] "Discours Préliminaire des Editeurs," *Encyclopédie*, vol. I, p. i. — The discourse covers 45 pages in folio.

[24] Because the table was contained first in Diderot's *Prospectus* and a year later in d'Alembert's "Discourse," it seems arbitrary to attribute it to one or the other of the joint authors. Yet, Cournot refers to it as d'Alembert's synopsis, without citing any evidence in support of the attribution. Antoine-Augustin Cournot, *Essai sur les fondements de nos connaissances et sur les caractères de la critique philosophique* (Paris: L. Hachette, 1851), p. 258. It is known, however, that d'Alembert had presented the synoptic table in a speech to the French Academy. Jeremy Bentham likewise attributed the "encyclopedical table" to d'Alembert. See the title page and Section VII of his "Essay on Nomenclature and Classification," *Chrestomathia*, Part II. It seems plausible to assume that d'Alembert was responsible for mathematics and the natural sciences, Diderot for art and literature.

classification system of the French encyclopaedists. Thus History, Poetry, and Philosophy are the three categories of human understanding, or learning.

History, according to Diderot, "consists of facts" concerning god, man, and nature, and therefore is Sacred History, Civil History, and Natural History. Sacred History may be Ecclesiastic History or the History of the Prophets. Civil History may be civil proper (presumably political and social) or Literary History. Natural History may treat of the Uniformities in nature, the Deviations (observed) in nature, and the Uses made of nature.

Philosophy, or its "synonym," Science, is (in an analogous tripartition) Science of God, Science of Man, and Science of Nature. Emulating Bacon's distinctions, Diderot and d'Alembert divide the Science of God into Natural Theology, Revealed Theology, and the Science of Good and Evil Spirits (angels and demons).[25] The Science of Man has two parts: Logic, stemming from the capacity of Comprehension (entendement) and directed towards truth; and Ethics (morale), related to the Will and directed towards virtue. Again following Bacon, the encyclopaedists divide Logic into the Arts of Thinking, Retaining the Thoughts, and Communicating Thoughts. Each of these is subdivided: the Art of Thinking, into Apprehending (perception), Judgment (propositions), Reasoning and Method (induction and demonstration); the Art of Retaining, into the Science of the Memory itself and the Science of the Aids to Memory; and the Art of Communication, into the Science of the Instruments of Discourse (grammar), the Science of the Quality of Discourse (rhetoric), and the Mechanics of Poetry (versification). Ethics is divided into General Ethics, dealing with the reality of good and evil, the necessity of fulfilling one's duties, and the necessity of being good, just, and virtuous, and into Particular Ethics, which can be Natural Jurisprudence (concerned with the duties of man segregated, especially his duty of self-conservation), Economy (the science of the duties of man in the family), and Politics (the science of his duties in society).

Natural Science—the third part of Philosophy—has three divisions: Physics (or natural philosophy), Mathematics, and General Metaphysics. Physics has three subdivisions: General Physics, Par-

---

[25] In the tabulation the term "pneumatology" appears, denoting the science of good and evil spirits. Further down one finds, among the fields of "mixed mathematics," the science of pneumatics, a branch of physics, dealing with the mechanical properties (such as density, elasticity, pressure) of air and other gases or fluids. But let the reader be warned that Bentham (see below) uses both these terms as synonyms for the science of the spirit or soul, that is, psychology.

ticular Physics (physical astronomy, meteorology, cosmology, botany, mineralogy, zoology), and Chemistry (chemistry proper, metallurgy, alchemy, and natural magic). Mathematics is likewise divided into three subject areas: Pure Mathematics (arithmetic, numerical or algebraic, elementary as well as infinitesimal; and geometry, elementary or transcendent), Mixed Mathematics (mechanics, static as well as dynamic, geometric astronomy, optics, acoustics, pneumatics, and probability [the analysis of chance]), and Physical Mathematics. General Metaphysics (or Ontology) has two major subdivisions: the Metaphysics of Bodies and the General Physics of extension, impenetrability, movement, the void, and so forth.[26]

Poetry, in Diderot's and d'Alembert's system, as in Bacon's, is of three kinds—narrative, dramatic, and parabolic—and has always the character of fiction: narrative of an imaginary past, dramatic of an imaginary present, and parabolic of things abstract and intellectual. The word "poetry" is meant to include all fine arts—the works of the musicians, painters, sculptors, and engravers no less than those of the writers of tragedies, comedies, operas, pastorals, and poems of all sorts. In any case, in both Diderot's and d'Alembert's expositions, the fine arts constitute, along with history and philosophy (the sciences), one of the three categories of human knowledge. Perhaps it should be made clear that the French encyclopaedists have acknowledged that, in this respect as in most others, they have "imitated" the scheme "so carefully presented by Chancellor Bacon."[27]

The synopsis by the encyclopaedists was criticized by Cournot, first for accepting the Baconian scheme after a century and a half of progress in scientific research had made it obsolete in many respects, and second, for several classificatory details that seemed unreasonable. In particular, Cournot chided d'Alembert for listing botany four

[26] A reader who compares this description with the schematic table of Diderot's *Prospectus* will notice a reversal in the order. The table shows General Metaphysics first, Mathematics second, and Physics third. Diderot's discussion, however, proceeds along the route taken in the text above. The encyclopaedic table has sometimes been reproduced with mistranslations or misplacements of entries and captions. For example, Gendzier, ed., *Diderot's Encyclopedia*, pp. 42-43, presents the table showing General Metaphysics at the top, together with the Knowledge of God, instead of with Natural Philosophy, a part of the Knowledge of Nature. That Gendzier consistently translates *science* as "knowledge" whenever it did not refer to natural science is another concession to linguistic parochialism.

[27] Despite such acknowledgments, Diderot appended to the reproduction of his "prospectus" in the first volume of the *Encyclopédie* (immediately following d'Alembert's "Discours") some "Observations on the Division of the Sciences of Chancellor Bacon," in which he pointed out in detail the differences between the two schemes.

places away from zoology, with physical astronomy, meteorology, and cosmology in between; for having the mathematical theory of chance follow acoustics and pneumatics;[28] and for placing natural history in a category entirely different from the natural sciences, physical and biological.[29]

[28] On the meaning of pneumatics see above, note 25.

[29] Antoine-Augustin Cournot, *Essai sur les fondements de nos connaissances et sur les caractères de la critique philosophique* (Paris: L. Hachette, 1851) vol. 2, p. 260.

CHAPTER 6

THE MAPPING OF THE SCIENCES

STEPPING OUT from the enchanted circle of learning, after our somewhat disenchanting exploration of its central and some of its peripheral curios, we proceed to a survey of the pertinent literature of the nineteenth century. The works of eight philosophers of science, engaged in mapping the sciences in what they thought to be the best of all possible orders, will be reviewed. A few words, however, should first be said about a philosopher who, although he offered no enumerative or taxonomic system, must not be entirely left out of this survey: I refer to Kant.

Kant's Architectonics

Immanuel Kant (1724-1804) has had a pervasive influence on classifiers of science, chiefly through his work on epistemology and methodology. He himself was a classifier only in the sense that he made fundamental distinctions in the analysis of knowledge.

Kant's analyses of the distinctions between analytic and synthetic, phenomena and noumena, intuition and perception, theoretical and practical, immanent and transcendent, empirical and transcendental, and many other contraries and contradictories laid the groundwork for the reflections of generations of classifiers and taxonomists of the branches of learning. His pronouncements on the architectonics of pure reason—architectonics as "the art of systems," as the method of forming "common cognition into science," of obtaining systematic "unity of diverse cognitions under an idea"—became guiding principles for most philosophers of science.[1]

Hegel's Dialectic Triads

The contribution of Georg Wilhelm Friedrich Hegel (1770-1831) to the classification of sciences was more direct than that of Kant, but whether it was fruitful has remained an open question. In 1817 he published a book titled (in literal translation from the German)

---

[1] Immanuel Kant, *Critick of Pure Reason*, translated by Francis Haywood (London: William Pickering, 1848), p. 574.

"Encyclopaedia of the Philosophical Sciences in Outline."[2] In this book he presented a system characterized by consecutive tripartitions. Everything is subject to triadic ordering, dictated by the formula, originally proposed by Fichte, of thesis-antithesis-synthesis; everything follows the perpetual law of thought commanding the dialectic rhythm of preliminary affirmation—negation (contradiction)—reunification. Thus Hegel's total system is divided into three parts, and every part is again divided into three, ad infinitum. According to Hegel, the three branches of Philosophy are Logic, Nature, and Mind.[3]

Logic is treated under the three heads of Being, Essence, and Notion. Under the third head (which is partly what most other philosophers understand by Logic), Hegel considers (1) the subjective forms of conception, judgment, and syllogism; (2) their realization in objects as mechanically, chemically, or teleologically constituted; and (3) the ideas of life, science, and the interpenetration of thought and objectivity.

Philosophy of Nature is divided into Mechanics, Physics, and Organics. The latter consists of Geology, Botany, and Animal Physiology—the three kingdoms of nature.

The Philosophy of Mind deals with the "subjective" mind, the "objective" mind, and the "absolute" mind. The first of these divisions is subdivided into Anthropology, Phenomenology (Consciousness, Self-Consciousness, and Reason), and Psychology in the narrower sense. The second division is subdivided into Philosophy of Law, Moral Philosophy, and Political Philosophy. The third is subdivided into Philosophy of Art, Philosophy of Religion, and History of Philosophy (Philosophical Theory).

Hegel's system has been praised as the greatest advance in the classification of philosophic and encyclopaedic thought; but it has also been condemned as an ideological swamp.[4]

---

[2] Georg Wilhelm Friedrich Hegel, Encyklopädie der philosophischen Wissenschaften im Grundrisse (Heidelberg: A. Oswald, 1817; 3rd rev. ed., C. F. Winter, 1830); English translation, Encyclopedia of Philosophy, translated and annotated by Gustav Emil Mueller (New York: Philosophical Library, 1959).

[3] The German word Geist has sometimes been rendered in English as "Spirit," which makes Hegel's philosophizing sound almost mystical. See, for example, Robert Flint, Philosophy as Scientia Scientiarum and A History of Classifications of the Sciences (New York: Scribner's, 1904), pp. 155-156.

[4] An example of praise may be quoted: "this glory . . . cannot fairly be denied to it [Hegel's Encyclopaedia], that there, for the first time, appeared a system of such a character and scope, so vast in its range of conception, so rich in suggestion and doctrine, and so skilfully constructed, as to present to the mind something like what a Science of the Sciences ought to be." Ibid., p. 157.

Bentham's Neologisms

Two features characterize the classification scheme presented by Jeremy Bentham (1748-1832). The first is his insistence that all proposed divisions of disciplines are at the same time divisions of arts and of sciences—art relating to practice and performance, science relating to the underlying knowledge needed for attainment.[5] He regarded it as nonsensical to call some of the branches "art" and others "science," because each is both art *and* science.

The second feature characterizing Bentham's classification scheme is his propensity to coin new words. He is probably the most prolific neologist in philosophy, and his linguistic creativity is beyond all bounds in his "Essay on Nomenclature and Classification."[6] As a crusader against ambiguous words—and, alas, few words have escaped promiscuity in usage—he found it impossible to impose logical orderliness on the classification of the learned disciplines by using their usual designations. Hence he invented dozens of new words, derived from Greek roots, to denote the branches of learning. Unfortunately, or perhaps fortunately, his terminological innovations have not been accepted.

A sample of Bentham's classification will suffice to give the reader a taste of the proposed nomenclature. Bentham distinguishes Coenoscopic and Idioscopic Ontology.[7] He divides the latter into Somatology and Pneumatology,[8] which may be either Alegopathematic or Pathematoscopic, later renamed Nooscopic and Pathoscopic Pneu-

[5] "As between *art* and *science*, in the whole field of *thought* and *action*, no one spot will be found belonging to either to the exclusion of the other. In whatever spot a portion of either is found a portion of the other may be seen likewise." Jeremy Bentham, *Chrestomathia* (London: Payne and Foss, 1816), p. 9. — Chrestomatic means conducive to useful learning.

[6] Jeremy Bentham, "Essay on Nomenclature and Classification," in *Chrestomathia*, pt. II (London: Payne and Foss, 1817). The full title of the work reads as follows: *Chrestomathia; Part II. Containing Appendix No. V. Being an Essay on Nomenclature and Classification: Including a Critical Examination of the Encyclopedical Table of Lord Bacon, as Improved by d'Alembert; and the First Lines of A New One, Grounded on the Application of the Logical Principle of Exhaustively Bifurcate Analysis to the Moral Principle of General Utility.*

[7] Coenoscopic Ontology is "that part of the science [of being] which takes for its subject those properties which are considered as possessed in common by all the individuals belonging to the class which the name ontology is employed to designate: i.e., by all beings" (p. 177). Idioscopic Ontology is "that branch of art and science which takes for its subject such properties as are considered as peculiar to different classes of beings . . ." (p. 179).

[8] Somatology treats of "body, matter, or corporeal substance" (p. 179). Pneumatology treats of the "spirit, i.e., *incorporeal substance*, in the sense in which it is used as synonymous to *mind*" (p. 180). Bentham reminds us that the linguistic kin and synonym, "Pneumatics," has been used also as the science of "the gaseous state" (p. 180). See also above, Chapter 5, note 25.

matology, respectively.[9] The latter is divided into Aplopathematic (or, alternatively, Aplopathoscopic) and Thelematoscopic Pneumatology.[10] Bentham tells the reader that Thelematoscopic Pneumatology is equivalent to Ethics—at last a word in the customary vocabulary, and perhaps a good point to stop this truncated exhibit of Bentham's "Encyclopedic Table."

Bentham does not really classify existing branches of learning into a taxonomic system, but he invents branches that *ought* to exist if the universe of learning were redesigned and ordered in a logically optimal system. The major principle of a strictly logical system of division is "exhaustive bifurcation," and Bentham applies this principle rigorously in the construction of his "encyclopedical tree."

Ampère's Columns

André Marie Ampère (1775-1836), best known for his work in electricity and magnetism, wrote an *Essai sur la philosophie des sciences, ou Exposition analytique d'une classification naturelle de toutes les connaissances humaines.*[11] He attempted to stay within the domain of learning that existed at his time but tried to arrange its contents into five columns with the captions "branches," "sub-branches," "sciences of the first order," "sciences of the second order," and "sciences of the third order." His scheme was displayed in a simplified form by Cournot in his *Essai sur les fondements de nos connaissances*[12] but will be presented here with an even greater simplification by concentrating on the main divisions and some of the better-known disciplines, no matter whether they are, for Ampère, sciences of the first, second, or third order.

The sciences are grouped into two domains: the Cosmological Sciences and the Noological Sciences.[13] Each is divided into four main

[9] Alegopathematic means "unnoticed" sensation or feeling; Nooscopic means "regarding intelligence." Pathematoscopic and Pathoscopic Pneumatology stand for "Psychological Pathology" (pp. 195-198; also Table V).

[10] Aplopathoscopic means "regarding mere sensations"; Telomatoscopic means "regarding volition." Bentham, p. 197. — Strangely enough, in Bentham's text as well as in a footnote the word "telomatoscopic" is misspelled "thelomatoscopic."

[11] (Paris: Bachelier, 1834).

[12] Antoine-Augustin Cournot, *Essai sur les fondements de nos connaissances et sur les caractères de la critique philosophique* (Paris: L. Hachette, 1851), vol. 2, pp. 261-265.

[13] There are at least two ways to interpret this division: The realm of phenomena (or bodies) versus the realm of the mind (or forms); or, in the language of Alfred North Whitehead, the domain of sense objects versus the domain of thought objects. Ampère retained an inconsistency of long standing when he placed mathematics in the first domain; traditionally it had been, and still is, so closely linked with physics, particularly with mechanics, that it takes a really open-minded thinker to assign mathematics, with logic, to the domain of the mind.

branches. The Cosmological Sciences comprise I. the Mathematical Sciences (with arithmology, geometry, mechanics, uranology); II. the Physical Sciences (with physics, chemistry, technology, geology, mineralogy, oryctotechnics (that is, the technology of extractive industries); III. the Natural Sciences [read: the Biological Sciences] (with botany, agriculture, zoology, zootechnics [probably including animal husbandry]); and IV. the Medical Sciences (with pharmaceutics, hygienics, nosology [description of diseases], therapeutics, practical medicine, diagnostics).

The Noological Sciences comprise V. the Philosophical Sciences (with psychology, logic, metaphysics, ontology, natural theology, ethics); VI. the Dialectical Sciences (with glossology, literature, bibliography, literary criticism, technesthetics, pedagogy); VII. the Ethnological Sciences (with ethnology, archaeology, history, chronology, philosophy of history, hierology, symbolics, disputation[14]); and VIII. the Political Sciences (with nomology, legislation, jurisprudence, military art, social economy, statistics, theory of wealth, politics, international law, diplomacy).

It is not surprising that Ampère's classification, proposed in 1834, looks far more familiar to us than most of the earlier schemes. Ampère definitely liberated the classification system from the triadic division of learning based upon its supposed sources in memory, imagination, and reason; and he insisted on the separation of the biological sciences from the physical sciences (though assigning the term "natural" sciences to the former) and arranged for a wider separation of metaphysics from physics and other natural sciences by placing it with the philosophical sciences. That Ampère still had psychology, along with logic and ethics, among the philosophical sciences is no anachronism; the emancipation of psychology as a theoretical as well as experimental discipline (natural or social science, depending on the particular emphasis) came much later.

The choice of the compound expression "philosophical sciences" should be mentioned as a signpost in the semantic transition from the usage of "philosophy" and "science" as synonyms to a differentiation in their meanings, allowing one of the words to modify the other. If some sciences can be singled out as philosophical, other sciences are evidently regarded as nonphilosophical.

The distinctions, under the heading of "Political Sciences," between social economy and theory of wealth, on the one hand, and between social economy and politics, on the other, have historical

[14] Ampère's term "controverse" was rendered in English as "disputation" in the translation of Cournot's work An Essay on the Foundations of Our Knowledge by Merritt H. Moore (New York: Liberal Arts Press, 1956), p. 495.

explanations. John Stuart Mill had distinguished between social economy and political economy, and Jeremy Bentham had proposed to specify the deductive part of economics as chrematology, or theory of wealth.

The complete table of classification of sciences by Ampère, with its differentiation between sciences of the first, second, and third order, would elicit several more critical or explanatory comments. Having suppressed these exercises in hairsplitting, I can spare the reader (if I have not yet lost all potential readers) further commentaries on Ampère's fourth and fifth columns.[15]

Comte's Positive Philosophy

Auguste Comte (1798-1857) regarded all previous attempts to classify the branches of learning as failures. Although he accused some of the earlier classifiers of lacking adequate knowledge of the sciences they undertook to distinguish, he remarked that their efforts could not possibly have succeeded, because "our principal scientific conceptions" had not sufficiently "matured" from the most primitive, the "theological stage," via "the metaphysical stage" to the final, the "positive stage." In this last stage, reasoning and observation are duly combined in the study of the "laws of phenomena," that is, of "their invariable relations of succession and resemblance." Comte assumed that at the time of his writing most sciences had reached or approached the positive stage, so that he might succeed in the endeavor in which his predecessors had failed.

He presented his system in a work of six volumes, *Cours de philosophie positive*, published between 1830 and 1842 and stretching over almost 4,800 pages.[16] Harriet Martineau, British classical economist, was brave enough to produce a free English translation and

[15] One historian of science who kindly read the manuscript of this chapter chided me for the attention accorded to Ampère, whom he regards as a crank whose philosophical attempts should not be taken seriously.

[16] Auguste Comte, *Cours de Philosophie Positive*, vol. I (Brussels: Rouen, 1830); vols. II-VI (Paris: Bachelier, 1835-1842). Much confusion in research involving this work has been caused by the *Societé Positiviste* in Paris by publishing in 1893 a 5th edition with the notation on the title page that it was identical with the 1st edition, without warning, however, that the reproduction was with a different type-face and completely different pagination. For example, the first appearance of the word "sociologie" and an explanatory footnote by Comte is in Volume IV of the 5th edition on pages 200-201, whereas in the original edition the word and the footnote were on page 252. Many hours of search have been wasted owing to the failure of a simple warning concerning the changes in the page numbers. Incidentally, later reproductions—for example, a *réimpression anastaltique* (1968-1969)—are even more deceptive, because one thinks that the original edition of Comte's work has been so reproduced.

drastic condensation of *The Positive Philosophy*.[17] She cut the work from six volumes to two, from 4,779 pages to 864. The abridged version was so much more popular than its portly parent that it was retranslated into French and became a preferred substitute for Comte's original.[18]

For Comte—in sharp contrast to Bentham—the most general division of human activities is between "speculation and action," and consequently the most fundamental distinction of knowledge is between theoretical and practical.[19] It is only the former that Comte undertakes to examine and to classify. He divides theoretical knowledge into abstract science and concrete science; abstract (or general) science attempts to discover the general laws that regulate phenomena in all conceivable cases; concrete (particular or descriptive) science deals with the application of general laws "to the actual history of various existing entities [êtres]."[20] But even the abstract sciences employ two methods: the "historical" and the "dogmatic" approach.[21] As a science progresses, the historical approach becomes increasingly unsuitable, and the dogmatic approach becomes increasingly necessary, because new conceptions permit the presentation of earlier discoveries from a "more direct point of view."[22]

Comte finds that "the only really rational classification" distinguishes six fundamental sciences, though he speaks of 720 "possible classifications."[23] He proposes to order his six classes according to the degree of simplicity and generality, beginning with the most general and ending with the one that studies the most particular and complex phenomena.[24] The phenomena regarding "organized bodies"—human and social phenomena—are the most complex ones. (Miss Martineau translated "corps organisés" as "organic bodies,"

---

[17] *The Positive Philosophy of Auguste Comte*, freely translated and condensed by Harriet Martineau (London: Kegan Paul, Trench, Trübner & Co., 1853; 3rd ed., 1893).

[18] Auguste Comte, *La Philosophie d'Auguste Comte*, condensée par Miss Harriet Martineau. Traduction française de M. Charles Avezac-Lavigne (Bordeaux: Feret & Fils; and Paris: Dunod, 1871). There are also later abridged editions. See, for example, *La Philosophie Positive par Auguste Comte*, resumé par Jules Rig (Paris: J.-B. Baillière et Fils, 1880).

[19] In the original edition, vol. I, p. 61; in the reprint editions of 1893 and 1968, p. 50; in the Martineau translation, p. 16. All further page references will be given in the text, the first number referring to the original French edition, the second to the reprinted 5th edition, and the third to the English (Martineau) edition. — A special "brava" to Jessica Kennedy, who found the cited passages in all different editions.

[20] Comte, vol. I, p. 71; p. 58; p. 18.

[21] Ibid., p. 77; p. 63; p. 18.

[22] Ibid., p. 78; p. 64; p. 19.

[23] Ibid., p. 85; p. 70; p. 20.

[24] Ibid., p. 88; p. 72; p. 21.

which may convey Comte's ideas regarding physiology but probably not those regarding social phenomena. If he had meant organic, he could have written *organiques*.) Incidentally, when Comte puts mathematics at the top of his classification, he concedes that it does not quite fit his formulations regarding "phenomena" (even though "concrete mathematics" has traditionally been considered a "part of natural philosophy"), but it does fit his formula stressing "generality."

The six fundamental sciences in Comte's system of positive philosophy are I. Mathematics, II. Astronomy, III. Physics, IV. Chemistry, V. Physiology (or Biology), and VI. Social Science (or "Social Physics"). The titles of his six volumes reflect this division of the sciences (or "philosophies"), although Comte treats the first five sciences, or philosophies, in the first three volumes and devotes the remaining three volumes to social philosophy.[25]

The subdivisions of the six fundamental sciences are so much closer to the designations of our time that we no longer find them quaint. That Comte speaks of "concrete mathematics" where we say "applied mathematics" does not rate much emphasis. Comte's treatment of astronomy and physics may be dated, but most of the terms are familiar to us. Perhaps the designation "barology," the science of weight, is an exception.[26] This term was coined only in the middle of the nineteenth century and did not stay long in the physics texts. Its further subdivision, however, into statics and dynamics, both applied to solids, liquids, and gases, is neither archaic nor avant-garde. Of the other four parts of physics enumerated by Comte, namely, thermology, acoustics, optics, and electrology, the first and the last appellations, though perfectly clear, have been superseded by newer ones.[27] Needless to say, Comte did not foresee the development of modern physics, which could not be fitted into the partitions he enumerated. This statement applies with equal force to Comte's sub-

---

[25] Volume I: *Les préliminaires généraux et la philosophie mathématique* (746 pp.). Volume II: *La philosophie astronomique et la philosophie physique* (724 pp.). Volume III: *La philosophie chimique et la philosophie biologique* (845 pp.). Volume IV: *La partie dogmatique de la philosophie sociale* (747 pp.). Volume V: *La partie historique de la philosophie sociale, en tout ce qui concerne l'état théologique et l'état métaphysique* (775 pp.). Volume VI: *Le complément de la partie historique de la philosophie sociale, et les conclusions générales* (942 pp.).

[26] Comte, vol. II, p. 465; p. 361; Martineau, vol. I, p. 192.

[27] The word "thermology" was in fact coined by Comte (1835). The *Oxford English Dictionary*—only in its complete edition, not in the "Universal" or any abridged editions—informs us that William Whewell changed the word to "thermotics." John Stuart Mill, in his *Logics* (1846) went back to "thermology." This term was still used by Herbert Spencer (1858).

divisions of chemistry, but the words he used in his discourse on chemical philosophy have, by and large, not lost currency.

Comte realized that biology was underdeveloped relative to the "inorganic" sciences. He explained this by pointing to the greater complexity of the "organic sciences." No one can reasonably reproach Comte for not foreseeing the revolutions that were to come in this field during the next 125 years. He was bold enough to propose a new subdivision, "bionomy," which was to denote "dynamical biology." The three divisions he proposed for biology were "biotomy, biotaxy, and pure bionomy, or physiology proper."[28] Comte used "anatomic philosophy" as an alternative designation for biotomy,[29] and "biotaxic philosophy" as an equivalent of biotaxy.[30] Dynamical biology was treated in three lessons on "vegetative life," "animal life," and "cerebral," that is, "intellectual and moral, functions." Thus, any similarity to the biology of our days seems to be purely coincidental.

Comte's ideas are more idiosyncratic with regard to the social sciences than to the other disciplines. He uses "social philosophy" and "social physics" as synonyms for "social science." The term "sociology," coined by Comte as a possible substitute, was introduced only in Volume IV, page 252, with a footnote apologizing for the neologism. Comte used the new term only sparingly in the text and not at all in the titles of the lessons on social philosophy or social physics. Miss Martineau used the term in the chapter titles of the English edition, and the French retranslation, as well as other French abridgments of the work, replaced "social physics" and "social philosophy" in many places with "sociology."[31]

Since the term "sociology" was thus used as equivalent to "social physics," "social philosophy," and "social science," its meaning included the disciplines of political science, political economy (economics), and social anthropology, in addition to what in our day is understood to constitute sociology. Comte was very explicit in his view that no part of social science had attained a state of maturity qualifying it to the status of positive philosophy. He felt sure, however, that "positive social doctrine" would "impart a homogeneous and rational character to the desultory politics of [his] day" and

[28] Comte, vol. III, p. 476; p. 375; Martineau, vol. I, p. 328.

[29] Comte, vol. III, p. 487; p. 384; Martineau, vol. I, p. 331.

[30] Comte, vol. III, p. 537; p. 425; Martineau, vol. I, p. 340.

[31] For example, the heading of the 26th lesson, which is the first devoted to the detailed discussion of social science, refers to "Social Physics" in the original French edition (vol. IV, p. 1), but to "Sociology" in the French abridged version by Jules Rig, vol. II, p. 1.

would "connect this co-ordinated present with the whole past, so as to establish a general harmony in the entire system of social ideas, by exhibiting the fundamental uniformity of the collective life of humanity."[32]

This program may sound more ambitious than what most present-day professors of the social sciences would think possible to achieve (except, perhaps, some generalists in pure economic theory). But Comte's optimism regarding the possibility of coping successfully with "the complex and special nature of social phenomena" becomes even more remarkable when we read his expectation that "the great discovery of cerebral physiology had opened a rational access to the analysis of these phenomena."[33]

Cournot's Series and Levels

Antoine-Augustin Cournot (1801-1877), French philosopher, mathematician, and mathematical economist, proposed a new classification of learning in general and of the sciences in particular. He did this in a chapter on "la coordination des connaissances humaines" in his major work on the philosophy of science, published (in 1851) in two volumes.[34] Cournot followed the practice of earlier taxonomists of the sciences of providing a "synoptic classification" in tabular form. With regard to substance, he borrowed much from, and acknowledged his debt to, Ampère.[35]

One of Cournot's major points was that the importance of theoretical sciences (including "speculative sciences") does not depend on the importance of the corresponding applied sciences ("technical and practical") or vice versa. That in actual fact their developments may have depended on each other should not induce us to merge them in our classification; they should be shown in separate columns ("series"), though placed in the same sequence, parallel to each other. This principle of organization led Cournot to develop a matrix of disciplines, with three columns and with many rows grouped into five major "levels."[36]

The three columns are 1. the Theoretical Series, 2. the Cosmolog-

[32] Comte, vol. IV, p. 178; p. 142; Martineau, vol. II, p. 35.

[33] Comte, vol. IV, p. 225; p. 179; Martineau, vol. II, p. 44.

[34] Antoine-Augustin Cournot, *Essai sur les fondements de nos connaissances et sur les caractères de la critique philosophique* (Paris: L. Hachette, 1851). English translation under the title *An Essay on the Foundations of Our Knowledge*, by Merritt H. Moore (New York: Liberal Arts Press, 1956). In my page references the first is to the French, the second to the English edition. (Occasionally I use my own rendition into English.)

[35] Cournot, vol. 2, pp. 268, 270; Moore, pp. 499, 503.

[36] Cournot, vol. 2, p. 268; Moore, p. 499.

ical and Historical Series, and 3. the Technical or Practical Series. The five groups (or "families") are I. the Mathematical Sciences, II. the Physical and Cosmological Sciences, III. the Biological Sciences and Natural History proper, IV. the Noological and Symbolic Sciences, and V. the Political Sciences and History proper.[37]

The three "series" and five "groups" provide fifteen boxes, some of which are quite crowded, but one of which is empty. The mathematical sciences are strongly represented in the theoretical column and in the practical column, but "cosmological and historical mathematics" is a null class. What are the sciences that fill the other boxes in the cosmological and historical series? The group "physical sciences" is represented in this column by astronomy, geophysics, meteorology, geology, physical geography, mineralogy, and other earth sciences. The group "biological sciences and natural history" has botany, zoology, anthropology, ethnology, and linguistics in the historical series. From the "noological and symbolic sciences" we find hieroglyphics, palaeography, philology, mythology and religious symbolics, dogmatic theology, and ethography. And the "political sciences and history proper" supply the largest number of disciplines, including archaeology, iconography, numismatics, historical chronology, political geography, history (ecclesiastic, political, civil, military, commercial, of civilization, of arts, of sciences, etc.), biography, and bibliography.

The sciences in the theoretical series need not be enumerated. Cournot, of course, parades the whole battalion of more or less traditional sciences, but he is quite progressive in his separation of historical from theoretical branches. For example, he displays the "theory of institutions" in the group of political sciences, whereas, the "history of institutions" is shown in the second column. That he has given an ostentatious place[38] to "chrematology, or theory of wealth" is hardly surprising when we recall his *Researches into the Principles of the Theory of Wealth*, first published in French in 1838, thirteen years before the work under review here.

Spencer's Three Basic Classes

Herbert Spencer (1820-1903) showed great irritation at Comte's "Positive Philosophy," taking exception especially to the misleading use of the adjective "positive" and to the "serial order" in which

[37] Moore renders this as "Historical Sciences," which is quite in conformance with general French and German practice, but not in correspondance with Cournot's emphasis on the differences between the fundamental approaches in history and "the sciences." Cf. Cournot, vol. 2, pp. 267, 271; Moore, pp. 499, 503.
[38] In the bottom line of the column of the theoretical series.

the sciences were classified. In his *Genesis of Science*[39] and in a later essay Spencer argued against Comte's hierarchy of sciences on both logical and historical grounds. The sciences, he wrote, in the "succession specified by M. Comte *do not* logically conform to the natural and invariable hierarchy of phenomena; and there is no serial order whatever in which they can be placed, which represents either their logical dependence or the dependence of phenomena."[40]

Another of Spencer's criticisms of Comte's system is that it divides each science into an abstract and a concrete part—for example, abstract mathematics versus concrete mathematics, or abstract physiology versus concrete zoology and botany—and, moreover, confuses abstract with general and concrete with particular.[41] "Abstractedness," according to Spencer, "means *detachment from* the incidents of particular cases. Generality means *manifestation in* numerous cases."[42] Spencer's own scheme, in Kantian fashion, provides first a distinction between science that "treats of the forms in which phenomena are known to us"—logic and mathematics—and science that "treats of the phenomena themselves." The latter is subdivided into sciences that treat the phenomena "in their elements"—mechanics, physics, chemistry, and so forth—and those that treat phenomena "in their totalities"—astronomy, geology, biology, psychology, sociology, and so forth.[43] This yields three basic classes: Abstract Science, Abstract-Concrete Science, and Concrete Science. The first provides the "laws of the *forms*," the second, the "laws of the *factors*," and the third, the "laws of the *products*."[44]

Spencer recommends his classification as serving the purposes of any "true classification," namely, to group together the like and to separate the unlike.[45] "The distinction between the empty forms of things and the things themselves, is a distinction which cannot be exceeded in degree. And when we divide the Sciences which treat of realities into those which deal with their separate components

[39] Herbert Spencer, "Genesis of Science," *The British Quarterly Review*, vol. 20 (July and October 1854), pp. 108-162. Reprinted in Spencer, *Essays: Scientific, Political, and Speculative*, vol. II (New York: D. Appleton and Company, 1899), pp. 1-73.

[40] Herbert Spencer, "Reasons for Dissenting from the Philosophy of M. Comte," first published as an annex to the *Classification of the Sciences* (New York: D. Appleton and Company, 1864), p. 39. Reproduced in *Essays: Scientific, Political, and Speculative*, pp. 129-130.

[41] *Classification of the Sciences*, pp. 6-7.

[42] Ibid., p. 7.

[43] Ibid., p. 6.

[44] Ibid., pp. 24-25.

[45] Ibid., pp. 3-4.

and those which deal with their components as united," we make another fundamental distinction.[46] Spencer proceeds to classify a large number of disciplines, traditional (such as mechanics) and nontraditional (such as astrogeny) into the slots provided by his scheme. That he failed to see developments in the various sciences that had taken place at the time he wrote, and to foresee developments that were still to come, caused him to make several misclassifications which, in the view of some critics, discredit his whole scheme. He evidently did not see that several of the sciences that he characterized as concrete had developed their abstract-deductive systems and, therefore, would either have to be divided into two separate sciences or be placed into the class of abstract-concrete sciences.

Pearson's Grammar of Science

Karl Pearson (1857-1936) first published his *Grammar of Science* in 1892. It became one of the most influential books among natural scientists who wanted to show that they were comfortable with "modern" philosophy of science.[47] Pearson's firm allegiance to empiricism, his righteous condemnation of everything that smacked of metaphysical speculation, his insistence that the real scientist tries only to "describe" and never to seek causal explanations, and similarly simple-minded rules of scientific etiquette made him for decades a most popular guide to many "men of science." The last chapter of his book deals with "The Classification of the Sciences."[48] It deserves our attention.

Pearson presents brief reports on the systems of Bacon, Comte, and Spencer. He contrasts the idea, "common to Bacon and Spencer," of the divisions of knowledge being "like branches of a tree that meet in one stem," and of all sciences therefore springing from one root, with "the view of Comte, who arranges the sciences in a series or staircase."[49] Pearson rejects Comte's reductionist position, according to which each of the six sciences is subordinate to one that is less complex, and in turn dominates another, a more complex one. He finds that "we have in Comte's staircase of the intellect a purely fanciful scheme, which is . . . worthless from the standpoint of modern science."[50] He agrees with Spencer's distinction between abstract

---

[46] Ibid., p. 24.

[47] Karl Pearson, *The Grammar of Science* (London: Adam and Charles Black, 1892; 2nd ed., 1900). — Page references refer to the 2nd edition.

[48] Ibid., pp. 504-532.

[49] Ibid., p. 508.

[50] Ibid., p. 510.

and concrete sciences and, particularly, with setting logic and pure mathematics, with their "conceptual notions of geometrical space and absolute time" apart from the "perceptual" domain.[51]

In his own classification, Pearson divides the concrete sciences into exact (or precise) sciences and descriptive (or synoptic) sciences.[52] Having ruled earlier that *all* concrete sciences be descriptive, he prefers the designation "synoptic" as the opposite of "exact" or "precise." What for Spencer was the category of "abstract-concrete sciences" is for Pearson the group of precise branches of concrete sciences; what for Spencer was the category of "concrete sciences" is for Pearson the group of synoptic branches of concrete sciences. Pearson gives us astronomy and meteorology as examples of precise and synoptic sciences, respectively. (He chastises Spencer for having misclassified astronomy.) Pearson realizes, however, that several sciences "where we have not yet succeeded in analyzing complex changes into ideal motions, or have only done so in part," and which are therefore still synoptic, may eventually become precise. In other words, what is at present a synoptic science may in time, perhaps quite soon, as it is "conceptualized" by "simple formulae or laws," develop into a precise science.[53]

Pearson warns his readers—as most classifiers have done before him—that, because of this always ongoing development, any classification inevitably reflects the stage in which each branch of knowledge happens to be at the time the system is being prepared—and therefore must become obsolete before long. The abstract sciences are abstract by nature, but the concrete sciences are "still synoptic" or "already exact," according to the stage of idealization attained at the time they are entered into the classification scheme.

Pearson attempted to make his classification more methodical by references to time, space, and general relations, by distinctions between quantitative and qualitative aspects and several other characteristics, which however prove to be more cumbersome than helpful. Little is lost, therefore, if we skip some supposedly explanatory distinctions and present only the fields of knowledge grouped in the various categories. Under Abstract Science Pearson enumerated no fewer than eighteen fields, but he added "et cetera" after each cluster in order to make it clear that his was an open-ended system. Some of his entries in the catalogue of Abstract Science are kinematics, theory of strain, theory of observation and description (a part of logic), geometry, trigonometry, descriptive geometry, theory of func-

[51] Ibid., p. 511.
[52] Ibid., p. 519.
[53] Ibid., pp. 520-522.

tions, calculus of fluxions and calculus of sums (differential and integral calculus), arithmetic, algebra, theory of probability, statistics, logic, orthology (a part of grammar), and methodology.[54]

Concrete Sciences are divided into those dealing with inorganic and those dealing with organic phenomena. Pearson provided tabulations and discussions for both. He classified the concrete sciences for inorganic phenomena into two groups: those that had been "reduced to ideal motions," that is, the "precise physical sciences," and those "not yet reduced to ideal motions," that is, the "synoptic physical sciences." Among the former, the "precise" ones, Pearson listed the theories of light, heat, electricity, dispersion, absorption, transmission, conduction, and radiation; theoretical chemistry, spectrum analysis, solar and sidereal physics; the theories of elasticity, plasticity, cohesion, sound, crystallography, hydromechanics, aeromechanics, the tides, and the kinetic theory of gases; and finally, mechanics, planetary theory, and lunar theory. Among the "synoptic physical sciences" Pearson listed nebular theories, evolution of planetary systems, geology, physical geography, meteorology, mineralogy, and chemistry.[55]

Pearson's classification of the organic portion of Concrete Science is rather idiosyncratic: there is, first, a division based on the distinction between space and time. The sciences dealing with organic phenomena with an emphasis on space (or localization) are Chorology (regarding geographical distribution of living forms), Ecology (regarding habits in relation to situation and climate), and Natural History (in the old sense). All other fields are oriented towards time, that is, "change or growth," and deal either with recurring or non-recurring phenomena, that is, they are either Biology or History. None of the branches of knowledge of organic phenomena qualifies, in Pearson's view, for the category of precise sciences; all are (still) synoptic sciences.[56] The "historical group of sciences" treats "generally of all life" and is divided into (1) a general part, dealing with evolution of species, the genesis of life, philogeny, palaeontology, the origin of species, the theories of natural and sexual selection, and (2) a part dealing with the "descent of man" regarding his "physique" (cranology and physical anthropology), his "mental faculties" (history of language, philology, the histories of philosophy, science, literature, art, etc.) or his "social institutions" (archaeology, folklore, the histories of customs, marriage, ownership, religions, states, laws,

[54] Ibid., p. 518.
[55] Ibid., p. 523.
[56] Ibid., p. 524.

etc.). That Pearson's Biological Sciences has, in its division of zoology, all sciences of man, including, besides the theories of sex and
heredity, all of "sociology," with the fields of morals, politics, economics, and jurisprudence, is quite in line with intellectual history
but still somewhat bizarre for a scheme acclaimed and accepted in
the twentieth century.[57] However, we shall see in the next chapter
that the philosophers for a "Unified Science" likewise gave the biological sciences a scope wide enough to embrace the social sciences
as well as the "humanistic sciences."

Biological Sciences is divided, first, into Botany and Zoology, with
the latter including the "sciences special to man,"[58] and, second,
into types captioned as "Functions and Actions," "Growth and Reproduction," and "Form and Structure." Under the first of these
captions we find Psychology and Physiology. Psychology is subdivided into a general group, dealing with the theory of instinct and
the genesis of consciousness, and a group "special to man," either
as an "individual" (psychics, physiology of thought) or as "group"
("sociology," including morals, politics, political economy, jurisprudence). Under the caption "Growth and Reproduction" the table
lists embryology, theory of sex, theory of heredity. Finally, under
the caption "Form and Structure" are morphology, histology, and
anatomy. The reader will have noted the peculiarity of a classification
that sees economics as a part of sociology, which is a part of psychology, which is a part of biology.[59]

Pearson finally discusses some of the "cross-links" between disciplines; for example, aetiology, linking biology with physics, for
which he proposes the designation "Biophysics,"[60] a term now generally accepted; and applied mathematics, linking abstract science
with concrete physical science. In his own summary of his classification, Pearson stresses that he sees the universe of learning in
"three fundamental divisions": Abstract Sciences, Physical Sciences,
and Biological Sciences.[61]

[57] Believe it or not, there are live economists who propogate this view. The announcement of a new book by Morris A. Copeland, *Essays in Socioeconomic Evolution*
(New York: Vantage Press, 1981), states that the author "considers economics to be
a natural science, a branch of biology."

[58] Pearson, *Grammar of Science*, p. 526.

[59] Psychology, in the course of the centuries, has been assigned to the greatest variety
of foster homes, from metaphysics to biology to social sciences. As we shall see later,
the classifiers in the Library of Congress have placed it together with philosophy and
religion.

[60] Pearson, p. 528.

[61] Ibid., p. 532.

Peirce's Taxonomic Arrangement

Charles Sanders Peirce (1839-1914) produced an elaborate classification of the sciences in a number of manuscripts written between 1896 and 1903; they are included in Volume I of his *Collected Papers*.[62] A student of the naturalist Louis Agassiz, Peirce borrowed from the classification schemes employed in zoology, but he adapted them for his own purposes when he distinguished the consecutive divisions and subdivisions as branches, subbranches, classes, subclasses, orders, suborders, families, and subfamilies.[63] For Peirce, science has two branches, Theoretical Sciences and Practical Sciences. The latter are evidently in the nature of *how-to* knowledge, and many of them may be merely the not-verbally-described knowhow of craftsmen. Thus Peirce's list of examples includes goldbeating, pigeon-fancying, printing, and bookbinding, which few philosophers of the nineteenth and twentieth centuries would catalogue as sciences. Several other inclusions, on the other hand, would be favorably received by present-day curriculum builders, especially "pedagogics, . . . surveying, . . . [and] librarian's work."[64]

The branch "Theoretical Sciences" has two subbranches: "Sciences of Discovery" and "Sciences of Review." Peirce does not offer a classification of the latter, but he describes them as the products of those who arrange "the results of discovery, beginning with digests, and going on to endeavor to form a philosophy of science." He cites the works of Humboldt, Comte, and Spencer, and states that the "classification of the sciences belongs to this department."[65]

The Sciences of Discovery are grouped into three classes: Mathematics, Philosophy, and Idioscopy (Bentham's term for sciences based on sense observation), with the last divided into two subclasses: Physical Sciences and Psychical Sciences (or Human Sciences). The first two classes and the two subclasses of the third class are divided into three orders each. Mathematics can be (1) of Logic, (2) of Discrete Series, or (3) of Continua and Pseudo-Continua. Phi-

---

[62] *Collected Papers of Charles Sanders Peirce*, edited by Charles Hartshorne and Paul Weiss (Cambridge, Mass.: Harvard University Press, 1931-1935). The essential statements on the classification of the sciences are in the papers collected under the heading of "Minute Logic" (1902) and in his essay, "A Syllabus of Certain Topics of Logic" (1903). A useful paraphrasing of Peirce's statements is contained in Thomas A. Goudge, *The Thought of C. S. Peirce* (Toronto: University of Toronto Press, 1950), pp. 44-50. Goudge presents also a chart that gives a complete overview of "Peirce's classification of the Sciences"; the chart folds out after page 48.

[63] *Collected Papers*, vol. 1, par. 238.

[64] Ibid., par. 243.

[65] Ibid., pars. 180-182.

losophy can be (1) Phenomenology,[66] (2) Normative Sciences, or (3) Metaphysics. Physical Sciences are (1) Nomological, or General, Physics, (2) Classificatory Physics, or (3) Descriptive Physics. Psychical Sciences are (1) Nomological Psychics, or Psychology, (2) Classificatory Psychics, or Ethnology, or (3) Descriptive Psychics, or History.[67]

At this point it may help to mention that Peirce does not regard any of his orders of science as independent of the others. For example, "Normative Science rests largely on phenomenology and on mathematics";[68] Metaphysics is based on phenomenology and normative science. Likewise, Descriptive Psychics "endeavors . . . to describe individual manifestations of mind" and "to explain them on the principles of psychology and ethnology. It borrows from . . . other branches of physical and psychical science."[69] This recognition of the interdependence of sciences may attenuate the shock of most historians when they learn that they primarily profess the science of descriptive psychics.

Proceeding now to the suborders, we find ourselves confronted with twenty-four disciplines, partitioned in clusters of two, three, or four, from eight of the twelve orders. Phenomenology and the three orders of mathematics are not so subdivided. There are three Normative Sciences: aesthetics, ethics, and logic;[70] three kinds of Metaphysics: ontology, religious metaphysics, and physical metaphysics (which discusses the real nature of time, space, matter, etc.); three kinds of Classificatory Physics: crystallography, chemistry, and biology; two kinds of Descriptive Physics: geognosy and astronomy; four kinds of Nomological Psychics: introspective psychology, experimental psychology, physiological psychology, and child psychology; three kinds of Classificatory Psychics: special psychology, linguistics, and ethnology proper; and three kinds of Descriptive Psychics: history proper, biography, and criticism.

Many of these suborders are divided into families, but we shall

---

[66] This is not what Husserl meant by the term. According to Peirce, "Phenomenology ascertains and studies the kinds of elements universally present in the phenomenon; meaning by the *phenomenon*, whatever is present at any time to the mind in any way" (par. 186).

[67] Ibid., pars. 183-189.

[68] Ibid., par. 186.

[69] Ibid., par. 189.

[70] "All thought being performed by means of signs, logic may be regarded as the science of the general laws of signs" (par. 191). That Peirce, despite this view, characterizes logic as a normative science may not sit well with most logicians of our time.

take the space to list only the unusual ones. Thus, logic is divided into speculative grammar ("the general theory of the nature and meanings of signs, whether they be icons, indices, or symbols"), critic (formal logic), and methodeutic (methodology).[71] Linguistics has two families: word linguistics and grammar. Ethnology is either of social development or of technology. History proper divides into monumental history, ancient history, modern history, political history, history of sciences, and history of social development. And criticism can be literary or art criticism.

It bears notice that Peirce, a philosopher of science born and educated in the United States (with degrees from Harvard in 1859 and 1863), resisted the practice, increasingly fashionable in Anglo-American teaching, of restricting the word "science" to mathematical or natural or experimental or nomological sciences. To Peirce, humanistic disciplines, such as classical history or modern literature, were also sciences.

[71] Ibid., par. 191.

CHAPTER 7

Unified Science and the Propaedia

ONLY TWO twentieth-century efforts to renovate the classification of learning will be examined here. Both were of encyclopaedic character. The first originated from a movement, led by a group of eminent philosophers, to integrate all areas of learning into an all-embracing unified science. The second was a new conception of the circle of learning, designed to form the foundation of the fifteenth edition of the *Encyclopaedia Britannica*.

Carnap's and Neurath's Unified Science

In 1935 a project for an encyclopaedia was launched that had at least two things in common with Leibniz's projects: first, that it was to be founded on the notion of what Leibniz called "General Science" and the proponents of the new project called "Unified Science," and, second, that the project failed to materialize beyond preliminary essays. The new project for an "International Encyclopedia of Unified Science" was announced at a congress in Paris, and a committee for the organization of the work was formed consisting of Rudolf Carnap, Philipp Frank, Joergen Joergensen, Charles W. Morris, Otto Neurath, and Louis Rougier.[1] Another congress, held in 1937, again in Paris, was entirely devoted to the project, and some of the papers delivered at that congress were published in a series entitled *Foundations of the Unity of Science: Toward an International Encyclopedia of Unified Science*.[2]

[1] See Otto Neurath (1882-1945), "Une Encyclopédie internationale de la science unitaire," in *Actes du congrès international de philosophie scientifique, Sorbonne, Paris 1935* (Paris: Hermann et cie., 1936), pt. II, "Unité de la Science," pp. II.54-II.59. Plans had previously been laid at a congress held in 1934 at Charles University in Prague for a series of annual congresses devoted to the unity of science. The proceedings of that preliminary congress were published in the 1935 *Erkenntnis* and also as a separate volume under the title *Einheit der Wissenschaft* (Leipzig: F. Meiner, 1935). The 1936 congress was held in Copenhagen and was devoted to the problem of causality; proceedings were published in 1937 *Erkenntnis* and as a separate volume.

[2] Chicago: University of Chicago Press, vol. 1, nos. 1-5, 1938; vol. 2, nos. 6-10, 1939. Editions combining all ten numbers were published in 1955 and 1969. In the 1955 edition, the title pages and tables of contents are very confusing. The volume numbers sometimes refer to the *Encyclopedia*, sometimes to the volumes in the combined edition, so that vol. 2 of the 1955 edition contains vol. 1, nos. 6-10 of the *Encyclopedia*.

The first issue of the series contained papers and statements by Otto Neurath, Niels Bohr, John Dewey, Bertrand Russell, Rudolf Carnap, and Charles W. Morris. The major programmatic statements were those by Otto Neurath and Rudolf Carnap. According to Neurath, the work was not to be "a series of alphabetically arranged articles; [but] rather . . . a series of monographs" (with a "highly analytical index" to make the encyclopaedia useful as a reference work), "each monograph . . . devoted to a particular group of problems." The aim was "to integrate the scientific disciplines, so to unify them, so to dovetail them together, that advances in one will bring about advances in the others."[3] "The *Encyclopedia* is to be constructed like an onion. The heart of this onion is formed by twenty pamphlets which constitute two introductory volumes. . . . The first 'layer' of the onion . . . is planned as a series of volumes which will deal with the problems of systematization in special sciences and in unified science—including logic, mathematics, theory of signs, linguistics, history and sociology of science, classification of sciences, and educational implications of the scientific attitude."[4] Unfortunately, not even this "first layer" has come into being.

The promised monograph on classification of sciences would have been of special interest for this chapter. Neurath makes us curious when he states that "the plan of this *Encyclopedia* could not be based on a generally accepted classification of the sciences—indeed, the collaborators may perhaps find a new way to assemble systematically all the special sciences," for they "know very well that certain frontiers of sciences are unsatisfactory. . . ."[5]

Carnap's part in the heart of the onion includes a section on "The Main Branches of Science."[6] He uses "the word 'science' . . . in its widest sense, including all theoretical knowledge, no matter whether in the field of natural sciences or in the field of the social sciences and the so-called humanities, and no matter whether it is knowledge found by the application of special scientific procedures or knowledge based on common sense in everyday life." His "first distinction . . . is that between *formal science* and *empirical science*. Formal

---

The table of contents of the first volume lists only the six papers included in the first entry of "Part I," so that there is no table of contents in the two volumes that would name the authors of nine of the major papers.

[3] Otto Neurath, "Unified Science as Encyclopedic Integration," in *International Encyclopedia of Unified Science*, vol. 1, nos. 1-5, 1955 ed., p. 24.

[4] Neurath, pp. 24-25.

[5] Neurath, p. 25.

[6] Rudolf Carnap (1891-1970), "Logical Foundations of the Unity of Science," in Otto Neurath, Rudolf Carnap, and Charles Morris, eds., *Foundations of the Unity of Science: Toward an International Encyclopedia of Unified Science* (Chicago: The University of Chicago Press, 1939; bound ed., 1969), vol. I, pp. 42-62.

science consists of the analytic statements established by logic and mathematics; empirical science consists of the synthetic statements established in the different fields of factual knowledge." Carnap takes " 'physics' as a common name for the nonbiological field of science, comprehending both systematic and historical investigations within this field, thus including chemistry, mineralogy, astronomy, geology (which is historical), meteorology, etc."[7] He is convinced, as were Comte, Cournot, Spencer, and Pearson before him, that the distinction between physics and biology has to be based on the distinction between "organisms and nonorganisms," though he leaves it to the biologists "to lay down a suitable definition for the term 'organism.' "[8] Like Comte, he holds that "biology presupposes physics, but not vice versa." And, like Pearson, he holds that "the whole rest of science may be called *biology (in the wider sense)*."[9]

Carnap proceeds, again like Pearson, to the "possibility of dividing biology in the wider sense into two fields": one, "biology in the narrower sense" containing "general biology, botany, and the greater part of zoölogy,"[10] the other, a field for which "there is no name in common use." He refused to call it either "mental sciences" (because of this term's association with "metaphysical dualism") or "behavioristics" (because of the narrow sense in which behaviorism had been limited to "overt behavior which can be observed from outside" [Carnap recognized that one needs to deal also with "internal behavior," with "dispositions to behavior" and with "certain effects upon the environment"]). Whatever its name, "this second field" divides into "two parts dealing with individual organisms and with groups of organisms," respectively.[11] "Compared with the customary classification of science, the first part would include chiefly psychology, but also some parts of physiology and the humanities. The second part would chiefly include social science and, further, the greater part of the humanities and history." However, it "has not only to deal with groups of human beings but also . . . with groups of other organisms." Carnap decides to use the designations "psychology" and "social science" as the names of the two parts "because of lack of better terms."[12]

[7] Ibid., p. 45
[8] Ibid.
[9] Ibid., p. 46.
[10] Ibid., p. 47.
[11] The distinction between individual and group has a long history. I may refer the reader to Francis Bacon's distinction between "man segregate" and "man congregate," discussed above in Chapter 4 under the heading "Moral Philosophy." The distinction between individual and group was also made by Pearson when he divided "psychology special to man" into "psychics" and "sociology" (see above, Chapter 6).
[12] Ibid., pp. 47-49.

Traditionalists, especially British and American, are probably shocked by Carnap's scheme. Not many biologists would expect their science to include each and every field that has to do with organisms, life, mental states, psychology, social studies, history, and all the humanities. Few psychologists would be willing to accept parts of the humanities among their responsibilities. Many social scientists would balk at being put in charge not only of "the greater part of the humanities" but also of the social behavior of ants and bees, notwithstanding the growing interest in sociobiology, ethology, and other novel fields. To mention the strong resistance most scientists and scholars would offer to Carnap's ideas on classifying the branches of learning is not to deny that these ideas have respectable precedents and can be the basis for a consistent and coherent system.

The plans for the *Encyclopedia* were described in the following outline: Volumes I and II. Foundations of the Unity of Science; Volume III. General Problems and Procedures of Unification of Science; Volume IV. Logic and Mathematics; Volume V. Physics; Volume VI. Biology and Psychology; Volume VII. The Social and Humanistic Sciences; Volume VIII. History of the Scientific Attitude.[13] Alas, the project had to be dropped. As one of the editors wrote in the 1969 edition of the *Foundations of the Unity of Science*, "there are no plans at this time to proceed further with the *International Encyclopedia of Unified Science*."[14]

Britannica 3, Mortimer Adler and the Propaedia

For the fifteenth edition of the *Encyclopaedia Britannica* (1974) a board of editors, chaired by Mortimer J. Adler (born 1902), developed a classification of intellectual knowledge covering the entire "circle of learning" (*enkyklios paideia*). It should be recalled that *Britannica 3* consists of three parts: a one-volume *Propaedia*, presenting an "Outline of Knowledge"; a nineteen-volume *Macropaedia*, offering "Knowledge in Depth," with 4,207 long articles on all the topics included in the Outline; and a ten-volume *Micropaedia*, a "Ready Reference and Index," with 102,214 short entries. It is in the *Propaedia* that the "circle of learning" is exhibited.

The circle of learning is divided into ten "segments," or parts, forty divisions, and 189 sections. The segments are Part One: Matter and Energy, Part Two: the Earth, Part Three: Life on Earth, Part Four: Human Life, Part Five: Human Society, Part Six: Art, Part Seven:

[13] Charles Morris, "On the History of the International Encyclopedia of Unified Science," in Otto Neurath, Rudolf Carnap, Charles Morris, eds., *Foundations of the Unity of Science*, 1969 ed., p. xi.

[14] Ibid., p. vii.

Technology, Part Eight: Religion, Part Nine: the History of Mankind, and Part Ten: the Branches of Knowledge. At first sight it is surprising to see the "branches of knowledge" listed as one of the segments or parts of knowledge. The explanation, furnished in the introduction to the *Propaedia* and in the text of "Part Ten" (written by Mortimer Adler), is that this tenth segment is actually considered as a discourse very different from the other nine. The first nine provide knowledge about things natural, human, and social, the tenth provides "knowledge about knowledge."[15]

To help the reader comprehend this distinction, the introduction offers a graph showing a large circle with nine sectors and one small circle in the center. "Knowledge about knowledge" is given this "central position" in the circle of learning. The editors wanted to emphasize the "distinction between (a) what we know about the world of nature, of man and society, and of human institutions *by means of* the various branches of learning or departments of scholarship; and (b) what we know about the branches of learning or departments of scholarship—the various academic disciplines themselves." In other words, "Part Ten examines the nature, methods, problems, and history of the various branches of knowledge or scholarly disciplines, the actual content of which is set forth in Parts One through Nine."[16] Put differently, Parts One to Nine "cover *what we know* about the knowable universe" and "Ten covers what we know about the sciences or other disciplines *whereby we know* that which we know."[17]

It is thus Part Ten of the *Propaedia* that presents the classification of learning. There are five divisions subdivided into from two to seven sections:

Division I.
Logic:

1. History and philosophy of logic
2. Formal logic, metalogic, and applied logic

Division II.
Mathematics:

1. History and foundations of mathematics
2. Branches of mathematics
3. Applications of mathematics

---

[15] *Encyclopaedia Britannica*, 15th ed. (1974), vol. 1, *Propaedia*, p. 692.
[16] Ibid., pp. 6-7.
[17] Ibid., p. 692.

Division III.
Science: 1. History and philosophy of
                           science
                        2. The physical sciences
                        3. The earth sciences
                        4. The biological sciences
                        5. Medicine and affiliated
                           disciplines
                        6. The social sciences and
                           psychology
                        7. The technological sciences

Division IV.
History and
the Humanities: 1. Historiography and the study
                           of history
                        2. The humanities and
                           humanistic scholarship

Division V.
Philosophy: 1. The nature and the divisions
                           of philosophy
                        2. History of philosophy
                        3. Philosophical schools and
                           doctrines

The classifiers of the *Propaedia* are faithful to the philosophical tradition of dismissing the narrow concept of science, adopted in British and American schools and universities, that restricts it to the physical, geological, and biological sciences and thus excludes the social and technological sciences. On the other hand, they do not accept the wide concept of science current in all German-speaking countries, in the Slavic countries, in Japan, and probably everywhere but in English-speaking countries. Thus, the propaedists, if I may so refer to the encyclopaedists of *Britannica 3*, shun such expressions as "historical science," "cultural science," and "juridical science." The first two of these three presumed nonsciences are given a comfortable berth in Part Ten, Division IV, History and the Humanities; no special place, however, is provided for jurisprudence, apart from occasional references in subsections of Political Science.[18] The exclusion of jurisprudence as a separate branch of learning is strange, because Part Five, Human Society, includes "Law" as Division V. Thus law is recognized as a social institution, but jurisprudence not

---

[18] Ibid., p. 749.

as a branch of knowledge. A similar neglect or snub is accorded to education: though treated as Division VI of Part Five, as an institution of human society, it is not included in Part Ten among the branches of knowledge. Deans and professors in schools of law and schools of education may smart under the indignity implied in the propae-dists' classification. Professors of theology have probably become used to being exiled from the modern tree of knowledge.

PART TWO

The Departments of Erudition

It is chiefly for the sake of variety, and thus for aesthetic purposes, that the title of Part Two differs from that of Part One. No serious difference in meaning is intended. The following three chapters, just as the previous six, are about classifications of higher learning and erudition. Part One treated of the branching and twigging proposed by philosophers and encyclopaedists. Part Two will discuss the divisions in the organizations of academic institutions: learned academies, research libraries, and universities.

CHAPTER 8

ACADEMIES OF SCIENCES:
CLASSES AND SECTIONS

IT IS NOT SURPRISING that the divisions, classes, or sections in which
the academies of sciences in various countries are organized reflect
the major classes and subclasses, orders and suborders, in which
philosophers and encyclopaedists had divided the universe of learning,
for, in many instances, the same philosophers and encyclopaedists,
influential classifiers or sciences, were the promoters, organizers, or
reorganizers of the academies. Once in place, the organization schemes
of the academies have not changed quite so speedily as the classification
systems of the dominant schools of philosophy of science: numerous
proposals for reclassification were skipped by the academicians. On
the other hand, in some countries changes in the organization of the
academies were subject more to political than to philosophical
influences. This point will be illuminated in connection with
reorganizations in France in 1803, 1816, and 1832.

A Few Noteworthy Distinctions

I shall not talk about the Athenian Academy of Plato and the
academies of later Greek philosophers.[1] These were largely *teaching
institutions*, where great masters held forth or conducted colloquia
for their disciples. The designation "academy" for a teaching institution
still exists, for example, for secondary ("preparatory") schools and
for military colleges in the United States, and for riding schools in
England and elsewhere. Academies as teaching institutions do not
concern us here.

The academies surveyed in this chapter are multidisciplinary
institutions, usually honorary societies, for the cultivation and
promotion of sciences (in the international sense of "learned
disciplines," including literature and arts). Traditionally, members
are elected on the basis of their scholarly achievements and professional
standing. I stress the multidisciplinary character of the academy of

---

[1] The word "academy" is derived from Academe, the name of a garden—an olive
grove—in a suburb of Athens, where Plato taught until his death in 348 B.C. Athenian
academies continued for nine centuries, until abolished by Emperor Justinian in A.D.
529.

sciences because this distinguishes it from the specialized academy and from the professional association or learned society serving only one particular or a few related branches of learning.

Several differences among academies of sciences in various countries should be noted. First, customs and procedures in the selection of members may be different. As a rule, new members are nominated by their peers in their particular discipline and elected by the academy at large, though in the final selection the relative weights of influence of section and plenum may vary considerably. In countries, however, where governments exercise strong control over cultural affairs, political decisions may prevail. The original idea was, of course, for academies of sciences to have full autonomy even in countries in which the government provided all or most operating funds. In Western Europe and in the United States the academies are completely independent and governments do not influence the selection of members. In the United States there are, in addition, numerous academies, though not the most respected, in which would-be members nominate themselves by applying for admission.

Differences exist also with regard to membership fees and membership salaries: the member may pay a small annual fee to the academy; the member may receive an annual salary or grant from the academy; or the member may neither pay a fee nor receive a compensation.

These differences are connected with the academies' roles as promoters or sponsors of research. Where the academy undertakes in-house research and employs the academician as principal investigator in charge of a research staff for all sorts of projects, the academician will receive a salary. (Indeed, the incomes of academicians in some countries, for example in the Soviet Union, exceed by large differentials those of their colleagues in other research institutes and in the universities.) Where membership in the academy is merely a highly coveted honor, members will be prepared to pay annual fees; they do their research and writing outside the academy, though they may occasionally contribute to the published proceedings or transactions.

It may be helpful to distinguish two ideal types: one, the academy as an assemblage of research institutes with sizable staffs of technical and clerical personnel; the other, the academy as an honorary society of elected savants. The first type has the academician come every day to his office, laboratory, or library in an academy building to conduct his research; the second has the academician come once every six months to attend a meeting, listen to a paper, and perhaps participate in the discussion. In actual fact, many academies fall between these extreme types. Broadly speaking, the academies in socialist countries are ordinarily closer to the first type, whereas the academies in Western Europe, England, and the United States come closer to the second.

My survey will cover ten countries: Italy, France, England, Germany, Russia, Sweden, Belgium, the Netherlands, Austria, and, in greater detail, the United States. The academies in these countries show considerable continuity of development. My major objective will be to report on their organization in divisions, classes, categories, and sections for different branches of learning; but wherever historical events and political or philosophical trends appear to have influenced the schemes of academic organization, I shall be glad to have brief narrative accounts interrupt the monotony of my enumerative exercise.

ACADEMIES IN EUROPE

The order in which I shall report on the academies in nine European countries is determined by chronological priorities: the dates of the founding of the academies that have survived, or the successors of which have survived, to our days. To fix a date for the founding is not always simple, because in some countries private academies preceded the establishment of national or royal academies, and the former were not always recognized officially as predecessors. For the reader's convenience, the basic data for the chronology may be summarized here: Italy: Accademia Nazionale dei Lincei, Rome, 1603; France: Académie française, Paris, 1635; England: Royal Society, London, 1660; Germany: Preussische Akademie der Wissenschaften, Berlin, 1711; Russia: Imperatorskaya Akademiya Naük, St. Petersburg, 1725; Sweden: Kungliga Vetenskapsakademien, Stockholm, 1741; Belgium: (Société littéraire, 1769), Académie impériale et royale des sciences et belles-lettres, Brussels, 1772; the Netherlands: (Hollandsche Maatschappij der Wetenschappen, Haarlem, 1752), Koninklijke Institut, Amsterdam, 1808; Austria: Akademie der Wissenschaften, Vienna, 1847.

Italy

There is a record of a renaissance of learned academies in the fifteenth and sixteenth centuries in Florence, Naples, and Rome, but none of these has survived. The oldest academy of those still in active operation is the Accademia Nazionale dei Lincei, established in Rome in 1603. Galileo Galilei was among its early members. Its statutes and official name have been changed several times in the course of political events: for example, after 1847 it was called the Accademia Pontificia dei Nuovi Lincei; after 1870, the Reale Accademia dei Lincei; and after 1926, under Mussolini's regime, the Reale Accademia d'Italia. In 1944, on Benedetto Croce's proposal, the original name was restored.

The organization too has been changed, though the division into two "classes" has been of long standing: "Physical, Mathematical and Natural Sciences" and "Moral, Historical and Philological Sciences." Class One is divided into five categories with two or more sections each: Category I. Mathematics and Mechanics; II. Astronomy, Geodesy, and Geophysics; III. Physics and Chemistry; IV. Geology, Palaeontology, and Mineralogy; and V. Biological Sciences (with sections for botany, zoology, physiology, and pathology). The categories add to their designations the words "and Applications." Class Two has seven categories: I. Philology and Linguistics; II. Archaeology; III. Art Criticism and Literary Criticism; IV. History, Historical Geography, and Anthropology; V. Philosophical Sciences; VI. Juridical Sciences; and VII. Social and Political Sciences.[2]

This is a rather straightforward classification; the one thing to note is that—in contrast to Anglo-American nomenclature but in conformance with international linguistic practice—history, philology, philosophy, jurisprudence, and so forth, are all referred to as sciences.

France

The Académie française was established by Louis XIV in 1635; an Académie des inscriptions et belles-lettres[3] was founded in 1663, and an Académie des sciences in 1666. The new Directorium of the French Republic established in 1795 the Institut national des sciences et arts, divided into three classes: Class One, "Sciences physiques et mathématiques"; Class Two, "Sciences morales et politiques," and Class Three, "Littérature et beaux-arts." Class One was subdivided into ten sections: Mathematics, Mechanical Arts, Astronomy, Experimental Physics, Chemistry, Natural History and Mineralogy, Botany and Plant Physics, Anatomy and Zoology, Medicine and

---

[2] *Annuario della Accademia Nazionale dei Lincei 1976* (Rome: Accademia Nazionale dei Lincei, 1976), pp. 31-33.

[3] The main task of the group concerned with "inscriptions" was to formulate and approve the inscriptions on public monuments. In 1701 this group was renamed "Académie royale des inscriptions et médailles." — In English translation the original name is rendered as "Academy of Inscriptions and Literature." In at least one German translation the name is given as "Akademie der Inschriften und schönen Wissenschaften." This is symptomatic for the refusal of any semantic separation between "letters" and "science." Article "Akademie" in *Meyers Konversations-Lexikon*, 4th ed. (Leipzig and Vienna: Bibliographisches Institut, 1890), vol. 1, p. 248.

Surgery, and Agronomy and Veterinary Art. Class Two was subdivided into six sections: Analysis of Sentiments and Ideas, Ethics, Social Science and Legislation, Political Economy, History, and Geography. Class Three was subdivided into eight sections: Grammar, Classical Languages, Poetry, Antiques and Monuments, Painting, Sculpturing, Architecture, and Music and Speech (*Déclamation*).[4]

A reorganization of the Institut national in 1803, when Napoleon was Consul of France, resulted in a change of name to "Institut de France" and an increase in the number of classes from three to four, essentially by separating the humanities into French Literature, Classical Literature, and the Fine Arts, each in a different class, and abolishing the class for Moral and Political Sciences. One cannot help suspecting political reasons for this change. After the downfall of Napoleon, under Louis XVIII, another reorganization created four academies as parts of the Institut de France; a fifth academy, that of Moral and Political Sciences, was added in 1832 under the regime of Louis Philippe of Orléans. The five parts of the Institute were now I. The Académie française (not subdivided); II. The Academy of Inscriptions and Literature (not subdivided); III. The Academy of Sciences (with eleven sections); IV. The Academy of Fine Arts (with five sections); and V. The Academy of Moral and Political Sciences (with the following five sections: 1. Philosophy, 2. Ethics, 3. Legislation, Public Law, and Jurisprudence, 4. Economics, Statistics, and Finance, and 5. History and Geography).[5] A separate Academy of Medicine, outside the Institut de France, was created in 1731, suppressed in 1793, and revived in 1820.

England

The history of the learned academies has been quite different in Britain. The two most prestigious groups are the Royal Society and the British Academy, the former founded in 1660, the latter in 1901, that is, 240 years apart. Neither of the two has the word "science" in its official name. It is a matter of record, however, that the beginnings of the Royal Society were closely related to the promotion of experimental natural philosophy (physics) and to the discoveries of Isaac Newton. On the other hand, there was also a movement promoting Johann Comenius's ideas of Pansophia (universal knowledge, all-

[4] *Institut National des Sciences et Arts* (Paris: Baudouin, 1795), pp. 4-5. For a detailed history of the Academy up to the mid-19th century see [Fontanier] Pellisson et d'Olivet, *Histoire de l'académie française* (Paris: Didier et cie., 1858), 2 vols.

[5] D. Maclaren Robertson, *A History of the French Academy 1635-1910* (New York: G. W. Dillingham, 1910), pp. 128-129. Erroneously this source names Section 5 "General History and Philosophy."

embracing learning); several English poets, including John Dryden, were among the early members of the Society, and the diarist Samuel Pepys, elected in 1664, became its president. Thus, a presumption that the Royal Society was chiefly devoted to experimental physics would be patently wrong.

The record of the papers presented to the Society shows a rather wide distribution over many branches of learning. In an historical account, published in 1812, the papers were classified in the following scheme: I. Natural History (botany, zoology, mineralogy, geography and topography); II. Mathematics; III. Mechanical Philosophy (astronomy, optics, dynamics, mechanics, hydrodynamics of liquids and gases (pneumatics), acoustics, navigation, electricity, magnetism); IV. Chemistry (chemistry proper, meteorology, chemical arts and manufactures); V. Other Subjects (weights and measures, political arithmetic, antiquities, and miscellanea).[6] The papers on political arithmetic and antiquities may have been merely occasional digressions[7] and, moreover, in later years the focus may have been put more sharply on mathematics and the natural sciences, resulting in a clearly felt need for an academy of social and cultural sciences.

This need was most clearly perceived when representatives of major European and American academies met in 1899 in Wiesbaden to draw up a scheme for the organization of an "International Association of Academies." The Royal Society represented the United Kingdom but considered itself not competent to represent the country with regard to "historical, philosophical, and philological studies." A group convened by the Royal Society considered that the Society "might propose to enlarge its scope so as to include the representation of the subjects in question" or, alternatively, "if it preferred to maintain the restriction of scope," might support the creation of a new body.

[6] Thomas Thomson, *History of the Royal Society* (London: Robert Baldwin, 1812), pp. vii-viii.

[7] The bias in favor of "natural things" and practical inventions and experiments was quite explicit in a statement by the first curator of the Royal Society, describing its objectives as "To improve the knowledge of naturall [sic] things, and all useful Arts, Manufactures, Mechanick practices, Engynes and Inventions by Experiments (not meddling with Divinity, Metaphysics, Moralls, Politicks, Grammar, Rhetorick or Logick)." Quoted from Charles Richard Weld, *A History of the Royal Society with Memoires of the Presidents* (London: J. W. Parker, 1848), vol. I, p. 146. The inclusion of "all useful Arts, Manufactures," etc., among the original agenda of the Royal Society should remind us of the existence of a separate Society of Arts. Founded in 1754, almost a century after the Royal Society, its name was expanded in 1909 to Royal Society of Arts. From the beginning, its chief purpose has been the encouragement of the arts, manufactures, and commerce. It has published a monthly journal, arranged expositions, and awarded prizes for technical improvements, for example, for the manufacture of tapestry, carpets, and porcelain.

The Royal Society chose not to expand its scope. Thus, in 1902, a royal charter was granted for "The British Academy for the Promotion of Historical, Philosophical, and Philological Studies."[8]

The Academy began with four sections: I. History and Archaeology; II. Philology in its Various Departments; III. Philosophy; and IV. Jurisprudence and Economics. At present (1978) it is organized in fourteen sections: 1. Ancient History; 2. Medieval History; 3. Biblical, Theological, and Religious Studies; 4. Oriental and African Studies; 5. Literature and Philology, Classical; 6. Literature and Philology, Medieval and Modern; 7. Philosophy; 8. Jurisprudence; 9. Economics and Economic History; 10. Archaeology; 11. History of Art; 12. Social and Political Studies; 13. Modern History, 1500-1800; and 14. Modern History from 1800.

Germany

The early history of German academies of sciences was closely associated with the untiring efforts of Leibniz, for whom the establishing of learned academies was a matter of great personal concern. He approached emperors, kings, and princes as well as fellow scholars all over Europe for their help and cooperation in this cause. His plea for the creation of a German Imperial Academy of Science (1676) was not successful.[9] But he did prevail upon King Friedrich I of Prussia to help set up, in 1700, the Societas Regia Scientiarum in Berlin and then, in 1711, the Preussische Akademie der Wissenschaften (Royal Prussia Academy of Sciences [with Leibniz as president]). This was followed in 1751 (35 years after Leibniz's death) by the Akademie der Wissenschaften (Academy of Sciences) at Göttingen and in 1759 by the Bavarian Akademie der Wissenschaften.

The Bavarian Academy of Sciences had four classes. I. History; II. Philosophy; III. Literature (added in 1778); and IV. Physics.[10] The academies at Berlin and at Göttingen, and also several later German academies, were divided into two classes: I. Philosophy and Historical Sciences; and II. Mathematics and Natural Sciences. The order was reversed in some of the academies but it did not connote any ranking. Each class was subdivided into sections and commissions.

After the second world war and the splitting up of the nation into

---

[8] *Proceedings of the British Academy 1903-1904* (London: British Academy, 1904 [?]), pp. vii-ix.

[9] On Leibniz's projects see above, Chapter 5.

[10] Lorenz Westenriede, *Geschichte der Baierischen Akademie der Wissenschaften, Part 1: 1759-1777* (Munich: Akademischer Bücher Verlag, 1784); *Part 2: 1778-1800* (Munich: Joseph Lindauer, 1807).

West Germany (the Federal Republic of Germany) and East Germany
(the German Democratic Republic), and the splitting up of Berlin
into an eastern and a western sector, we find the Berlin Academy of
Sciences in the East, and a Berlin Academy of [Fine] Arts (Kunstakademie) in the West. (This Kunstakademie had been founded in
1696, earlier than the Academy of Sciences.) In West Germany the
Bavarian Academy of Sciences in Munich and the Göttingen Academy have remained active, as has the Heidelberg Academy (founded
in 1909), and two new academies were established: the Academy of
Science and Literature in Mainz (in 1949) and the Rhineland-West-
phalia Academy of Sciences in Düsseldorf (in 1950, renamed in
1970). The classes or sections of the academies at Munich, Göttingen,
and Heidelberg have remained unchanged. Mainz has three sections:
I. Mathematics and Natural Sciences, II. Philosophy and Social Sciences, and III. Literature. Düsseldorf has two sections: I. Philosophy,
and II. Natural, Technical, and Economic Sciences.

The Academy of Sciences of the German Democratic Republic in
East Berlin includes many specialized research institutes: twenty-
five "central institutes," fifteen "institutes," and six "research centers." This system of research institutes within, or affiliated with,
academies (or with classes or sections of academies) is a relatively
recent development, especially where it involves research staff of
persons who are not elected members of the academy. Individual
institutes of the academy may have several hundred employees of
various ranks and qualifications who do research in a routine fashion.
The Berlin Academy itself, that is, the roster of academicians, is now
divided into six sections: 1. Mathematics, Physics, and Technological Sciences; 2. Chemistry, Geology, and Biology; 3. Mining, Metallurgy, and Geology Applied to Mining; 4. Medicine; 5. Languages,
Literary and Fine-Art Sciences (*Kunstwissenschaften*); and 6. Philosophy, History, Political Science, Juridical, and Economic Sciences.

Russia and the Soviet Union

Since the system of large research institutes attached to the academy is most highly developed in the socialist countries, it may be
appropriate to turn next to the Soviet Union. This order of presentation is justified also by the chronological sequence, for it was in
1725—fourteen years after the foundation of the Prussian Academy
at Berlin—that Empress Catherine (after plans previously approved
by Peter the Great) founded the Imperatorskaya Akademiya Naük
(Imperial Academy of Sciences) at St. Petersburg, the first academy
in Russia. Despite all the changes during the next 250 years, the

Academy of Sciences of the Union of Soviet Socialist Republics in Moscow is regarded as its descendant. Indeed, the Moscow Academy itself gives 1725 as the year of its foundation. Its latest reorganization was in 1963; it is subordinate to the Council of Ministers of the U.S.S.R. and, in 1973, controlled the activities of more than 260 scientific institutions—including councils, commissions, research stations, laboratories, naval institutes, observatories, and museums— and eleven scientific societies.[11] To give just two examples: the Department of Economics includes twenty-two institutes, councils, and so forth, and the Department of Literature and Linguistics includes sixteen.

The Academy itself is divided into four sections, each subdivided into departments, and one separate Siberian department. The four sections are I. Physical-Technical and Mathematical Sciences; II. Chemistry and Biological Sciences; III. Earth Sciences; and IV. Social Sciences. Section I has five departments, 1. Mathematics; 2. General Physics and Astronomy; 3. Nuclear Physics; 4. Physical and Technical Problems of Energy; 5. Mechanics and Control Processes. Section II also has five departments: 1. General and Technological Chemistry; 2. Physical Chemistry and Technology of Inorganic Materials; 3. Biochemistry, Biophysics and Chemistry of Physiologically Active Compounds; 4. Physiology; 5. General Biology. Section III has only two departments: 1. Geology, Geophysics and Geochemistry; 2. Oceanology, Atmospheric Physics, and Geography. And Section IV has four departments: 1. History; 2. Philosophy and Law; 3. Economics; 4. Literature and Linguistics.

Sweden

The history of the Kungliga Vetenskapsakademien (Royal Academies of Sciences) at Stockholm is complicated by the fact that much of the time it consisted of several independent academies. It began as a small private group of scholars. Even after its confirmation as a royal institution in 1741, it continued as a cluster of separate academies. In 1799 the Royal Academy was organized into seven classes; and at present it consists of the following twelve classes: I. Mathematics, II. Astronomy, III. Physics, IV. Chemistry, V. Mineralogy, Geology, and Physical Geography, VI. Botany, VII. Zoology, VIII. Medical Sciences, IX. Technical Sciences, X. Economic, Statistical, and Social Sciences, XI. Geophysics, and XII. Other Sciences and

[11] *The World of Learning: 1974-75*, (London: Europa Publications, 25th ed., 1974), vol. 2, p. 1,184. — The reader should bear in mind that "scientific" is used in the international sense, which comprises all branches of academic learning and research, including the humanities (called in Russia the "humanistic sciences").

Scientific Research of Outstanding Merit. Attached to the Royal Academy are observatories, museums, institutes, and committees. Of the latter the most influential are the Nobel-Prize committees for physics, chemistry, and economics.[12]

Belgium

The political history of Belgium is reflected in the history of its Academy of Sciences. It was officially founded by Empress Maria Theresa in 1772—when Belgium was part of Hapsburg Austria—as the Académie impériale et royale des sciences et belles-lettres; however, a Société littéraire had been established in 1769, and this is usually given as the year of the founding of the Academy. The Academy was divided into three classes, the names of which were later accorded more conspicuous recognition by being included in the new title of the institution: Académie royale des sciences, des lettres et des beaux-arts de Belgique.[13]

The more detailed classification subdivides Class I into two sections, one for mathematical and physical sciences, and another for natural sciences; calls Class II "Letters and Moral and Political Sciences" and subdivides it into one section for history and letters and another for moral and political sciences; and subdivides Class III, Fine Arts, into six sections: painting, sculpture, engraving, architecture, music, and art history and criticism.[14]

The Netherlands

The earliest academy in the Netherlands was the Hollandsche Maatschappij der Wetenschappen (Society of Sciences) in Haarlem, established in 1752. The Academy of Sciences in Amsterdam goes back to 1808, when Louis Napoléon founded the Royal Institute of Sciences, Letters and Arts. In 1851 it became the Koninklijke Nederlandsche Akademie van Wetenschappen (Royal Netherlandish Academy of Sciences).[15] Its two divisions were then, and still are, I. Mathematical and Natural Sciences, and II. Historical and Literary

[12] Kungliga Vetenskapsakademien, *Årsbok 1968* (Stockholm: Almquist & Wiksell), pp. 22-24, 46-60.

[13] Académie royale des sciences, des lettres et des beaux-arts de Belgique, *Notices Biographiques et Bibliographiques, 1886* (Brussels: F. Hayez, 1887).

[14] *The World of Learning 1975-76* (London: Europa Publications, 26th ed., 1975), vol. 1, p. 145.

[15] Koninklijke Nederlandsche Akademie van Wetenschappen, *Jaarboek 1973* (Amsterdam: North-Holland Publishing Co., 1974).

Sciences.[16] The first division has at present nine sections: 1. Mathematics; 2. Physics (*Natuurkunde*) and Astronomy; 3. Chemistry; 4. Earth Science; 5. Technical Sciences; 6. Biology; 7. Medicine; 8. Biochemistry and Biophysics; and 9. Free Section (for borderline fields). The second division, embracing what German classifiers would call the social and cultural sciences and what some American classifiers might call social sciences, arts and humanities, is not strictly sectionalized but allows members to belong to more than one group of scholars.

Austria

No academy of sciences had a longer gestation period than the Austrian.[17] It was first recommended and promoted by Leibniz in 1712; then by Johann Christoph Gottsched in 1749; almost delivered by Empress Maria Theresa in 1750, and again in 1774; eventually moved forward by Prince Metternich in 1837; and finally established by Metternich[18] and Emperor Ferdinand of Austria in 1847—one year before the rebellion of 1848.

There were reorganizations in 1919, after the end of World War I and the termination of the Hapsburg monarchy; in 1938, after the beginning of the Nazi regime; and in 1947, after the collapse of the Nazi regime. The Academy's structure has also been changed repeatedly, though the division into two classes has always been retained: I. Mathematics and Natural Sciences, and II. Philosophy (for a time, however, Philology) and History. The subdivisions have been reshuffled several times; in 1947, the two classes had fourteen and twenty sections, respectively. The mathematical-and-natural-sciences class is divided into 1. Astronomy and Geodesy; 2. Mathematics; 3. Physics; 4. Geophysics; 5. Chemistry; 6. Mineralogy; 7. Geology and Palaeontology; 8. Physical Geography; 9. Botany; 10. Zoology; 11. Anatomy; Histology and [Physical] Anthropology; 12.

---

[16] The Dutch names are "I. Wis- en natuurkundige wetenschappen, II. Geschied- en letterkundige wetenschappen." Dutch translators into English have a tendency to suppress the linguistic characteristics of their own language by avoiding literal translation and replacing them by English renditions that fit English rather than Dutch institutions. Thus, in the *World of Learning* the Dutch "Akademie van Wetenschappen" is rendered as "Academy of Arts and Sciences," and the Dutch "Geschied- en letterkundige wetenschappen" (historical and literary sciences) is rendered as "Philology, Literature, History and Philosophy" (suppressing the word "sciences").

[17] Richard Meister, *Geschichte der Akademie der Wissenschaften in Wien, 1847-1947* (Vienna: Holzhammer, 1947).

[18] It is not easy to decide whether Prince Metternich should be given credit as successful promoter and founder, or charged as chief procrastinator. See Meister, pp. 64-67.

Physiology; 13. Medicine; and 14. Technical Sciences. The philo-sophical-historical class is divided into 1. Philosophy and Pedagogy; 2. History; 3. Roman Law and History of Ancient Laws; 4. History of German Law; 5. Church Law and Church History; 6. Civil Law, Criminal Law, and Legal Procedure; 7. Public Law, Constitutional Law, Administrative Law, and International Law; 8. Economic Sci-ences and Sociology; 9. Ancient History and Antiquity; 10. Classical Archaeology and History of Art;[19] 11. Music Science;[20] 12. General and Indo-Germanic Linguistics; 13. Classical, Medieval-Latin and Byzantine Philology; 14. German Philology; 15. Romance Philology; 16. English Philology; 17. Slavic Philology; 18. Oriental History; Philology and Antiquity; 19. Ethnography and Prehistory; and 20. Geography. The degree of fragmentation, especially in the juridical and cultural sciences, is extraordinary: no fewer than five sections deal with law, and seven sections with languages and literatures.

At present, thirty-eight commissions are attached to the Acad-emy—four to the class of mathematical and natural sciences, twenty-seven to the class of philosophical and historical sciences, and seven jointly to both. In addition, the Academy operates sixteen institutes—for example, for brain research, comparative-behavior research (in-cluding animal sociology), high-energy physics, solid-state physics, socio-economic development research—and six international pro-grams—for example, a hydrological program and a program on "Man and the Biosphere."[21]

ACADEMIES IN THE UNITED STATES

In the United States the number of learned societies called acad-emies or serving as academies is so large that a statistical account might present a better picture than a historical narrative. The reason for the proliferation is that most of the academies in the United States are private and local (rather than official national organizations char-tered or sponsored by emperors, kings, or princes) and require no official authorizations by state or local governments. By confining the story to academies with truly national membership and with truly pansophic, or at least multidisciplinary scope, a narrative be-comes manageable. For example, the highly prestigious New York Academy of Sciences, founded in 1817, may be excluded because more than one-third of its members are residents of New York; the

---

[19] An earlier classification had *Kunstwissenschaft* in the title of a section. It included the history, as well as the theory, of fine arts.

[20] *Musikwissenschaft* includes history, as well as theory, of music.

[21] Österreichische Akademie der Wissenschaften, *Almanach für das Jahr 1975* (Vienna: Akademie der Wissenschaften, 1976), pp. 629-653.

National Academy of Education, the National Academy of Engineering, both founded in 1964, and the Institute of Medicine, founded in 1970, may be excluded because their interests are not sufficiently broad.[22]

American Philosophical Society

The oldest organization with the character of an academy with continental (or even international) as well as pansophic scope is the American Philosophical Society Held at Philadelphia. It was started by Benjamin Franklin in 1743 and was designed for the promotion of "useful knowledge" with the focus on the observational and experimental sciences. In 1769 it established six committees: 1. Geography, Mathematics, Natural Philosophy and Astronomy; 2. Medicine and Anatomy; 3. Natural History and Chemistry; 4. Trade and Commerce; 5. Mechanics and Architecture; 6. Husbandry and American Improvements. A seventh committee was added in 1815: History, Moral Science, and General Literature. The regrouping of 1936 showed four classes: I. Mathematical and Physical Sciences; II. Geological and Biological Sciences; III. Social Sciences, and IV. Humanities. This general scheme has survived even the latest reclassifications, which modernized the subdivisions of each class and added a fifth class for members at large.

The new classification, officially adopted in 1976 and slightly altered in 1980, is given here in full: Class I. Mathematical and Physical Sciences: 1. Mathematics; 2. Astronomy; 3. Physics; 4. Chemistry and Chemical Biochemistry; 5. Engineering; 6. Physical Earth Sciences. Class II. Biological Sciences: 1. Biological Earth Sciences; 2. Zoology, Anatomy; 3. Botany, Microbiology; 4. Experimental Psychology; 5. Physiology, Biological Biochemistry, Pathology; 6. Medicine, Pharmacology, Surgery. Class III. Social Sciences: 1. Economics, Finance, Statistics, Sociology; 2. History since 1715;

---

[22] Some of these specialized academies recognize the importance of an interdisciplinary membership, or they may emphasize in their system of classes or sections the transdisciplinary vision of their organizers. To give just one example, the National Academy of Education has five sections: I. the history and philosophy of education, II. the politics, economics, sociology, and anthropology of education, III. the psychology of education, IV. the study of educational practice; and V. a group of members at large.

Several reference works list the academies in the United States, for example, *The World of Learning; Scientific, Technical and Related Societies of the United States;* and *Directory and Proceedings of the Association of Academies of Science.* The largest number of academies in the United States are chiefly interested in natural history; an examination of the academies subdivided in sections shows a conspicuous prevalence of sections for biology, or zoology and botany.

3. Jurisprudence and Political Science. Class IV. Humanities: 1. Philosophy, Education; 2. Ancient, Medieval, Cultural History; 3. Cultural Anthropology; 4. Archaeology, History of Art; 5. Languages and Literary History. Class V. Fields of endeavor not included within the previous four classes in which candidates have achieved equivalent distinction in their profession or occupation: 1. Administration; 2. the Creative Arts; 3. Banking, the Law, and Public Affairs.

This classification scheme takes account of the fact that several fields of learning, for example, chemistry, the life sciences, and the earth sciences, have come to overlap so much that they can no longer be assigned either to the physical or to the biological sciences. Thus, several fields had to be split in the middle before they could be placed in one of the classes. For example, "physical earth sciences" are distinguished from "biological earth sciences," and "chemical biochemistry" from "biological biochemistry." The difficulty of dividing psychology between the biological and the social sciences is not completely overcome in the new classification. The problem of differentiating creative writers and artists from scholarly writers on literature and art has been solved by having the latter in the subdivision "Letters and Fine Arts" in Class IV and the producers of literature, art, and music in Class V, thus separating the critics and the doers.

American Academy of Arts and Sciences

The second-oldest American academy, The American Academy of Arts and Sciences was founded in Boston in 1780, "to cultivate every art and science which may tend to advance the interest, honor, dignity, and happiness of a free, independent, and virtuous people." At present it is organized in four classes with five or six sections each, as follows: Class I. Mathematical and Physical Sciences: 1. Mathematics, 2. Physics, 3. Chemistry, 4. Astronomy and Earth Sciences, and 5. Engineering Sciences and Technology; Class II. Biological Sciences: 1. Molecular Biology, 2. Cellular and Developmental Biology, 3. Physiology and Experimental Psychology,[23] 4. Evolutionary and Environmental Biology, and 5. Medicine; Class III. Social Arts and Sciences: 1. Social Relations, 2. Economics, 3. Political Science, 4. Law, 5. Public Affairs and Business Administration, and 6. Educational and Scientific Administration; Class IV.

---

[23] It may be a mere oversight that Psychology other than physiological and experimental has no explicitly assigned place in this scheme. Clinical Psychology may be included with Medicine, but Social Psychology may have to be accommodated under Social Relations; this does not seem to be a very satisfactory solution.

Humanities: 1. Philosophy and Theology, 2. History and Archaeology, 3. Philology and Criticism, 4. Literature, and 5. Fine Arts.

This classification scheme has been found unsatisfactory by one past president of the Academy. He pointed especially to "serious shortcomings" in Class IV. "For example, the section entitled 'Philology and Criticism' includes such divers scholars as linguists and literary critics."[24] He seemed to prefer a division into five classes—the natural sciences (which would include most of what is now in Classes I and II); the practical sciences (technology, medicine, and architecture, thus joining sections or parts of sections now spread over Classes I, II, and IV); the social sciences (most of what is now in Class III); the humanities (philosophy, history, and criticism); and the arts (literature, sculpture, painting, theatre, dance, and music).[25] I suppose he would, to be consistent, want to move law from Class III to the proposed class of practical sciences.

National Academy of Sciences

One academy received a charter from the United States Congress: the National Academy of Sciences, set up in Washington in 1863 to serve as an independent adviser to the Federal Government in science and technology. Its history of reorganizations and reclassifications of disciplines is interesting, both because of the frequency of change and because of the considerations behind these changes.[26] At the outset, in 1863, the Academy was divided into ten sections: 1. Mathematics; 2. Physics; 3. Astronomy, Geography, and Geodesy; 4. Mechanics; 5. Chemistry; 6. Mineralogy and Geology; 7. Zoology; 8. Botany; 9. Anatomy and Physiology; and 10. Ethnology. In 1872, the sections were abolished; there were committees working on reorganization and producing plans, which were considered and deferred in 1885, 1892, 1894. The second of these plans proposed seven sections, with one for "Anthropology, including Sociology, Economic Science, etc." The 1894 proposal substituted for this a section labeled "Miscellaneous." The scheme adopted in 1899 had six sections: Astronomy was merged with Mathematics; Engineering (replacing Mechanics) with Physics; Chemistry kept its original independence; Geology became linked with Palaeontology; Zoology, Botany,

---

[24] Victor F. Weisskopf, "Report of the President," in American Academy of Arts and Science, *Records 1975-1976*, p. 8.

[25] Ibid., p. 7.

[26] Frederick W. True, *A History of the First Half-Century of the National Academy of Sciences, 1863-1913* (Washington: National Academy of Sciences, 1913); and Edwin Bidwell Wilson, *History of the Proceedings of the National Academy of Sciences, 1914-1963* (Washington, D.C.: National Academy of Sciences, 1966).

Anatomy, and Physiology became one comprehensive section, Biology; and Anthropology was added. Other disciplines that lost separate listing in the new organization were Geography and Geodesy. The change from "Ethnology" to "Anthropology" was probably only a change in name.

The next change, in 1911, added Psychology, but only as a part of a section together with Anthropology; and it split the previously united Biology into three separate sections, Botany, Zoology with Animal Morphology, and Physiology with Pathology. This arrangement with eight sections lasted only until 1914, when Mathematics and Astronomy became independent sections. Another divorce came in 1919, when Physics and Engineering separated. The next split occurred in 1932: Physiology and Pathology dissolved their marriage, each linking up with newcomers—Physiology with Biochemistry, Pathology with Bacteriology. There were now eleven sections.

In 1942 Palaeontology lost its listing, leaving Geology as the sole owner of the title to the section. In 1948 another divorce restored the independence of Anthropology and gave Psychology its separate berth. In 1951 a thirteenth section was established: Geophysics. In 1954 Physiology and Biochemistry were separated and became independent sections. In 1957 Microbiology replaced Bacteriology as section-partner of Pathology.[27] In 1965 Applied Biology was added as a fifteenth section, and a year later an analogous addition was made by forming a section for Applied Physical and Mathematical Sciences. Four changes were made in 1968: Anatomy was dropped from the section for Zoology, and Pathology from the section for Microbiology; and two new sections were added, one for Medical Sciences and another for Genetics. A nineteenth section was established in 1971—and this marked a real change of heart—for "Social, Economic, and Political Sciences." It was split in 1974, into one section for Social and Political Sciences and another for Economic Sciences.[28]

A major reorganization occurred in 1975, when the twenty sections, for which a new numbering system had been adopted in 1974, were renumbered and some of them renamed; and three new sections were added, two of them by splitting the section for Medical Sciences into three parts, and one by creating a section for Population Biology, Evolution, and Ecology. In this reorganization Zoology lost its status as a separate class, and so did Microbiology, (which had been given this status only in 1968, when it shed Pathology as a partner). The

[27] Wilson, pp. 21-23.
[28] National Academy of Sciences, *Annual Reports, 1965-66*, p. 231; *1966-67*, p. 242; *1968-69*, p. 241; *1971-72*, p. 199; *1974-75*, p. 202.

line-up of the twenty-three sections—divided into five categories, indicated by the first digit of a numerical code—is as follows: 11. Mathematics, 12. Astronomy, 13. Physics, 14. Chemistry, 15. Geology, 16. Geophysics; 21. Biochemistry, 22. Cellular and Developmental Biology, 23. Physiological Sciences, 24. Neurobiology, 25. Botany, 26. Genetics, 27. Population Biology, Evolution, and Ecology; 31. Engineering, 32. Applied Biology, 33. Applied Physical and Mathematical Sciences; 41. Medical Genetics, Hematology, and Oncology, 42. Medical Physiology, Endocrinology, and Metabolism, 43. Medical Microbiology and Immunology; 51. Anthropology, 52. Psychology, 53. Social and Political Sciences, 54. Economic Sciences.

The history of organizational changes is interesting in that it reflects the Academy's flexibility in acknowledging changes in the division and specialization of physical and biological disciplines and, at the same time, its rigidity and procrastination in recognizing the existence, let alone the developments, of the social sciences. For example, although the plan of 1892 had proposed a section (one out of a total of seven) for "Anthropology, including Sociology, Economic Science etc.," and Anthropology was actually recognized in 1899 (perhaps in deference to its branch, "Physical Anthropology"), it took until 1911 for Psychology to be admitted (as a section-partner with Anthropology) and until 1972 for Social, Economic, and Political Sciences to be allowed in. They had not been represented in the National Academy for the first 109 years of its life.

The present organization still reflects the bias against social and cultural disciplines. There are seven sections for pure and applied physical sciences and engineering (12-16,31,33) and eleven sections for biological and medical sciences (21-27,32,41-43). Against these eighteen sections, representing natural sciences, technology, and medicine, there are the separate sections for Mathematics (11), a formal science, Anthropology (51) and Psychology (52), sciences that straddle the natural and social sciences, and only two sections (53 and 54) for the social sciences proper. Perhaps it is unrealistic to expect a better understanding of highly specialized fields of scientific inquiry only a few years after their "official" recognition.

The imbalance in the organization and composition of the National Academy of Sciences (NAS) was slightly alleviated in 1916 by the establishment of an affiliated organization, the National Research Council (NRC), in which, in 1919, "Psychology and Anthropology" became one of seven scientific divisions. The NRC was founded at the request of the Government (President Woodrow Wilson) and was designed to study and advise on matters related to national defense, national security, and welfare. The NRC has functioned, so to speak, as the business arm of the NAS, employing for its research activities and for the preparation of its reports not just members of the Academy but nonmember specialists and research staff, part-time and full-time, as well as temporary consultants. Engineering was one of the divisions from the beginning. (In the NAS, we recall, there was in 1863 a section on Mechanics, replaced in 1899 by a section for Physics and Engineering, until in 1919 Engineering became an independent section.) In the NRC, Industrial Research was joined to the Division of Engineering from 1932 to 1972. (By that time, there was a separate National Academy of Engineering [NAE], established in 1964 and living in close symbiosis with the NAS. Thus, under the same roof, there are three organizations for engineering: the NAE, Section 31 of the NAS, and a division of NRC.) The division "Anthropology and Psychology" was renamed "Division of Behavioral Sciences" in 1963.

A major reorganization of the NRC in 1973 gave it four discipline-oriented assemblies and four problem-oriented commissions. The four assemblies are for Engineering, Life Sciences, Physical Sciences, and Behavioral and Social Sciences. The four commissions are on Human Resources, International Relations, Natural Resources, and Sociotechnical Systems. Thus, the social sciences are, at last, "in business." Indeed, the Assembly for Behavioral and Social Sciences (ABASS) has been the fastest-growing part of the NRC.[29]

American Council of Learned Societies

No attempt, however, had been made to close the schism between "the two cultures": the humanities and the arts had not found places in the National Academy. This situation became conspicuous in 1919 (soon after the end of World War I) when a French group, chiefly interested in philology, archaeology, and history, proposed the establishment of an "International Union of Academies." The National Academy of Sciences, because of its restrictive definition of science and the consequent exclusion of humanistic disciplines, could not represent these branches of learning in the International Union of Academies. Thus, a new organization, the American Council of Learned Societies (ACLS)—embracing initially thirteen learned societies—was formed in 1919, to be the counterpart of the initial ten foreign academies. The ACLS represented the social sciences and the humanities in the International Union of Academies. This Union in-

[29] Constance Holden, "ABASS: Social Sciences Carving a Niche at the Academy," *Science*, vol. 199 (17 March 1978), pp. 1183-1187.

cluded in 1976 the academies of sciences or equivalent organizations of thirty-two countries.

The ACLS grew from the thirteen member associations in 1920 to forty-two in 1976. These constituent learned societies represent social sciences (including anthropology, economics, history, geography, political science, psychology, and sociology), humanities (including archaeology, ancient history, linguistics, oriental studies, philology, and philosophy) and also comprehensive academies (American Philosophical Society, American Academy of Arts and Sciences). Among the more recent members are the Society of the History of Technology, the American Society for Legal History, the American Psychological Association, and the American Society for Theatre Research.[30]

The ACLS does its work chiefly through committees. Over the years, several of these committees have been sponsored jointly with other organizations, especially with the Social Science Research Council.

Social Science Research Council

In accordance with a proposal made in 1922, noting excessive specialization and stressing the desirability of "cooperative and coordinated research in the social sciences," the Social Science Research Council (SSRC) was established in 1923 and incorporated in 1924. The founding of the National Research Council (NRC) had undoubtedly given a strong impetus to the social scientists, partly by providing a model of the institutionalization of cooperative research, partly by organizing a committee for research on human migration, a project in which social scientists were asked to participate.[31]

The SSRC is composed of seven professional organizations in as many fields of the social sciences (anthropology, economics, history, political science, psychology, sociology, and statistics), and their representatives make up the board. They are joined by "at-large members," from allied fields. This is in accord with the view that "the societies which at present constitute the Council do not regard themselves as covering the whole field of social science."[32]

[30] American Council of Learned Societies Devoted to Humanistic Studies. *Directory of Constituent Societies of the American Council of Learned Societies*, May 1978.

[31] Social Science Research Council, *Third Annual Report, 1926-27* (New York: Social Science Research Council, 1927), pp. 15-16. For a "History and Purposes of the Social Science Research Council" see *Fifth Annual Report, 1928-29* (New York: Social Science Research Council, 1929), Appendix A, pp. 39-41.

[32] *Fifth Annual Report, 1928-29*, p. 40.

The SSRC has several standing committees as well as ad hoc committees, charged with research tasks that usually straddle two or more social sciences. Specialists of the pertinent disciplines are appointed to these committees. In many of the projects the SSRC cooperates with other organizations.

Neither the SSRC nor the ACLS are academies in the traditional sense: they do not elect individual scholars in recognition of their scientific achievements. Their membership consists of learned societies, most of which are quite open-ended, that is, they can be joined by any individual interested in that field of study. It is chiefly in the promotion of scholarly research that these organizations of organizations share some of the characteristics of academies.[33]

American Association for the Advancement of Science

Another multidisciplinary organization in the United States should not remain unmentioned in this survey, even if it is not an academy— to which eminent scholars are elected in recognition of their scientific achievements—but an association that every interested person may join: the American Association for the Advancement of Science (AAAS), founded in 1880. Although it has "open admission" to membership, it does have a system of elected fellows.

The AAAS, after many changes in its sectional organization, has now (1979) twenty-one sections: A. Mathematics; B. Physics; C. Chemistry; D. Astronomy; E. Geology and Geography; G. Biological Sciences; H. Anthropology; J. Psychology; K. Social and Economic Sciences; L. History and Philosophy of Science; M. Engineering; N. Medical Sciences; O. Agriculture; P. Industrial Science; Q. Education; R. Dentistry; S. Pharmaceutical Science; T. Information, Computing, and Communication; U. Statistics; W. Atmospheric and Hydrospheric Sciences; and X. General.

Faithful to the current Anglo-American usage of the word "science," the AAAS has provided slots for natural, social, technological, medical, and other practical sciences, but not for cultural disciplines,

---

[33] A paragraph from Section III of the Statutes of the International Union of Academies may be quoted in this context: "The word *Académique* applies first and foremost to the learned bodies properly called academies and having a national character; it includes also, either in default of academies or side by side with these latter and in agreement with them, the scientific institutions which may be considered as assimilated to academies by reason of their national character, their scientific purposes, and the nature and method of their work, and which in each of the countries affiliated with the Union have decided or shall decide to form a group and to assure themselves a joint representation." Quoted from Council of Learned Societies, *Bulletin*, no. 2 (December 1922), p. 4.

with the exception of the history and philosophy of science, and perhaps Section X, General.

American Association for the Advancement of the Humanities

The fact that the disciplines that would in non-English-speaking countries be called "cultural sciences" were left out of most academies and associations for the promotion of advanced studies in the United States led eventually to the establishment of an American Association for the Advancement of the Humanities (AAAH). The founding of the AAAH in 1977 trailed the founding of the AAAS by almost one hundred years.[34]

The AAAH has among its objectives to "promote public understanding of the humanities" and to help humanists to "address issues of public concern."[35] Noteworthy is its aim to "strengthen ties among humanists" and to "reduce their fragmentation in specialized disciplines." In line with this aim, there is no sectional organization, no classification of fields of study and inquiry. But the editor of the *Humanities Report* promises to publish "occasional special reports examining fields of inquiry within the humanities."[36]

[34] There could not have been an AAAH much earlier, because the present meaning of humanities did not exist before 1930 and was not widely accepted before the 1950s. Traditionally, humanistic studies were studies in classical Greek and Latin, and of the history of classic Greece and Rome. See Chapter 3 in Volume I of this work.

[35] The promotional aims of the AAAH incited the writing of a review in *The New Republic* with the title "The Humanities Hustle."

[36] *Humanities Report*, vol. 3 (January 1981), p. 3.

CHAPTER 9

LIBRARIES:
CLASSIFICATION SYSTEMS

CLASSIFYING men and women by the branches of learning in which they have specialized is in several respects different from classifying books and articles by the subject matter with which they deal. One difference lies in the fact that persons may themselves select the group to which they "belong," whereas publications have to be grouped by others judging their contents (often only by their titles). These two kinds of classifications may serve quite different purposes: the sections to which members of an academy belong help the staff decide who should be invited to which conferences or committee meetings; the classes in which books are listed help the library staff decide in which stacks to shelve the books so that they can be found when they are wanted.

For all uses, problems of overlapping interests of multidisciplinary and interdisciplinary competence (of persons) and coverage (of publications) present difficulties, but they may call for different solutions in grouping persons and in cataloguing books. When finer distinctions of subject-matter areas are required, which is imperative in cataloguing and other library operations, it will often be found that classification schemes designed for publications are not suitable for classifying the members of academies and universities by the branches of learning they profess.

Philosophical Harmony versus Practical Needs

Despite these and other differences, the classification schemes used in libraries have long been modeled after academic and encyclopaedic systems. This was perhaps not true of schemes used in the catalogues of libraries in antiquity, particularly the library of Alexandria, founded by King Ptolemaeus Philadelphus of Egypt (283-247 B.C.) with Aristotle as one of the advisers. A hundred years after its establishment, the library had a collection of 400,000 scrolls in all languages of the period. The Greek poet Kallimachos (Callimachus in Latin) became one of the librarians; his catalogue is probably the most widely researched of the early products of librarianship.[1] According to the most reliable sources, the *Pinakes* of Kallimachos were compiled in 2,310 scrolls, of which only some fragments now exist. The classification system does not really satisfy the requirements nowadays insisted upon in a library catalogue. In some instances, the scrolls are classed by the state (city) in which the author resided; in other instances, by the major vocation or avocation of the writer (dramatist, poet, etc.); within the special catalogues the order was sometimes chronological, sometimes alphabetical. Still, one can identify an overall principle of classification in divisions for laws and lawmakers, philosophers, poets, historians, orators and rhetoricians, and miscellaneous works. Within literature, epic and dramatic works were distinguished.[2] As far as the focus of this chapter is concerned, we may say that the catalogue of the library of Alexandria does not yet qualify as a classification by subject group.

One of the earliest, perhaps the first, bibliographic subject classification in print was that by Conrad Gesner, who in 1548 catalogued, not the books contained in one particular library, but all the 15,000 books in Latin, Greek, and Hebrew that he knew to exist somewhere.[3] Gesner arranged the literature into twenty-one subject groups: 1. Grammar and Philology, 2. Dialectics, 3. Rhetoric, 4. Poetry, 5. Arithmetic, 6. Geometry and Optics, 7. Music, 8. Astronomy, 9. Astrology, 10. Divination and Magic, 11. Geography, 12. History, 13. Useful and Mechanical Arts, 14. Natural Philosophy, 15. Metaphysics and Pagan Theology, 16. Moral Philosophy, 17. Domestic or Social Philosophy, 18. Civil and Military Arts, 19. Law, 20. Medicine, and 21. Christian Theology.

This scheme—which incidentally seems to have no obvious place for psychology (or "the science of the human soul")—was undoubtedly derived from the curricula of medieval universities. Its signif-

---

[1] Some scholars took pains to deny his status as chief librarian and bibliographer. Max Arthur Lincke, *De Callimachi vita et scriptis* (Halle: University of Halle-Wittenberg 1862).

[2] Victor Garthausen, *Die Alexandrinische Bibliothek: Ihr Vorbild, Katalog und Betrieb* (Leipzig: Deutsches Museum für Buch und Schrift, 1922), pp. 3-6, 24-26.

[3] His *Bibliotheca Universalis . . .* (Zürich: Christophorus, 1545) had been an author index, arranged alphabetically by the authors' Christian names. His *Pandectarum sive partitionem universalium . . . libri xxi* (Zürich: Christophorus, 1548) contained the subject classification. Of the twenty-one books announced in the title the one on Medicine was not published as planned but was replaced by a bibliography of Galen's works; the twenty-first, on Christian Theology, was published separately in 1549 with no fewer than 25,000 subject headings (with multiple listings of most titles). See Theodore Besterman, *The Beginnings of Systematic Bibliography* (London: Oxford University Press, 1935), pp. 14-20, 64.

icance lies in the fact that it preceded Bacon's classification of learning by sixty years; moreover, it was not only a classification scheme
but an actual catalogue of published works.

As a rule, librarians followed the systems that some philosophers
had developed for their own, often quite impractical, purposes. This
is a matter of record, for example, in the case of the early classification
scheme of the Library of Congress of the United States.

Thomas Jefferson's personal library became the nucleus of the
collection of the Library of Congress after its first collection had been
destroyed by the fire of 1812. Jefferson had arranged his collection
around the Baconian system of three main sources of knowledge—
Memory, Reason, and Imagination—with forty-four divisions within
these categories.[4] "The Librarian refined the forty-four somewhat,
locked them into a printed book catalogue, and froze the Library of
Congress's classification scheme for a hundred years. As late as Theodore Roosevelt's time, the Library's cataloguers were dutifully sorting
hundreds of thousands of volumes into the same forty-four com-
partments in which the earliest titles had sat on the shelves at Mon-
ticello."[5]

Although librarians generally recognized that the practical requirements of a library and "theoretical harmony" of its catalogue
with a system first presented in 1605 were hardly compatible, the
Baconian scheme seemed indestructable. When Melvil Dewey in
1873 developed a streamlined classification scheme in nine major
classes for the library of Amherst College, he found it appropriate
to reassure his readers that "in filling the nine classes of the scheme
the inverted Baconian arrangement of the St. Louis Library has been
followed."[6]

The Dewey Decimal System

The Dewey system, expanded and amended several times, became
the most widely used classification scheme for libraries, except perhaps for an earlier French system developed by Gustav Brunet in
1865. The Dewey system, first used by American college and university libraries, soon became the most popular system in public
libraries and was made the basis for the classification adopted in

[4] We may recall that Ephraim Chambers' *Cyclopaedia* (1728) had an arrangement
of the universe of learning in forty-seven classes.

[5] Charles A. Goodrum, *The Library of Congress* (New York: Praeger Publishers,
1974), p. 15.

[6] Melvil Dewey, *Classification and Subject Index for a Library* (Amherst, Mass.,
1876), p. 10. — The 18th edition appeared in 1971 (Lake Placid Club, N.Y.: Forest
Press, 1971).

1905 by the International Institute of Bibliography in Brussels. (The Brussels classification was printed in a catalogue of over 2,000 pages.) This "Extended Dewey System," as it has often been called, became the standard classification for libraries and booksellers on the European continent, especially in France and Italy.[7] In the United States, it has been used by more libraries than any other system.

Dewey's invention "was not really in the classification scheme; rather it was a winning idea of numbering a classification" that appeared practical to cataloguers and to users of libraries. "The impossibility of making a satisfactory classification of all knowledge as preserved in books has been appreciated from the first, and nothing of the kind attempted. Theoretical harmony and exactness has been repeatedly sacrificed to the practical requirements of the library or to the convenience of the departments in the college."[8]

Because of its numerical arrangement, in which each major class was assigned one hundred numbers, and each subclass ten numbers, in three digits, the scheme was called the "Dewey Decimal" system. The first hundred numbers, 000 to 099, were given to "General Works," and the next nine hundreds were assigned to the following nine classes: 100, Philosophy and Related Disciplines; 200, Religion (previously Theology); 300, Social Sciences (previously Sociology); 400, Languages (previously Philology); 500, Pure Sciences (previously Natural Sciences); 600, Technology, Applied Sciences (previously Useful Arts); 700, The Arts (previously Fine Arts); 800, Literature; 900, General Geography and History. The General Works, numbered below 100, include general bibliographies, encyclopaedias, general-interest periodicals, and so forth.

The second digit allows each of the nine classes to be divided into nine subclasses. Social Sciences, for example, is divided into (using the latest designations) 310, Statistics; 320, Political Science; 330, Economics; 340, Law; 350, Public Administration; 360, Social Pathology and Services (previously Associations and Institutions); 370, Education; 380, Commerce and Communication; 390, Customs and Folklore. The subdivisions of Languages, after "410, Linguistics," are English, German, French, Italian, Spanish, Latin, Classical Greek, and "490, Other Languages." The same eight languages and language groups are distinguished in the 800 class, Literature, by the same second digits. Natural or Pure Sciences is divided into 510, Mathematics; 520, Astronomy; 530, Physics; 540, Chemistry; 550, Sci-

[7] Ernest Cushing Richardson, *Classification, Theoretical and Practical* (Hamden, Connecticut: Shoe String Press, 1964, reprinted from the 3rd ed., New York: H. W. Wilson Co., 1930), p. 118.

[8] Dewey, *Classification*, Preface, p. 4.

ences of Earth and Other Worlds (previously Geology); 560, Paleontology; 570, Life Sciences (previously Biology); 580, Botany; 590, Zoology.

The fact that the numerical scheme—from 000 to 999—has only 1,000 integral numbers may give the impression that the expansion of the classification is rigidly limited. This is not so, for the use of decimals allows indefinite subdivision of each subclass. As a matter of fact, the eighteenth edition of Dewey's *Classification* (1971) contained 18,980 entries. Class 6, Technology, was most densely populated with 5,694 entries (not titles of books, but names of subdivisions), followed by Class 3, Social Sciences, with 3,430 entries, and Class 5, Natural Sciences, with 2,830 entries. It was Class 5, however, that showed the most rapid expansion between the seventeenth and eighteenth edition, a "built-in expansion," analogous to a rapid division of cells.

Alternative Systems

Several of the large research libraries developed their own classification systems. Libraries and faculties evidently valued a show of their independence and superior wisdom above the advantages of uniform classification. Thus, the Cutter system[9] was developed for the Boston Athenaeum in 1879; the Rowell system[10] for Berkeley in 1894; the Richardson system[11] for Princeton in 1901; the Brown system[12] for smaller libraries in 1906; and the Bliss system[13] for libraries of all types.

The Cutter system is usually referred to as a system of "expansive classification." Its first version was prepared in 1870, its "Sixth Expansion," in 1891-93; the seventh expansion contained about 10,000 subdivisions. The twenty-six major classes are designated by capital letters from A to Z, which are followed by lower-case letters for various subdivisions:

[9] Charles Ammi Cutter, "Classification on the Shelves with Some Account of the New Scheme Prepared for the Boston Athenaeum," *Library Journal*, vol. 4 (1879), pp. 234-243; idem, *Expansive Classification* (Boston: C. A. Cutter, 1891).

[10] Joseph Cummings Rowell, *Classification of Books in the Library* (Berkeley: University of California, Library Bulletin No. 12, 1894).

[11] Ernest Cushing Richardson, *Location of Books in the Library of Princeton University* (Princeton, N. J., 1901); idem, *Classification* (3rd ed.), pp. 133-138.

[12] James Duff Brown, *Subject Classification* (London: Grafton, 1906); idem, *The Small Library: A Guide to the Collection and Care of Books* (London: Grafton, 1907), pp. 84-88.

[13] Henry E. Bliss, "A Modern Classification of Libraries with Simple Notation, Mnemonics, and Alternatives," *Library Journal*, vol. 35 (1910), pp. 351-358.

A, General Works; B, Philosophy; C, Christianity and Ju-
daism; D, Ecclesiastical History; E, Biography; F, History;
G, Geography and Travels; H, Social Sciences; I, Demotics,
Sociology; J, Civics, Government, Political Science; K, Leg-
islation, etc.; L, Sciences and Arts together; M, Natural His-
tory; N, Botany; O, Zoology; P, Anthropology and Ethnology;
Q, Medicine; R, Useful Arts, Technology; S, Constructive
Arts (Engineering and Building); T, Manufactures and Han-
dicrafts; U, Art of War; V, Recreative Arts, Sports, Games,
Festivals; W, Art; X, Philology; Y, English and American
Literature; Z, Book Arts.

We shall see later that the classification system of the Library of
Congress follows, with some exceptions, the Cutter notations of capital letters from A to K. The Cutter system has been praised for the
"painstaking intelligence of subdivision and the full description of
exact meaning of what is intended to be included under the subdivision."[14]

The Richardson system uses numerical notations with a four-digit
base. The ten major classes are as follows: 0000-0999, General Works;
1000-1999, Historical Sciences; 2000-2999, (Old) Languages and Literature; 3000-3999, Modern Languages and Literature; 4000-4999,
Arts; 5000-5999, Theology; 6000-6999, Philosophy and Education;
7000-7999, Sociology; 8000-8999, Natural Sciences; 9000-9999,
Technology.

The Brown system, designed chiefly for small libraries, has a philosophically more intelligent division of fields than most other systems
have. It is one of the rare classifications that recognizes that mathematics is not a natural science but belongs either in a class by itself
or together with other "general" disciplines such as logic. The latter
arrangement was chosen by Brown. As to notation, he uses one capital letter followed by an arabic number. Here is an outline of the
system:

A, Generalia: A0, Generalia; A1, Education; A3, Logic; A4,
Mathematics; A5, Graphics; A6, General Science; B, C, D.
Physical Science: B0, Physics; C0, Electricity; C1, Optics;
C2, Heat; C3, Acoustics; C8, Astronomy; D0, Physiography;
D3, Geology; D7, Chemistry; E, F, Biological Science; E0,
Biology; E1, Botany, F0, Zoology; G, H, Ethnology and Med-
icine; I, Economic Biology, Domestic Arts; J, K, Philosophy

[14] Richardson, *Classification*, p. 122.

and Religion; J0, Metaphysics; J1, Esthetics, Psychology; J2, Ethics; J3, Philosophy; J4, Theology; L, Social and Political Science; L0, Social Science; L1, Political Science; L2, Government; L4, Law; L8, Commerce and Trade; M, Language and Literature; M0, Language; M1, Literature; M7, Palaeography, Bibliography; N, Literary Forms. N0, Fiction, N1, Poetry, N2, Drama; N3, Essay and Miscellanea; O-W, History and Geography; O0, Universal History; O1, Archaeology; O2, Universal Geography; O3, Africa; P, Oceania and Asia. P0, Oceania and Australasia; P29, Asia; Q, R, Europe (South, Latin, etc.); S, T, Europe (North, Teutonic, Slavonic); U, V, British Islands; W, America; X, Biography.

The Bliss system, designed several years after the Library of Congress had developed its classification, followed Brown in joining Logic and Mathematics in its "general" class, which however contains also Philosophy and History of Science. Bliss followed Richardson in separating Religion from Philosophy. And he innovated in linking Psychology with Education in one class, and in making Political Science, Jurisprudence and Law, and Economics, each a separate class in addition to Social Sciences (which include Sociology and Philanthropy) and Cultural Antropology. The outline looks like this:

A. General Science and Philosophy: Science in General, History of Philosophy, Metaphysics, Logic, Mathematics, Metrology, and Physical Sciences in General; B. Physics; C. Chemistry and Chemical Technology; D. Astronomy; E. Geology, including Physical Geography, Meteorology, Mineralogy, and Economic Geology; F. Biology; G. Botany; H. Zoology; I. Physical Anthropology and the Medical Sciences; J. Psychology and Education; K. Cultural Anthropology: Ethnology, Ethnography, Folklore; L. Religion and Religions; M. History: Accessory Sciences, General History, and Ancient History; N. Europe, Medieval and Modern; O. America; P. Africa, Asia, and Australasia, etc.; Q. Social Sciences: Sociology, Philanthropy, Ethics; R. Political Science; S. Jurisprudence and Law; T. Economics; U. Useful and Industrial Arts: Recreative Arts, Pastimes; V. Fine Arts; W. Philology: General Linguistics, Non-Aryan and Unclassified Languages, Semitic Languages; X. Indo-European Languages and Literatures severally; Y. English Language and Literature; Z. Alternative for Theology and Religion.

In Richardson's opinion, the Bliss system "represents the freest adjustments of subjects to the results of modern science of any of the modern systems."[15]

The System of the Library of Congress

When the Library of Congress began in 1901 to revamp its system of classification—with its first outline finished in 1904 and the first complete scheme published in 1910—it had to choose between a numerical and an alphabetical notation. Any numerical notation system, be it decimal, centesimal, or millesimal, suffers from a natural constraint: it allows for only nine or ten basic classes in an expanding universe of learning. The Library of Congress chose the English alphabet with its twenty-six letters—or twenty-four letters, once the ambiguous letters *I* and *O* were omitted—for denoting basic classes. By adding a second letter, followed by (now up to four) numerals, the coding system is almost infinitely subdivisible.

The cataloguing scheme of the Library of Congress (LC) is readily available in virtually every library and, thus, it would be wasteful to reproduce it here in its entirety. On the other hand, only a very few of us—with the exception of librarians—have actually seen enough of the classification to be familiar with the LC code outside our own fields of specialization. I shall therefore present enough of it to have most of the major branches of learning on exhibit. In a few classes, subdivisions will be shown in greater detail:

A General Works, Polygraphy. *AE* General Encyclopaedias, *AG* Dictionaries . . .

B Philosophy, Psychology, Religion. *BC* Logic, *BD* Speculative Philosophy: 95-131 Metaphysics, 143-236 Epistemology, 240-241 Methodology, . . . *BF* Psychology, *BH* Aesthetics, *BJ* Ethics, *BL* Religions, Mythology, Rationalism, *BM* Judaism, *BP* Islam, Bahaism, Theosophy, *BR* Christianity

C Auxiliary Sciences of History. *CC* Archaeology, general, . . . *CJ* Numismatics, . . . *CT* Biography

D History, general and Old World. *DA* Great Britain, *DB* Austria, Czechoslovakia, Hungary, *DC* France . . .

E-F History, America. *E*, 184- . . . United States, general, *F* 1-975 United States local history, . . . 2511 Brazil, . . .

G Geography, Anthropology, Recreation. *GA* Mathematical

---

[15] Ibid., p. 148.

Geography, *GB* Physical Geography, *GC* Oceanography, *GN* Anthropology, *GV* Recreation, 561-1197 Sports

H Social Sciences. *HA* Statistics, *HB* Economics, *HC* Economic history and conditions, national production, *HD* Land, Agriculture, Industry, 4801-8942 Labor, *HE* Transportation and Communication, *HF* Commerce, *HG* Finance, 1501-3542 Banking, . . . *HJ* Public finance, . . . *HM* Sociology, *HN* Social history, . . . *HQ* The Family, Marriage, Woman, . . . *HV* Social pathology, Social and public welfare, Criminology, *HX* Socialism, Communism, Anarchism

J Political Science, Official Documents, . . . *JC* Political Theory, Theory of the state, . . . *JK* United States, . . . *JN* Europe, . . . *JS* Local governments, . . . *JV* Colonies, . . . Emigration, Immigration, *JX* International Law, International relations

K Law

L Education

M Music and Books on Music

N Fine Arts, Visual Arts. *NA* Architecture, *NB* Sculpture, *NC* Drawing, Design, Illustration, *ND* Painting, *NE* Print media . . .

P Language and Literature. *PA* Classical, *PB* Modern European, *PC* Romance, *PD* Germanic . . .

Q Science. *QA* Mathematics, 8-10 Mathematical logic, 76 Computer Science, *QB* Astronomy, *QC* Physics, *QD* Chemistry, *QE* Geology, . . . *QH* Natural History, 301-559 General biology, including life, genetics, evolution, 573-671 Cytology, . . . *QK* Botany, *QL* Zoology, *QM* Human anatomy, *QP* Physiology, *QR* Microbiology . . .

R Medicine. *RA* Public aspects, *RB* Pathology, . . . *RD* Surgery, . . .

S Agriculture. . . . *SB* Plant culture, . . . *SB* Forestry, . . . *SF* Animal culture, . . .

T Technology. *TA* Engineering, general, Civil engineering, general, *TC* Hydraulic engineering, . . . *TT* Handicrafts, . . . *TX* Home economics

U Military Science

V Naval Science

Z Bibliography and Library Science

The LC classification scheme does not pretend to be philosophically sound; it merely seeks to be pragmatic. The arrangements of some subjects are rather odd, but much that seems plausible at one time becomes peculiar or even "indefensible" as the branches of learning develop and multiply. The appearance of mathematics and mathematical logic (under the letter Q) in close union with empirical natural sciences is "traditional," even though it offends the convictions of virtually every philosopher from Bacon to Carnap, Nagel, and Adler. It would be too expensive to change the catalogue numbers on the volumes and in the catalogues of many hundreds of libraries just to please the sensibilities of philosophers of science (even though the philosophers are perfectly right). Psychologists have a stronger case if they are dissatisfied; they have become used to being shuttled back and forth between the natural sciences and social sciences, but they may gravely resent being placed under the letter B together with philosophy and religion, along with Judaism and Christianity. Perfectionists may also take exception to the arrangement under which the social sciences (under the letter H) have exiled cultural anthropology and political science; the former is placed together with geography and recreation (under the letter G) and the latter is given a separate home (under the letter J). A mere renaming would repair the anomaly of having a class "social sciences without cultural anthropology, social psychology, and political science": instead of calling the class "Social Sciences" one could designate it as "Statistics, Economics, Sociology," which would fully describe its contents. Renaming a class in the system does not require any change in cataloguing.

The LC classification has been adopted by the majority of large research libraries in the United States. This simplifies the reader's search for any particular title, which is catalogued under the same symbol in virtually all libraries that are likely to have the book in their collection. It also reduces the cost of cataloguing, because each library can purchase copies of the catalogue cards and instant access to the electronic computer files.

There is more to say about cooperative arrangements in cataloguing and about an eventual changeover of card catalogues to electronic catalogues, but this is no longer a matter of classification; it is one of the several tasks of library operation. This is a topic for one of the later volumes of this work.

CHAPTER 10

Universities:
Faculties and Departments

THE THEME "universities and the classification of higher learning" occurs at least three times in this work. In Volume I, the discussion of the types of knowledge invited an examination of the traditional division of learning into the sciences of nature, society, and human culture (Chapter 2). In Volume V, the discussion of higher education in the United States will have to include a more detailed report on the departmentalization of university teaching and university organization. Between these two occurrences of the theme is the present chapter, which may be regarded as a part of the intellectual history of organized knowledge.

One might expect to find the existing segmentation of colleges and universities into faculties, schools, colleges, divisions, departments, and other administrative units no less traditional—and perhaps more anachronistic—in its depiction of the different fields of knowledge than the classes and sections of most learned academies. Yet, the development of the two types of institutions was quite different, chiefly because for several centuries universities placed much emphasis on the universality or pansophic nature of higher learning. Although universities of earlier centuries recognized a division between faculties of philosophy and faculties of the learned professions—law, medicine, and theology—it is only in the last century that the specialization and fragmentation of advanced knowledge have made their marks on the universities and left us with the highly complex picture, mirrored in complex organizations, of institutions of higher education.

In view of these developments, different approaches have to be used in a study of the classifications of higher learning within universities. Only for about the last hundred years can the "accepted" classification be read off the organization charts of these institutions. For early periods, historical treatises, based on archival records and on reports and letters by contemporary observers, have to be consulted in order to find out what subjects were taught and which of them received major emphasis. For a middle period, before the departmentalization of the universities but after universities had started to publish catalogues of the courses offered, these official announcements can serve as the best source for a study of the taxonomy of the subjects taught.[1]

THE EARLY UNIVERSITIES OF EUROPE

The early history of universities has been told in many publications, but I cannot assume it to be so widely known as to make it superfluous to provide a sketch.

The Medieval Universities

I may begin this sketch with a quotation from an essay of mine: "In the middle ages, a learned man was regularly a divine: learning and religious thought were almost identical, formal education was offered only in church-schools, most universities were founded by ecclesiastic functionaries and chartered by the pope, and most teachers (magistri) were clerics."[2] The qualifications in this statement— "regularly," "almost," "most"—were necessary to allow for notable exceptions. The first university (or quasi university), at Salerno (now Italy) in the ninth century, was a school of medicine; and the second, at Bologna around A.D. 1000, was chiefly a school of law (civil as well as canon law); they included secular as well as ecclesiastic students. The transition of schools to universities involves the formation of a community or federation of teachers or students or both into a "whole" (universus) body, a universitas magistrorum or a universitas scholarium or a universitas magistrorum et scholarium.[3] These bodies had the character of guilds, chartered by ecclesiastic and/or secular authorities, usually the pope, the emperor, the king. The students' communities were often formed along national lines, so-called "nations," confederations of aliens on foreign soil, with privileges granting them various rights, including protection from restrictions by municipal authorities. Older than the term "universitas" was the designation "studium generale." This has sometimes been assumed to refer to general as distinguished from professional studies. Actually it meant to distinguish the institutions from merely local schools (cathedral school, monastic school) and to indicate that this was, as Rashdall explained, a place of higher education with a

---

[1] Much of the contents of this chapter is based on research by Mary Taylor Huber, my assistant.

[2] Fritz Machlup, "European Universities as Partisans," in Neutrality or Partisanship: A Dilemma of Academic Institutions (New York: Carnegie Foundation for the Advancement of Teaching, bulletin no. 34, 1971), p. 11.

[3] The university as a body of teachers and students offers a body of learning, hence, a universitas litterarum.

plurality of masters attracting or inviting students from all parts of Europe.[4] Where the status of *studium generale* was conferred by a papal or imperial charter, it included also the *ius ubique docendi*, the right of the graduates (*doctores*) to teach anywhere.[5]

The earliest universities in Europe evolved as *studia generalia* without papal bull or imperial charter. If a census of universities had been taken in the year 1200, it would have recorded Salerno, Bologna, and Reggio in (what is now) Italy; Paris and Montpélier in (what is now) France; and Oxford in England. During the thirteenth century another seventeen universities were established, so that a census taken in 1300 would show altogether twenty-three. The newcomers included Cambridge in England; eight in Italy (among them Vicenza, Padua, Pavia, Siena, and Naples); three in France (Orléans, Angers, and Toulouse); three in what is now Spain (among them Salamanca); and one in Portugal (Lisbon-Coimbra). The fourteenth century saw another twenty-two new universities, of which seven were in Italy, four in France, three in Spain, five in the Hapsburg countries and the German empire (Prague in 1347, Vienna in 1365, Erfurt in 1379, Heidelberg in 1385, and Cologne in 1388); two in Hungary (Pécs [Fünfkirchen] in 1367, and Buda in 1389); and one in Poland (Cracow in 1397).[6]

The Four Faculties

Even if some of the medieval universities began as professional schools—faculties of theology, law, or medicine—they usually added

---

[4] This is not the place to discuss the contributions of cathedral and monastic schools to those medieval notions of knowledge that were formalized in the medieval universities. The reader may find discussions of the ways in which classical culture came to influence the curricula of cathedral and monastic schools in Pierre Riché, *Education and Culture in the Barbarian West: Sixth through Eighth Centuries* (Columbia, S.C.: University of South Carolina Press, 1976); and of the historical relationships between cathedral and monastic schools and the early universities, in Hastings Rashdall, *The Universities of Europe in the Middle Ages*, new edition edited by F. M. Powicke and A. B. Emden (Oxford: Clarendon Press, 1936 [1st ed., 1895]). For a sociological interpretation of cathedral and monastic schools, see Émile Durkheim, *The Evolution of Educational Thought: Lectures on The Formation and Development of Secondary Education in France*, translated by Peter Collins (London: Routledge and Kegan Paul, 1969 [1st ed., in French, 1938]).

[5] Rashdall, *Universities*, pp. 6-14. This right was not always recognized. The University of Paris did not recognize degrees obtained elsewhere. Oxford retaliated and did not admit doctors from Paris.

[6] The exact year of the establishment of a university is sometimes difficult to determine, chiefly because some began to operate long before and others long after they received their official charter (papal bull or charter by the crown). For example, the University of Piacenza received its charter in 1248 but began operations only in 1398; the University of Pavia, on the other hand, when chartered in 1361, had been operating for about a century. I use the earlier of the two events if I state the year of the founding.

a fourth, a faculty of philosophy. All studies, professional or philosophical, were preceded by years of study of the liberal arts, divided into two curricula, the trivium, consisting of grammar, rhetoric, and dialectic (logic), and the quadrivium, consisting of music, arithmetic, geometry, and astronomy.[7] The professional schools considered themselves the "superior" faculties vis-à-vis the faculty of philosophy. Philosophy, in its early scope, consisted of ethics, physics, and metaphysics. Some universities actually began as faculties of philosophy. The first of these was the University of Paris, which emphasized from the start the study of logic and philosophy, regarded as the "science of sciences."

The study of dialectic and philosophy was sometimes linked with theology; for example, the Sorbonne, a Paris college founded circa 1257, concentrated on theology. It is worth noting that the perpetual battle between practical, career-oriented studies and purely intellectual, more speculative studies goes back to the very beginnings of the medieval university. The "Bologna-type" and the "Paris-type" university are the terms used by historians when they speak of the two opposite orientations. The two types differed also in another respect: Bologna was a "university of students," Paris a "university of masters." Incidentally, Bologna soon extended its scope. To its law faculty it added, before the year 1200, a faculty of medicine and, a little later, a faculty of philosophy. The student body at Bologna at that time has been estimated at the astonishingly high figure of 10,000; the majority were foreigners.

The two oldest British universities were of the Paris type; indeed, there were mass secessions of masters and students from Paris to Oxford and Cambridge. The size of the student bodies did not approach that of Paris, let alone Bologna; in 1257 Oxford had only approximately 3,000 students. Various religious orders—Dominicans, Franciscans, Carmelites, Benedictines, Cistercians—exercised a profound influence on the education offered. This was equally true of Cambridge, which was established by a migration from Oxford in 1209. Both these universities differed, and still differ, from continental European universities with respect to the institution of the various autonomous colleges, in the sense of residential communities of scholars. They replaced, and sometimes actually razed, private quarters, "halls" or inns. University College (founded in 1249), Balliol (1263), and Merton (1264), were the oldest colleges at Oxford;

---

[7] This division of the liberal disciplines goes back to Varro (116-27 B.C.), Saint Augustine (A.D. 354-430), Capella (*Satyricon*, before A.D. 439), and Cassiodorus (*De artibus et disciplinis liberarium litterarum*, before A.D. 550).

Peterhouse (1284), Pembroke (1347), Gonville and Caius (1348), and Corpus Christi (1352), were the oldest at Cambridge.[8]

With all the differences in organization and in emphasis on various disciplines, the similarities among medieval universities were much more important. All faculties of theology taught the scriptures and the writings of the church fathers; all faculties of law taught canon law and civil law (and some also Roman law); all faculties of medicine taught the little that was known at the time and much that was based on faith (such as how to exorcize demons and devils); and the faculties of arts (philosophy) were based on the same seven disciplines that make up the trivium and quadrivium.[9] There was much interuniversity migration of masters and of students. And, most important of all, all teaching and all learned discussion was in Latin.

Particularism and Partisanship

The similarities among the early universities were not so close as to amount to uniformity. Ideological, doctrinal, and theological dissension had existed all along and increased in the subsequent centuries as the number of universities on the continent of Europe increased and severe conflicts in secular and ecclesiastic matters arose or aggravated. Some of the universities were established with specific religious commitments, voluntary or imposed. The University of Toulouse, for example, was founded in 1229 by a papal bull for the purpose of combatting and suppressing Albigensianism, a heresy fought by Rome. (Strangely enough, this was thought to be compat-

---

[8] Two earlier colleges at Cambridge were later (in the 16th century) merged into Trinity College.

[9] Even the texts were largely the same. In a typical trivium, for grammar the texts by Donatus and by Priscian were used; for logic, Aristotle; for rhetoric and poetry, Tully. In a typical quadrivium, for arithmetic the text by Boethius; for geometry, Euclid; for music, Pythagoras, and for astronomy, Ptolemy. For the advanced study of philosophy, for ethics, Seneca; for physics, Aristotle; and for metaphysics, Peter Lombard. As documentation for this "reading list" (except for physics) I refer to an etching used as an illumination in Gregory de Reisch, *Margarita Philosophica* (Basel: 1508), reproduced in Ellwood P. Cubberly, *Syllabus of Lectures on History of Education* (Totowa, N.J.: Rowman and Littlefield, 1971), p. 85. The illumination named no author for physics; I filled the void with the one writer who is most often mentioned in treatises on ancient and medieval teaching of physics. That the picture named only one author for each subject (except for grammar) was possibly due to limitations of space in this remarkable medieval cartoon. From other sources we can learn that the *artes liberales* by Martianus Capella were widely used in the trivium, as were the texts by Alcuin. In the teaching of logic or dialectic the writings of Peter Abelard played a considerable role. See Theobald Ziegler, *Geschichte der Pädagogik mit besonderer Rücksicht auf das höhere Unterrichtswesen*, 4th ed. (Munich: C. H. Beck, 1917), pp. 24-31.

ible with the promised *libertas scholastica*). Such religious commitments were not confined to theologians, but extended to masters and students in all faculties, including law, medicine, and the liberal arts.[10] Indeed, it was the Faculty of Arts at the University of Paris that in 1339 prohibited the reading of the works of Occam, who had been expelled from the University by a papal ban in 1330. In 1346 the books of another scholar were burned on the grounds of the Arts Faculty in compliance with a demand by the pope.[11] In 1382, Oxford University "retired" John Wyclif and his followers for their "heretical" views. Expelled or exiled teachers often found refuge at other universities.

Expulsion was not the extreme sanction against subversive professors.[12] In 1415 John Hus, professor and rector at the University of Prague, was condemned by the Council of Constance and was burnt at the stake. In 1555, after an academic trial, the Anglicans Cranmer, Latimer, and Ridley, of Oxford, and John Hullier, of Cambridge, were burnt at the stake, a penalty that intimidated masters and fellows sufficiently to make them accept the fifteen articles of Catholic tenets in lieu of the forty-eight articles of the English Church. In 1600, Giordano Bruno, teaching at various universities after his expulsion from France, was tried by the Roman Church as defender of the Copernican heliocentric system and was burnt at the stake. In 1626 the University of Paris prescribed the death penalty for anyone who would publish without the University's authorization.

Several historical events and developments contributed to the divergent theological and political commitments of the universities: for example, the war between England and France (1338-1453); the papal schism, with one pope in Rome and another in Avignon (1378-1423); the feud between the Armagnacs and Burgundians in France (1404-1420); the rivalry for the throne of the Holy Roman Empire (1400-1420); the Hussite alienation and eventual break with the Roman Church (1414-1436); the reformation movements led by Luther, Zwingli, and Calvin leading to different Protestant creeds (1517-1555); the conflicts of Henry VIII with Rome, and the establishment of the Church of England (1534); the temporary return of Catholicism in England and the persecution of the Protestants (1555-1558); the

[10] Fritz Machlup, "European Universities," pp. 10, 11.

[11] Ibid., p. 12.

[12] Expulsions of subversive or disobedient professors occurred, to cite only a few more instances, at Cambridge in 1570 and 1596, at Oxford in 1662, 1730, and 1768, at Leiden in 1676, at Halle in 1723, at Göttingen in 1837, at Leipzig in 1849, and at Heidelberg in 1854.

Counter Reformation in continental Europe (1608-1648) and the Thirty Years' War (1618-1648).

Apart from all the burning issues relating to matters of religious and political power, there were genuine philosophical issues that split the universities and their faculties; foremost among such issues were (beginning in the 14th century) the controversies between nominalism and realism and (in the 17th century) between Cartesian and orthodox Aristotelian philosophy. Besides all these divisive elements, the increasingly national character of the universities, especially the substitution of national languages for Latin, tended to weaken the cosmopolitan character of higher learning.

The Dominance and Decline of Latin

In the seventeenth and eighteenth centuries the "reaction against abstract theological education"[13] and against the supremacy or monocracy of Latin gradually gained strength. The reaction can be best understood against the background of the most successful system of education by the Jesuit order, which had gained clear predominance almost everywhere in Europe. "In 1710 the order had no less than six hundred and twelve colleges, one hundred and fifty-seven normal schools [teachers' colleges], twenty-four universities, and two hundred missions. These institutions had a large patronage. In 1675 the College of Clermont numbered three thousand students."[14] The "plan of studies," first formulated in 1584 but based on a draft by St. Ignatius Loyola (1491-1556), included an absolute prohibition of the use of the mother tongue at school, with penalties for infractions. The lower course of instruction gave the first three years entirely to Latin grammar and syntax, the fourth year to Latin literature, and the last two years to Latin rhetoric. Of the six years of the higher course of instruction, the first two years were devoted to philosophy, which included psychology, logic, ethics, and mathematics, but chiefly the study of the works of Aristotle, and the next four years to theology, which meant the study of the Holy Scriptures, Hebrew, and the writings of the Scholastics.[15]

In the history of the movement against the predominance of theology and the exclusive use of Latin in elementary, secondary, and tertiary education, scholars in several countries should be mentioned: Michel de Montaigne (1533-1592) and René Descartes (1596-1650) in France; Johann Amos Comenius [Komensky] (1592-1671)

---

[13] Franklin V. N. Painter, *A History of Education* (New York: Appleton, 1886), p. 173.

[14] Ibid., p. 168.

[15] Ibid., pp. 169-172.

in Poland, Germany, Holland, England, and Sweden; Francis Bacon (1561-1626) and Isaac Newton (1642-1727) in England; and Gottfried Wilhelm von Leibniz (1646-1716) and several humanist writers and school reformers in Germany. Montaigne was one of the first French scholars who wrote in French (*Essays*, 1582, 1587, 1588) and advocated that French be used in teaching. Descartes wrote his famous *Discours de la méthode* (1637) in French. Bacon wrote his *Advancement of Learning* (1603) in English, though he later published a Latin edition (*De augmentis scientiarum*, 1623). Newton wrote his great work still in Latin: *Philosophiae Naturalis Principia Mathematica* (1687); moreover, his works were replete with theological discourse. Newton's role in the movement lay in his emphasis on mathematics and natural philosophy. The role of Leibniz was similar; in his outline of a "theoretical encyclopaedia" he gave eight of the sixteen parts to mathematics and physics.[16]

The work of Comenius was directly addressed to the reform in schooling and teaching. A German pedagogue, Wolfgang Ratich (1571-1635), had taken the lead (in 1612) advocating that everything be taught first in the mother tongue. Comenius recommended (in 1631) that "In languages the mother tongue is to come first, next the languages of the neighboring nations, then Latin as the language of the learned world. Theologians and physicians should study Greek."[17] His plan for school reform provided for a popular school for ages six to twelve, stressing reading, writing, arithmetic, singing, catechism, history, and geography; this would be followed by six years of Latin school, to teach grammar, physics, mathematics, ethics, logic, and rhetoric. Graduates of Latin school would be ready for university. Incidentally, because Comenius wrote for the educators and statesmen of several countries, his works were in Latin.[18]

It is interesting to read the pleas of the school reformers to reduce the role of the classical languages in the teaching programs of secondary schools and universities. As an example I mention the German Johann Matthias Gesner (1691-1761), professor of philology and education at the new and most progressive University of Göttingen. He charged that the existing system was plagued by pedantry and that the students were "tortured" by an excess load of Latin grammar.

---

[16] See above, Chapter 4.

[17] Quoted from Painter, *History*, p. 210.

[18] The works of Comenius included *Pansophiae prodromus* (1630), *Janua linguarum reserat* (1631), *Methodus linguarum novissima* (1649), *Eruditionis scholasticae janua* (1652), and *Orbis sensualium pictus* (1658). The latter was probably the first children's picture book: it added pictures to some of the words given in three languages.

Yet, he himself continued to lecture in Latin and to write in Latin.[19] Some of his contemporaries, however, began to publish their works in German, and some professors at the University of Halle, led by the jurist and philosopher Christian Thomasius in 1688, began to give their lectures in German. In France the replacement of Latin by the national language began in 1770, when Jean Darcet obtained a dispensation permitting him to offer his lectures at the Collège Royal (now Collège de France) in French.[20]

For the British universities it is not easy to cite any particular dates for the transition from Latin to English lecturing; in tutorial work in the colleges the changeover occurred earlier than in scheduled university lectures, and in Cambridge probably earlier than in Oxford. The disputations in college and the examinations by the university[21] were entirely in Latin. In the public disputation the student read his thesis in support of one of his propositions, was then challenged by other students acting as opponents, and had to respond in defense of his argument. Knowledge of formal logic as well as of conversational Latin was needed for this task.[22] The Latin was often quite poor, and one historian of Cambridge University came to the conclusion that "had the language of the discussions been changed to English, as was repeatedly urged from 1774 onwards, these exercises might have been kept with great advantage, but the barbarous Latin and the syllogistic form in which they were carried on prejudiced their retention."[23] After 1830 the disputation in Latin became "an elaborate farce," and in 1840 Cambridge discontinued this "public performance."[24]

Most lectures at Oxford around 1800 were still in Latin—to the

---

[19] Two of his works are *Institutiones rei scholasticae* (1715) and *Primae lineae isagoges in eruditionem* (posthumous). See Ziegler, *Geschichte*, pp. 273-278.

[20] Charles C. Gillispie, *Science and Polity in France at the End of the Old Regime* (Princeton: Princeton University Press, 1980), p. 135.

[21] In Cambridge, the college disputations, usually held at the end of the student's third year, and the college examinations, at the end of his fourth year, were required before the college would present the student's name for admission to the University's "senate-house examination," which had to be taken for the award of the B.A. degree.

[22] Walter W. R[ouse] Ball, *A History of the Study of Mathematics at Cambridge* (Cambridge: At the University Press, 1889), pp. 165 and 182. Ball quotes, on p. 182, a reminiscence of Augustus De Morgan, recorded in *A Budget of Paradoxes* (London: Longmans, Green, and Co., 1872), p. 305: "I was badgered for two hours with arguments given and answered in Latin—or what we call Latin—against Newton's first section, Lagrange's derived functions, and Locke on innate principles." — This nerve-shattering experience of the noted mathematician and logician took place at Trinity College in Cambridge in 1826.

[23] Ball, p. 183.

[24] Ibid., p. 183.

extent that there were any. There are several reports about the scarcity of lectures, at both Oxford and Cambridge.[25] These reports, however, have been called exaggerated. But that the use of Latin was on the decline from the middle of the eighteenth century is probably undeniable. A reading list for students of "moral philosophy and metaphysics" at Cambridge in the year 1730 included 157 items, of which 48 were in Latin. In the same year the Cambridge University Press published 16 books, of which 11 were in Latin; of the 19 books published in 1777, 8 were in English and 11 in Latin; and of the 19 books published in 1797, 12 were in English and 7 in Latin.[26]

A Sample Curriculum of 1650

In the middle of the seventeenth century the student at Oxford or Cambridge was assigned Greek and Latin works only. From a document preserved in the archives we have a specimen of a reading list for the entire four years of study; it is contained in the "Directions for a Student in the Universitie" prepared by Richard Holdsworth, a fellow of St. John's College and later (1637-1643) Master of Emmanuel College, Cambridge.[27] The listed works are for "afternoon study" during each of the twelve months of the year. (No vacations?) In the first year, the readings include Thomas Godwin, Marcus Junianus Justinus, Cicero's *Epistles*, Erasmus, Terence, Alexander Ross, Ovid's *Metamorphoses*, and the Greek Testament; in the second year, Lorenzo Valla (on Latin grammar and style), Franciscus Vigerius (on Greek grammar and style), Cicero's *De senectute*, *De amicitia*, *De oratore*, and so forth, Aesop's *Fables*, Florus, Sallust, Quintus Curtius, Virgil's *Ecologues* and *Georgics*, Ovid's *Epistles*, Horace, Martial, Hesiod, and Theocritus; in the third year, Nicolas Caussin's *De eloquentia*, Cicero's *Orations*, Demosthenes' *Orations*, Famianus Strada's *Prolusiones academicae*, Robert Turner's *Orationum*, Quin-

---

[25] If the account of Zachary Conrad von Uffenbach, a visiting scholar from Germany, was typical, no more than three or four university lectures were delivered during a whole winter at Cambridge, and these only "to the walls," that is, without attendance. Similarly, Edward Gibbon reported thus on his experience at Magdalen College, Oxford, in 1752: "A tradition prevailed that some of our predecessors had spoken Latin declamations in the hall; but of this ancient custom no vestige remained: the obvious methods of public exercises and examinations were totally unknown." See Christopher Wordsworth, *Scholae Academicae: Some Account of the Studies at the English Universities in the Eighteenth Century* (Cambridge: At the University Press, 1877), pp. 10 and 14-15.

[26] Ibid., pp. 129-132, 401-402, 412, and 416-417.

[27] A summary of Richard Holdsworth's "Outline of Studies" appears in Lawrence A. Cremin, *American Education: The Colonial Experience, 1607-1783* (New York: Harper & Row, 1970), pp. 204-205.

tilian's *Institutio oratoria*, Juvenal, Persius, Claudian, Virgil's *Aeneid*, and Homer's *Iliad*; and in the fourth year, Hans Cluver's *Historiarum totius mundi epitome*, Suetonius, Aulus Gellius, Macrobius Saturnus, Plautus, Cicero's *De officiis* and *De finibus*, Seneca's *Tragedies*, Lucanus, and Homer's *Odyssey*. Those who miss in this list such writers as Julius Caesar, Lucretius, and Aristotle may be reassured: these works were assigned for morning study. Indeed, Aristotle's *Organon*, *Physics*, and *Ethics* were studied for three months each in the third year, and *De anima*, *De caelo*, and *Meteorologica* for six months in the fourth year. The last three months of the last year were devoted to Christian theology.

The voluminous list of readings may reflect merely the educator's wishful thinking; it was, in all likelihood, a detailed blueprint for an ideal rarely, if ever, followed in reality. In this one respect, the seventeenth century may have been very similar to the twentieth: those long reading lists are more in the nature of pious hopes than of enforced requirements.

To complete this account, I have still to report what the student was directed to do in the morning hours during the first two years at college—besides pray at 5 a.m. The subjects of study were not fully reflected in the reading list. In the first year, the mornings of nine months were given to the study of logic, and another three months to ethics. In the second year, three months were devoted to physics, another three months to "Controversies in logic, ethics and physics," the third three-month period to metaphysics, and the last to "Controversies of all kinds." The heavy emphasis on controversies is understandable in view of the system of disputations, the chief educational technique employed at British universities for hundreds of years.

EARLY AMERICAN COLLEGES

When college-trained settlers in New England established the first college in American colonies, they created it in the image of an English college.

Harvard College

A gift of books and money from John Harvard made it possible in 1636 to found Harvard College (this name adopted in 1639) in Cambridge, Massachusetts, patterned after Emmanuel College in Cambridge, England. Designed for the training of Puritan clergymen, the curriculum was solidly oriented towards the cultivation of classical languages: "A Puritan minister must be able to expound the Sacred Scriptures from the original Hebrew and Greek, and be cognizant of what the Church Fathers, the Scholastic Philosophers, and the Reformers had written, in Greek and Latin."[28] Knowledge of Latin and Greek was required for admission, and "almost all textbooks, even the Greek and Hebrew grammars," were in Latin.[29] Adherence to the British model was not confined to the curriculum, but extended to the style of living, with teachers and students residing "in the same building under common discipline, associating not only in lecture rooms but at meals, in chambers, at prayers, and in recreation."[30]

In its early years, Harvard College had a carefully prescribed three-year curriculum, devised by President Dunster in 1642. The weekly schedule provided for three full days of language study: one day for Greek, one for the languages of the Holy Scriptures (Hebrew, Chaldee, and Syriac), and one day for rhetoric. Two days were given over to various subjects: logic and physics for first-year students; ethics and politics for sophomores; and arithmetic, geometry, and astronomy for third-year students. All three classes of students studied catechetical divinity on Saturday morning, and history, and the nature of plants, on Saturday afternoon.[31] No special time was set aside for the study of Latin; after all, mastery of Latin was a prerequisite of admission.

In the early 1650s Harvard College extended its program to four years, but the basic principles were not changed; indeed, they were still recognized in the curriculum a hundred years later, though that curriculum was enriched by a little more attention to mathematics

---

[28] Samuel Elliot Morrison, *Three Centuries of Harvard: 1636-1936* (Cambridge, Mass.: Harvard University Press, 1936), p. 3.

[29] Ibid., p. 30.

[30] Ibid., p. 12.

[31] Cremin, *American Education*, p. 214. The detailed time schedule looked like this:

	1st year	2nd year	3rd year
Monday } Tuesday }	Logic and Physics	Ethics and Politics	Arithmetic, Geometry, and Astronomy
Wednesday	Greek	Greek	Greek
Thursday	Hebrew A.M. Grammar P.M. Old Testament	Chaldee (Ezra and Daniel)	Syriac (New Testament)
Friday	Rhetoric	Rhetoric	Rhetoric
Saturday A.M.	Catechetical Divinity	Catechism	Catechism
P.M.	History, Nature of Plants	History, Nature of Plants	History, Nature of Plants

and surveying. One of the richest sources of erudition used at Harvard, in and after 1655, was Johann Heinrich Alsted's great *Encyclopaedia*, seven volumes published in Latin in 1630 in Germany.[32] Professors used this reference work for their lectures, and students for their preparation.[33] There was no organizational division of the college into departments or fields of concentration.

Tradition and Innovation

Almost all colleges established in colonial America were denominational.[34] And, as in Europe, all stuck to the classical curriculum, sometimes enriched by increasing doses of mathematics and natural philosophy, chiefly physics. There were no requirements for students regarding the breadth of interests or the distribution among different subject groups, nor any choice of a major subject. Each class of students progressed through a prescribed course, consisting chiefly of Philosophy (which usually included logic, physics, ethics, politics, and astronomy), Ancient Languages (Greek, Hebrew, etc.), Rhetoric, and Divinity. These curricula stayed virtually unchanged throughout the eighteenth and the early nineteenth century.

As an example of a particularly broad and rich program of instruction, I may cite the advertisement of King's College (later, Columbia University) of New York in 1754:

> it is . . . the Design of this College . . . to instruct and perfect the Youth in the Learned Languages, and in the Arts of *reasoning* exactly, and *writing* correctly, and *speaking* eloquently; and in the Arts of *numbering* and *measuring*, of *Surveying* and *Navigation*, of *Geography* and *History*, of *Husbandry*, *Commerce* and *Government*, and in the Knowledge of all *Nature* in the Heavens above us, and in the *Air*, *Water*, and *Earth* around us, and in the various kinds of *Meteors*, *Stones*, *Mines* and *Minerals*, *Plants* and *Animals*,

---

[32] For a description of this work, see above, Chapter 4.

[33] Cremin, *American Education*, pp. 215, 216.

[34] The College of William and Mary at Williamsburg, Virginia (established in 1693) was Anglican; Yale College at New Haven, Connecticut (1701), Congregational; the College of New Jersey, later Princeton (1746), Presbyterian; King's College at New York, later Columbia (1754), Anglican; Queen's College at New Brunswick, New Jersey, later Rutgers (1766), Dutch Calvinist; the College of Rhode Island in Providence, later Brown (1764), Baptist; Dartmouth College in Hanover, New Hampshire (1769), Congregational. The earliest exception was the College of Pennsylvania, in Philadelphia (1740), nondenominational from its inception. In addition to the nine colleges mentioned, another eighteen were established before 1800, most of them after 1776, hence no longer in the colonial provinces but in the United States.

and of everything *useful* for the Comfort, the Convenience and Elegance of Life, in the chief Manufactures relating to any of these Things; and finally to lead them from the Study of Nature to the Knowledge of themselves, and of the God of Nature."[35]

Actual course offerings corresponded to this array and were designed for three years of study, leaving the fourth year for metaphysics, logic, moral philosophy, law, government, and history (sacred and profane).

Historians of higher education pay homage to the innovative ideas of William Smith, partly carried out at the College of Philadelphia (later, the University of Pennsylvania). They included greater emphasis on natural sciences and "practical studies," giving nearly one third of the students' time to these fields and also to English and "English literature and other tool subjects."[36]

Admission to almost all colleges was based on a knowledge of Latin and Greek. By 1760 entering freshmen at Princeton were required also to understand the principal rules of "vulgar arithmetic." The president of the College personally examined each applicant and determined whether or not he should be admitted.[37] Yet, although the status of Latin and Greek remained strong at most colleges for another century, there was, by the time of the revolution, clear evidence of a gradual decline in the eminence of Hebrew and divinity studies, and a rise in the emphasis on natural philosophy and practical studies.[38] In the postrevolutionary period we see considerable broadening of the curricula in many institutions, for example, the establishment of courses in French, English, chemistry, agriculture, and mechanical arts. Symptomatic of anticlassical tendencies is the statement by Benjamin Rush, an eminent physician, in a paper for a contest of the American Philosophical Society in 1799: "While Greek and Latin are the only avenues to science, education will always be confined to a few people. . . . it is only by rendering knowledge universal, that a Republican form of government can be preserved in our country."[39]

[35] Louis Franklin Snow, *The College Curriculum in the United States* (Ph.D. diss., Columbia University, published by the author, 1907), p. 57.

[36] Frederick Rudolph, *The American College and University: A History* (New York: Vintage Books, 1962), p. 32.

[37] Alexander Leitch, *A Princeton Companion* (Princeton: Princeton University Press, 1978), p. 3. — From this source we can also get an idea of the scale of the operation. In 1803 a professor wrote to a trustee of the college: "We got another student today."

[38] Snow, p. 77; Rudolph, pp. 29-31.

[39] Rudolph, pp. 42-43.

In the first third of the nineteenth century the advocates of an "English-Scientific Course" to replace the classical curriculum made progress. Geneva College (later Hobart College), at Geneva, New York, is said to be the first college "in the English-speaking world" to introduce, in 1824, a special curriculum without Greek and Latin.[40] The graduates of this "English" course of studies received only a diploma, not a degree of bachelor of arts. For a B.A. degree the requirement of Latin or Greek was retained for another hundred years. Several other institutions were considering the adoption of an English-based curriculum, and some went at least as far as allowing some sort of trade-off between classical and modern studies. Thus, in 1826, Bowdoin College in Maine permitted the substitution of Italian and Spanish for Greek and Latin.[41] Other colleges accepted additional work in physics and modern languages in lieu of some requirements in the classical curriculum. When New York City College was established in 1832, it instituted parallel curricula of the classical and the "English-Scientific" type.

The program of studies at the University of Virginia, started in 1824 according to plans outlined in all details by Thomas Jefferson, constituted a giant step towards the elective system: it provided for eight separate "schools," each giving its own diploma to students who elected its course: 1. Medicine, 2. Ancient Languages, 3. Modern Languages, 4. Natural Philosophy, 5. Mathematics, 6. Chemistry and Materia Medica, 7. Moral Philosophy, and 8. Law. The acquisition of a diploma from any one of these schools was to entitle the winner to the designation "Graduate of the University of Virginia." It was expected, however, that each student would acquire diplomas from at least three schools. To students who did not attain diplomas, "Certificates of Proficiency" were awarded. In 1831 the University introduced the M.A. degree for those who earned diplomas in Ancient Languages, Mathematics, Natural Philosophy, Chemistry, and Moral Philosophy; and an M.D. degree for graduates of the School of Medicine. Finally, the traditional B.A. degree was instituted. The fact that Latin was taught may mislead us to assume that students could be admitted without prior knowledge of Latin; this was not

[40] Milton Haight Turk, "Without Classical Studies," *Journal of Higher Education*, vol. 4 (October 1933), pp. 339-346. According to its announcement, Geneva College was to provide "besides the regular Course of Study pursued in similar institutions, a totally distinct Course, in direct reference to the practical business of life, by which the Agriculturalist, the Merchant and the Mechanic may receive a practical knowledge of what genius and experience have discovered, without passing through a tedious course of classical studies." Turk, pp. 340.

[41] William T. Foster, *Administration of the College Curriculum* (Boston: Houghton Mifflin Co., 1911), p. 98.

the case, however; the university courses were merely designed to bring the students to a more advanced level.[42]

The Trend Towards Practical Courses

The fifty years between 1825 and 1875 were marked by heated controversies between advocates of reform and defenders of tradition. The latter supported the classical curriculum enriched by all of the liberal arts; the reformers fought for "useful" knowledge—more mathematical and physical sciences, vocational training, and modern languages—and in favor of selective rather than compulsory courses. Major antagonists were reformist Harvard and traditionalist Yale. The eloquent statement of the Yale faculty of 1828, setting forth the educational philosophy of classical and very broad education is worth quoting. It argues that the most important object of college education is "discipline . . . of the mind"[43] and that the Yale curriculum layed a foundation for a thorough education by exercising "all the important mental faculties. . . . From the pure mathematics, [the student] learns the art of demonstrative reasoning. In attending to the physical sciences, he becomes familiar with facts, with the process of induction, and the varieties of probable evidence. In ancient literature, he finds some of the most finished models of taste. By English reading, he learns the powers of the language in which he is taught to speak and write. By logic and mental philosophy, he is taught the art of thinking; by rhetoric and oratory, the art of speaking."[44]

The Yale report attacked the notion that an undergraduate college should provide professional and technical education; this position, a defense of a liberal-arts education, does not, however, imply a preference for breadth rather than depth. The educational philosophy embraced by the defenders of the traditional university curriculum underrated or understated the importance of concentration on a major subject and of developing an understanding of and a taste for research. But the development of the "research university" was

[42] Philip Alexander Bruce, *History of the University of Virginia: 1819-1919* (New York: Macmillan Co., 1920), vol. 1, pp. 327 and 332, and vol. 2, p. 138. — As to the emphasis on both classical and modern languages, Jefferson wanted students to know Latin and Greek, and to learn French, Spanish, Italian, and German, but if possible also Anglo-Saxon in order to build a firmer foundation for their knowledge of English. See Thomas Jefferson, *Crusade Against Ignorance: Thomas Jefferson on Education*, edited by Gordon C. Lee (New York: Teachers College Press, 1967), pp. 123-125.

[43] "The Yale Report of 1828," in Appendix A of Arthur Levine, ed., *Handbook on Undergraduate Curriculum* (San Francisco: Jossey Bass Publishers, 1978), pp. 544-556. The quoted words are from p. 545.

[44] Ibid., p. 546.

not under discussion at the time. The questions at issue were classical versus modern languages, liberal versus mechanical arts, compulsory versus selective courses. On these questions, the debate was heated, and in each case the reformers were gaining strength. Thus, Harvard University established in 1847 the Lawrence Scientific School. In general, the outcome was largely determined by the power of money. Private benefactors, who had acquired their wealth from mercantile enterprise, were prepared to endow educational institutions disseminating practical knowledge for use in industry and trade; and public funds, from state governments, provided support for institutions teaching practical knowledge for use in agricultural and mechanical arts.

The Morrill Act of 1862 gave a strong boost to vocational training on the tertiary level of education. Under this federal statute, each State was to receive the proceeds of a sale of public lands to endow, support, and maintain one or more colleges "where the leading object shall be, without excluding other scientific and classical studies, and including military tactics, to teach such branches of learning as are related to agriculture and mechanic arts." As a result, the cause of the vocational college—and of vocational schools within universities—triumphed. This was a purely American phenomenon; not that there were no technical schools, business schools, agricultural schools, teacher-training schools, and other vocational schools on the tertiary level of education in Europe; but, steeped in the classical-humanistic tradition, European countries refused to recognize them as "universities." Most Americans regard such semantic exclusiveness as sheer snobbism; present-day Europeans are inclined to agree and, in fact, in several countries American nomenclature has now been adopted in this as in other respects.

Parallel with the spread of vocational training on the third level of education was the spread of the elective system. Promoted by Harvard College and adopted by an increasing number of institutions, the elective system of undergraduate education became the general rule, though mildly qualified by "distribution requirements" among different subject groups.

The substitution of modern for classical languages proceeded along with the spread of the elective system. For a while, Latin remained a requirement for admission to, or graduation from, college, but eventually this was given up. And although modern foreign languages had first been promoted as substitutes for Latin and Greek, the time was to come when all language requirements in most colleges and universities were abolished.

Lest this be interpreted as an account of the decline of higher education in the United States, let it be noted that the most important upgrading of the American university remains to be reported: the institution of the research university in the last quarter of the nineteenth century. Because the research university came about in emulation of the commitment to research that had become characteristic of German universities, we shall now interrupt the story of higher education in the United States and revisit the European scene.

DEVELOPMENTS IN EUROPE

We interrupted the review of the European university after the description of an Oxford plan of study from the year 1650. This break was appropriate because it helped to show how the early American colleges were patterned after the British model. Having now reviewed the developments on the American academic scene over some two hundred years, it is time to take a look at the simultaneous developments on the old continent, particularly in Germany, for significant influences on institutions of higher education in the United States became evident in the second half of the nineteenth century. For the sake of greater continuity, however, it is preferable to return first to England.

Oxbridge

In England, the two old universities, Oxford and Cambridge, had been on different sides of several important issues during the sixteenth, seventeenth, and eighteenth centuries. Most of these issues were theological (the divorce of Henry VIII, the acceptance of articles of faith) or political (the battle between Crown and Parliament, the King and Cromwell, allegiance to William III or loyalty to James II, a Whig majority in Cambridge and a strong Tory force at Oxford); eventually, however, the issues became educational: early acceptance of Newtonianism in Cambridge but continued allegiance to classicism at Oxford. Thus, Oxford stuck to Aristotle as the major authority, whereas Cambridge dropped Aristotle in favor of Newton in natural philosophy and Locke in moral philosophy.

At Cambridge education became increasingly mathematical. With University teaching mainly mathematical in content, the cultivation of classical learning was left to the colleges. There it was encouraged by prizes and scholarships and tested by "written translations from and into Latin and Greek."[45] Recognizing the continuing existence

[45] Martin L. Clarke, *Classical Education in Britain: 1500-1900* (Cambridge: At the University Press, 1959), p. 69.

of, and respect for, classical learning, the University authorities, after prolonged academic bickering, introduced in 1824 the classical tripos, but only for students who had already taken mathematical honors.[46] It was not until after 1857 that students were permitted to take this examination in the classics as the sole requirement for a degree. By 1900, there was a wide choice of curricula at Cambridge, but Natural Sciences was the most popular tripos, followed by Classics and by Mathematics; the other options were less important. A more recent list enumerates triposes in the following subjects: 1. Mathematics, 2. Classics, 3. Moral Sciences, 4. Natural Sciences, 5. Theology, 6. Law, 7. History, 8. Oriental Languages, 9. Medieval and Modern Languages, and 10. Mechanical Sciences (Engineering).

At Oxford, a university statute in 1800 had provided for a single examination for the bachelor's degree. It covered grammar, rhetoric, logic, moral philosophy, and the elements of mathematics and physics. The candidates had to show their skill at Latin by sight translation from English. In 1807, two honors schools were established, one in *litteris humanioribus*, the other in mathematics and physics. The former was defined as Greek, Latin, rhetoric and moral philosophy ("in so far as they are derivable from the ancient authors") and logic. After 1830, they were redefined to include the histories of Greece and Rome, rhetoric and poetry, and moral and political science ("in so far as they may be drawn from writers in antiquity").[47] Latin literature took second place to Greek. After 1850, there were six "final honour schools": 1. *Litterae Humaniores* (Latin, Greek, logic, ancient history, philosophy), 2. Mathematics, 3. Jurisprudence, 4. Natural Science, 5. Modern History, and 6. Theology. Added later were 7. Oriental Languages and 8. English Literature. By 1900, *Litterae Humaniores* was still the largest by far.

Developments at both Oxford and Cambridge during the nineteenth century have been summed up in the following statement: ". . . so long as [secondary] school education remained predominantly classical, new honours schools could be established at the universities without seriously disturbing that unity of outlook which was given to the men of learning by their common classical back-

---

[46] "Tripos" is the word at Cambridge University for honors examinations. Originally the tripod was the three-legged stool on which an appointed bachelor of arts sat when he questioned a candidate for the degree. The word "tripos" was used also for humorous verses composed by the examining bachelor, and also for the list of candidates printed on the back of the sheet of verses. See *Oxford English Dictionary*.

[47] University of Oxford, *Oxford University Statutes*, translated by George R. M. Ward and James Heywood, vol. II (London, 1851), pp. 62 and 166, quoted from Clarke, *Classical Education*, p. 99.

ground."[48] Greek remained an entrance requirement at Oxford and Cambridge until the 1920s, and Latin, until around 1960.[49]

German Universities

The organization of most universities in continental Europe, and especially in Germany and Central Europe, differed in essential respects from that of the English universities. For several centuries, the recognition of separate "nations," quasi-autonomous communities of students coming from foreign lands, had imposed on the university an organization along ethnic lines. Of lasting importance, however, was the partition by subject groups, leading to an organization into four faculties (*facultates*) or orders (*ordines*): the three "superior" or professional faculties—Theology, Jurisprudence, and Medicine—and the "lower" faculty of Philosophy, comprising both natural and moral philosophy, mathematics and all other recognized areas of study.

With regard to academic degrees awarded by the universities, the German system differed significantly from the English and French. The University of Paris granted bachelor's degrees (*baccalarius*, later changed to *baccalaureus*), licences (*licentiatus*), and master's degrees (*magister*). Later, the doctor's degree replaced the master's degree. German universities, however, granted only doctor's degrees.[50] This suggests that all studies at German universities were of the postgraduate type, far more advanced than the work of most students at English and French institutions. Whether this was actually so has sometimes been questioned, but for the nineteenth century it seems to have been the case. It certainly was the official stance that the primary commitment of the university was to research and the creation of new knowledge. Indeed, the man in charge of the organization of the University of Berlin made research orientation a criterion of "higher education" [*Hochschule*] in general and part of the definition of the university.[51] Perhaps this higher level of German higher education explains why, in the last third of the nineteenth century, American scholars and scientists chose German universities

[48] Ibid., p. 127.

[49] Stanley J. Curtis and Myrtle E. A. Boultwood, *An Introductory History of English Education since 1800* (London: University Tutorial Press, 1966), p. 339.

[50] For a time the faculty of philosophy awarded only the degree of *magister*; later the system was made uniform in that all four faculties granted doctor's degrees.

[51] Wilhelm von Humboldt, "Über die innere and äussere Organisation der höheren wissenschaftlichen Anstalten in Berlin" (1810), in *Gesammelte Schriften*, vol. X (Berlin: B. Behr, 1903), p. 252. — Humboldt contrasted the "university" with the "school," the university dedicated to the generation of new knowledge, the school to the dissemination of received knowledge.

for their advanced studies and as models for the reorganization of American universities.

The four faculties of the German universities differed in numbers of students far less than one might expect on the basis of present-day proportions.[52] There was, however, a tradition of intellectual and political rivalry among the four faculties and, particularly, between the three "upper" faculties and the philosophical faculty. The philosopher's contempt for the professional faculties found a highly literate expression in Immanuel Kant's caustic epistle on "The Squabble Among the Faculties," in which Kant spoke of "the merchants [or hucksters] of the upper faculties—the clerics, the legal officers, and the physicians" and characterized them sarcastically as the "miracle men" of our society.[53]

In most of the universities, the faculty of philosophy included natural sciences and cultural sciences without any organizational subdivision.[54] The first exceptions occurred in the 1860s, when two universities (Tübingen and Strassburg) established a philosophical-historical faculty separate from a faculty of mathematical and natural sciences. In the 1890s, Heidelberg formed a separate faculty of natural sciences. Otherwise, the comprehensive faculty of philosophy remained the rule for German universities until the 1930s. One qualification needs to be made regarding the social sciences: at most German universities political science and political economy, and sometimes also sociology, were taught in the juridical, not in the philosophical, faculty.

By 1939 the situation had changed drastically: twelve out of eighteen universities had established separate faculties of natural sciences or of mathematical and natural sciences. By 1968 all eighteen (counting only the universities that had existed in 1939) had adopted the new organizational arrangement. A similar change had occurred regarding the social sciences. Back in 1850 there had been only two

[52] The official statistics of the State of Prussia showed for its ten universities in the summer semester of 1888 the following enrollments: 6,024 in the Faculty of Theology, 6,472 in the Faculty of Law, 8,750 in the Faculty of Medicine, and 7,944 in the Faculty of Philosophy.

[53] Immanuel Kant, Der Streit der Facultäten (Königsberg: Friedrich Nicolovius, 1798), pp. 27 and 37.

[54] My sources for the account of German universities were Wilhelm Lexis, A General View of the History and Organization of Public Education in the German Empire (Berlin: A. Asher & Co., 1904); World Universities (London: British Universities Encyclopedia, Atheneum Press, 1939); Handbuch der deutschen Wissenschaft, pt. I (Berlin: Druckhaus Tempelhof, 1949); The World of Learning, 1967-68 (London: Europa Publications, 1968); The World of Learning 1975-76 (London: Europa Publications, 1975).

German universities with separate faculties of the social sciences (Munich and Tübingen). The existence of the social sciences was given explicit recognition by several universities in the first quarter of the twentieth century by renaming the law faculty "Faculty of Law and Political Sciences." To make the picture more complicated, a few universities taught the social sciences, not in the law faculty, but in the philosophical faculty. By 1939 four German universities had established separate social-science faculties. This exception tended to become the rule after the second world war; the number of faculties of "economic and social sciences" or "economic and political sciences" increased. However, several universities have maintained the fusion between law and economics, or law and political sciences; and at least one (Heidelberg) continues to keep economics and other social sciences in the philosophical faculty.

The old tradition of only four faculties has definitely come to an end. In 1850, there had been only two German universities with more than four faculties, and by 1903 only three. This had completely turned around by 1939, when there were only three universities left that stuck to the four traditional faculties. By 1949 the only holdout was the University of Marburg; and in due course it gave in to the pressures of the age of greater specialization. At present, the German universities have between five and ten faculties, some of them previously regarded as vocational institutions of higher education but not of university character (because they did not require Latin). Several German universities have abandoned their division into faculties in favor of departmentalization after the American model. The one-time leaders have become followers.

Far more significant than the organizational changes in German universities is the fact that these institutions have long been dedicated to research—at least as much as to teaching, if not more so. It was this double allegiance to higher learning—generation of new knowledge as well as dissemination of received knowledge—that in the late nineteenth century attracted the attention and admiration on the part of American academics. It was chiefly in this respect that German universities were the model for the "research universities" in the United States.

AMERICAN UNIVERSITIES SINCE 1876

The choice of the year 1876 as the benchmark for a new generation of American universities was dictated by the founding of Johns Hopkins University in Baltimore, Maryland. This institution, the first genuine research university in the country with a postgraduate division more important than its undergraduate division, was designed by its first president, Daniel Coit Gilman.[55]

The Research University

The commitment to advanced studies and research was made explicit in Gilman's inaugural address, when he distinguished the objectives of a university from those of an undergraduate college. There had been graduate education, leading to the degree of doctor of philosophy, at several American institutions before the "new experiment" at Johns Hopkins University, but nowhere had the research mission of the university been given the emphasis it received at Hopkins. Professorial appointments were strictly confined to research-minded scholars and scientists with a record of significant publications and good promise of further research. No stress was put on teaching loads, class hours, credit points, and similar quantitative rules that elsewhere became integral parts of academic practice in the United States.

The upgrading of higher education took several forms. Students were encouraged to engage in research projects and were taught not to accept findings on authority, but to question them and seek new evidence. The Ph.D. degree became an attestation of original contributions to knowledge. Most professors were directors of laboratories, institutes, or seminars. To facilitate the publication of scholarly books, a university press, the first in the country, was organized. A medical school was established (in 1893), integrated with Johns Hopkins Hospital (opened in 1889), with all full-time professors dedicated to research, and with students selected on the basis of the highest standards of admission. The Johns Hopkins Medical School became a model for the country.

The Johns Hopkins idea of a university was much admired, and emulated in several respects; the success of its Ph.D.s was extraordinary.[56] Several established universities, for example, Harvard, Yale,

[55] Gilman was a graduate of Yale College, studied at the University of Berlin, and returned to Yale as librarian and professor of physical and political geography. He served as president of the University of California from 1872 and became president-elect of Johns Hopkins University in 1874. See his book *The Launching of a University, and Other Papers* (New York: Dodd, Mead & Co., 1906). The need for a research university had been clearly seen and proclaimed by some of the original trustees of the University. See George William Brown, *The Need of a Higher Standard of Education in the United States* (Baltimore: Steam Press of W. K. Boyle, 1869).

[56] ". . . the influence of Johns Hopkins on American higher education was out of all proportion to its size, wealth, or age. In 1926, J. McKeen Cattell found that of 1,000 distinguished American scientists, 243 were Hopkins graduates. Within twenty years

and Columbia, followed the Hopkins lead in developing strong and successful graduate schools of arts and sciences. A few new universities, especially the University of Chicago (1890), likewise became top-ranking research universities. Besides these private institutions, several state universities developed strength in their graduate programs; most prominent among them were the Universities of California, Michigan, Wisconsin, and Minnesota. By 1900 there were at least seven private and public universities granting Ph.D. degrees or other doctorates at annual rates sustained over several years.[57] By 1976, the number of such universities had increased to 184.

Not all institutions granting doctorates, today or in the past, are called "research universities." What qualifies a university to this designation? In casual talk, one would expect the following characteristics to be present: that the university grants a "considerable" number of doctor's degrees year after year; that a "large" percentage of its teaching staff have obtained doctor's degrees and have a "good"

---

of the founding of the Baltimore institution, over sixty American colleges and universities had three or more members of their staff holding Hopkins degrees. These young Ph.D.s were going out as dedicated missionaries all over the country to spread the university idea. In 1896, there were already ten of them at Harvard, thirteen at Columbia, and nineteen at Wisconsin." John S. Brubacher and Willis Rudy, *Higher Education in Transition: A History of American Colleges and Universities, 1636-1976*, 3rd ed. (New York: Harper & Row, 1976), p. 181.

[57] Various sources inform us that some 50 universities in the United States were granting doctorates in 1900. See, for example, Ernest Hollis, *Toward Improving Ph.D. Programs* (Washington, D.C.: American Council on Education, 1945), p. 21; or Robert L. Ebel, *Encyclopedia of Educational Research* (New York: Macmillan Co., 1969), p. 546. Other sources count only about 25. None of these figures is acceptable, because they include institutions that awarded only one or two doctor's degrees a year, or actually none at all—except one or more honorary degrees. Tables in the Education Reports for 1899-1900 and 1900-1901 list 52 and 56 universities, respectively, as "institutions conferring Ph.D. degrees" in these years. Of the 52 institutions in 1899-1900, 21 conferred only three or fewer degrees each, and another 15 no earned degree at all. Of the 56 institutions one year later, 26 conferred three or fewer earned degrees each, and another 14 conferred none. See U.S. Office of Education, *Report of the Commissioner of Education for the Year 1899-1900*, vol. II (Washington, D.C., 1901), p. 1876, and U.S. Office of Education, *Report of the Commissioner of Education for the Year 1900-1901*, vol. II (Washington, D.C., 1902), p. 1614. Most of the listed institutions conferred the doctorates on the basis of examinations, not research. Bernard Berelson, eliminating many of the institutions as not "legitimate" (for example, Taylor University in Upland, Indiana, which had awarded as many as 52 and 45 Ph.D. degrees, respectively, in the two years), reduces the number of doctorate-granting institutions to 25 in a table of "raw data" and, after further examination, to only 7. Bernard Berelson, *Graduate Education in the United States* (New York: McGraw Hill, 1960), pp. 26 and 93. The seven universities, in the order of the number of degrees conferred in 1901, were Johns Hopkins, Yale, Harvard, Chicago, Columbia, Pennsylvania, and Cornell.

record of publications; that the teaching loads of faculty members are "sufficiently light" to leave them "enough" time to pursue research; and that library and laboratory facilities are "adequate" for the pursuit of substantial research undertakings. These characteristics leave much leeway to subjective judgment. For systematic, statistical surveys, quantitative criteria for operational definitions were needed. They have been developed by the National Center for Educational Statistics (NCES) and the Carnegie Commission on Higher Education. The category of "doctorate-granting institutions" was divided into four subcategories: research universities I (51 in 1976), research universities II (47), doctorate-granting universities I (56), and doctorate-granting universities II (30). The major criteria are the size of federal financial support received and the number of doctorates awarded per year.[58]

Graduate, Undergraduate, Professional, and Vocational Instruction

Although the development of American graduate schools of arts and sciences was inspired by German models of advanced scholarship and research, two features distinguished most American universities from continental European models: their continuing commitment to *undergraduate* education and their proclivity to establish courses, curricula, and schools for *vocational* education.

The American undergraduate college, as we have seen, had developed first as a center for the "classical" education of young men. To this core were gradually added separate schools for training in the professions of law, medicine, and theology, which traditionally required "philosophical" preparation. In the first half of the nineteenth century, curricular experiments added scientific-vocational courses of study to the offerings of many undergraduate colleges. As the state universities of the Midwest developed after the Civil War, and as the elective system was adopted somewhat later, vocational instruction gradually achieved institutional recognition as a course

[58] To qualify for the subcategory "research universities I," the institution must have been among the largest fifty recipients of federal research funds in at least two of the three years between 1972 and 1974 and must have awarded at least fifty doctorates in 1973-1974. Research universities II must have been among the largest one hundred recipients of federal funds and must have awarded at least fifty doctorates in 1973-1974. The next two subcategories are made up of universities that were not among the largest one hundred recipients of research funds from federal agencies and have awarded fewer doctorates in the specified years. For exact specifications, see *A Classification of Institutions of Higher Education* (rev. ed.). A Report of the Carnegie Council on Policy Studies in Higher Education (New York: The Carnegie Foundation for the Advancement of Teaching, 1976), pp. xv-xvi.

of study just as legitimate as the traditional, classical undergraduate course. By the late nineteenth century, specialized schools for the "vocations" joined those for the older professions. It was within the context of these changes that a few established institutions followed the model of Hopkins and Chicago in adding graduate schools of arts and sciences. And these new universities, dedicated from the start to developing as pure research universities, soon established programs and facilities for undergraduate and vocational education along the "American plan," offering a more varied fare than the German or "Continental" menu.[59]

Of course, not all institutions of higher education were able or willing to dedicate themselves to all of these goals with equal strength. Many remained liberal arts colleges for undergraduates, and included "vocational" education only as single courses among their offerings, if at all. Institutions that subscribed to a comprehensive conception of educational mission varied in the extent of their commitment to its constituent areas of interest and levels of scholarship. A few universities emphasized graduate over undergraduate education in the schools of liberal arts and sciences, or professional and vocational training over classical and liberal studies. Others developed reputations for emphasizing undergraduate instruction as against graduate studies (notwithstanding the high standards of "excellence" in their pursuit) and the liberal arts and sciences as against professional and vocational work (however advanced the level of research and teaching).

[59] One institution attempted to set an example for dedication to exclusively *non-vocational* and exclusively *graduate* studies: Clark University (founded in 1887 in Worcester, Massachusetts), under the leadership of its first president, G. Stanley Hall, a former professor at Johns Hopkins, set out to be "exclusively what is called in Europe a Philosophical Faculty . . . devoted to a group of the *pure sciences*. . . ." After twelve years, the founder of Clark University, disturbed by Hall's lofty ideas, withheld funds, forcing the university to institute a college for undergraduate education. Brubacher and Rudy, p. 182.

Even Johns Hopkins felt pressure for greater emphasis on undergraduate instruction and programs in applied studies. By 1920, Hopkins had added to its faculties of philosophy and medicine, schools for engineering, higher studies in education, and hygiene and public health. It did, however, resist extremes of vocationalism. For this show of purity it got highest marks from Abraham Flexner, the indomitable guardian of intellectual idealism and fastidious critic of meretriciousness in (presumably) higher education. Abraham Flexner, *Universities: American, English, German* (London: Oxford University Press, 1930). — For a concise account of the complex institutional changes at Johns Hopkins University I am indebted to its archivist, Julia Morgan. (Personal communication, 16 November, 1979.) For the institutional history of the University prior to World War II, see John C. French, *A History of the University Founded by Johns Hopkins* (Baltimore: The Johns Hopkins Press, 1946).

Enrollment figures in the various programs of a few selected universities between 1880 and 1920 demonstrate how their relative emphases varied from one another and changed over time during this period. In 1880-1881, for example, nearly 75 per cent of the students at Johns Hopkins were pursuing graduate degrees, but at other universities—still vacillating in their commitment to graduate education—the proportion of graduate students in the liberal arts and sciences was far less: 11 per cent at Princeton, 7 per cent at both Harvard and Yale, 2 per cent at the University of Michigan. Twenty years later, in 1900-1901, the students enrolled in the liberal arts and sciences at Johns Hopkins were about equally divided between graduates and undergraduates; the proportion of graduates in the student body at the University of Chicago was 35 per cent; at Princeton, 13 per cent; at Harvard, 15 per cent; at Yale, 20 per cent; and at the University of Michigan, 8 per cent. By 1920-1921, the proportion of graduate students in the liberal arts and sciences at Hopkins had declined, but increased at Chicago so that they were at the same level—approximately 39 per cent of those enrolled were pursuing graduate degrees. These two institutions were still leading the field. At Harvard the proportion of graduate students was slightly up, to 17 per cent, at Yale a little down, to 15 per cent—counting only students in the liberal arts and sciences. At Princeton the proportion had dropped to 8 per cent, as low as Michigan's (which had remained at that level).

A different picture emerges if graduate and undergraduate enrollments in the liberal arts and sciences are combined and compared with total enrollments in the professional and vocational schools during the same period. For most of the forty years between 1880 and 1920, Michigan and Johns Hopkins had the highest proportion of professional and vocational students, Princeton and Chicago the fewest, with Harvard and Yale in between. Michigan's large proportion of vocational and professional students was distributed, by 1910, among six different schools, but Johns Hopkins' professional students were all in its medical school. Harvard had five professional schools in 1910, and Yale had seven. Princeton had, until 1910-1911, only a school of science, which was then amalgamated with its "academic" or liberal arts department. Chicago's small proportion of professional students was due less to design than circumstance—it was still a young university, just in the process of adding and developing its professional and vocational schools, with four of them in operation by 1910.

Schools of Applied Studies

The growth and development of applied studies at doctorate-granting universities has been much faster in the United States than in most other countries. This development calls for closer attention, because the inclusion of such schools in universities has greatly broadened the range of fields encompassed by the term "higher learning." Catalogues and organization charts of universities, displaying the arrangements of old and new fields among separate schools, colleges, and other administrative units of the institution, may serve as "authoritative" classification schemes of academic subjects.

Theology, law, and medicine have claimed to be "the learned professions" for at least 800 years and have not gladly seen this designation extended to engineering or architecture. Hardly anybody would claim agriculture or business to be professions in the traditional sense of the word. On the other hand, there is little reason to quarrel whether librarianship or education are professional or vocational fields of study. I shall stay out of such arguments and shall deal with all applied studies as one category.

The number of professional and vocational schools has much increased over the last hundred years, and particularly over the last twenty-five years. Even more impressive is the increase in scope: the fifty largest research universities (as defined by the Carnegie Commission) offer forty-two different applied fields of study, if the different appellations of their separate schools are taken as indications of different professions or vocations. Institutions differ greatly in their rates of expansion in applied studies. For example, Johns Hopkins has only five professional-vocational divisions (Medicine, Public Health, Engineering, International Studies, and Music), and Princeton has only three (Engineering, Public and International Affairs, and Architecture and Urban Planning). Harvard, on the other hand, which in 1900 had only three (Divinity, Law, and Medicine), now has another eight (Business, Fine Arts, Education, Public Health, Dentistry, Engineering, Design, Public-Affairs), or a total of eleven; and the University of California at Berkeley (and San Francisco), which in 1900 had nine "colleges," of which six were for applied studies, now has fifteen professional and vocational schools and colleges (Medicine, Law, Education, Agriculture, Environmental Design (formerly Architecture), Engineering, Library and Information Studies, Business Administration, Criminology, Forestry and Conservation, Nursing, Optometry, Public Health, Social Welfare, and Public Affairs).

In order to gauge the spread of vocationalism for a somewhat larger sample of institutions, I examined the descriptions of the fifty largest research universities in the United States to ascertain the number of their separate schools (divisions, colleges, faculties) of applied studies.[60] In tabulating these schools, I disregarded the semantic idiosyncrasies of the particular institutions and placed differently named divisions under a common heading descriptive of their programs of study. Thus, schools of commerce, business administration, management, and accounts and finance are all under the heading business schools; schools of librarianship, library service, library science, library and information sciences, etc., are all under library schools; schools of environmental design, urban planning, or architecture plus any cognate field are all under architecture. Much simpler have been the decisions to put jurisprudence under law, and applied science under engineering. Among the curiosities are a "School of Consumer and Family Sciences" and, at another university, a "School of Family Resources and Consumer Sciences," both evidently teaching what others have more prosaically named "home economics." The puzzlement raised by excessively imaginative nomenclature— for example, a "School of Applied Life Studies"—had to be resolved by consulting the school's catalogue; this particular school was concerned largely with physical education.[61]

The tabulation of the professional and vocational schools of the largest fifty research universities shows interesting similarities and differences.[62] Engineering is almost ubiquitous; virtually all universities in the sample have engineering programs under one name or another, for undergraduates or graduates or both.[63] The next most common vocational school among the fifty universities is the graduate or undergraduate business school. Only eight of the fifty have resisted the temptation to operate this cost-effective division (cheap per student; high ratio of student fees to instructional expenses). Yet, most of the eight exceptional institutions have good substitutes for

[60] On forty-eight of the fifty-one institutions listed as "research universities I" by the Carnegie Council on Policy Studies in Higher Education, adequate information is available in the 1979-1980 guide to the World of Learning. I considered a "division" as the equivalent of a separate school or college if it is headed by a dean. I omitted research centers, institutes, committees, and similar entities that are not independent from one or more schools or colleges.

[61] The course offerings included "Health and Safety," "Leisure Studies," "Rehabilitation-Education Services," in addition to physical education.

[62] I plan to supply the tabulation in the volume on Education. At this juncture I confine myself to a brief summary and discussion of significant findings.

[63] One exception is a large private university that, in the course of a recent reorganization, transferred its engineering school to another institution.

explicit programs in business, either in the form of schools of public and international affairs (which are more expensive) or of curricula built into schools of engineering (for example, "industrial engineering").

Schools of medicine are operated by forty-two of the fifty universities in the sample, despite their high cost. Of the eight institutions without medical schools, most are predominantly dedicated to engineering science (Princeton is an exception in this respect). Schools of education are fourth in frequency in the sample of fifty.

In the middle group of professional or vocational schools are architecture (at 23 of the 50 institutions), nursing (22), social work (20), dentistry (18), pharmacy (17), agriculture (17), fine arts (15), library science (14), journalism (14), veterinary medicine (13). Less frequent in our sample of fifty are public health (10), public affairs (9), music (8), forestry (8), home economics (7), allied health professions (6), divinity (6), applied earth sciences (4), physical education (4). The many applied fields represented by separate divisions at only one or two universities will be discussed presently; a few explanatory observations are needed here with regard to certain fields included in the list above.

The absence of a particular autonomous school of applied studies at any university does not imply that no courses in these fields are offered; they may be offered either in the college of arts and sciences or in a professional-vocational school that can accommodate the particular field in its program. Courses in education are sometimes offered in arts-and-science divisions; the same is true for general courses in fine arts, music, and architecture, in so far as the emphasis is on the theoretical and historical rather than the practical or performing aspects of these fields. Nursing is sometimes taught in the school of medicine, sometimes in the school of education, sometimes in the "university extension." Courses in journalism may be offered by the department of English in the college of arts and sciences. Several universities have home economics and physical education among their academic departments in the college. Finally, some institutions have departments of religion among the liberal arts, even though they may also have a separate divinity school.

The fact that only six divinity schools can be counted among the largest fifty research universities should not surprise us if we realize that the sample includes twenty-nine state universities, which—often for state-constitutional reasons—do not include preparation for religious ministry as part of their educational programs.[64] For reasons going back to the Morrill Act, most schools of agriculture, forestry, and veterinary medicine are operated by state universities; there are, however, a few private universities catering to these fields, some in state-supported schools, some without state support; for example, Duke and Yale have forestry schools.

Among schools of applied studies represented at only one or two of the fifty universities are some that are quite extraordinary in their excessive specialization: for example, a school of textiles (at North Carolina State), a school of hotel administration (at Cornell), and a school of travel industry management (Hawaii). On the other hand, some vocational or professional schools are represented at only one or two universities in the sample, simply because the demand for personnel trained in these specialties is relatively small. Thus, the sample contains only two schools each of mining, of marine sciences, and of optometry, and one school each of osteopathic medicine, of gerontology, and of fisheries. Altogether, sixteen schools are "unique"—with only one each in the list—and another five applied fields are represented by two special schools at the fifty universities.

Private universities have in general fewer schools of applied studies: the range in the sample under examination is from three to fourteen schools, the mode is seven. Public universities have typically a more vocational orientation: the range in the numbers is from five to fifteen, the mode, twelve.

This discussion of schools of applied studies has been confined to universities, public and private, and it has focused on the largest fifty *research universities*. Perhaps it is in order to call attention to the trend towards vocationalism and, particularly, practical-technical training in very large numbers of lower-level institutions of

[64] State colleges and universities have developed a wide variety of arrangements for teaching religion as an academic discipline. Milton McLean and Harry H. Kimber, in a study of programs in religion at twenty-five state institutions in 1960, found departments of religion, departments of philosophy and religion, and interdepartmental programs of religion fully integrated within their schools of liberal arts and sciences. Some state colleges and universities have "cooperative programs" in which separate schools of religion, or programs in religion, are partly funded, administered, or staffed by religious organizations. The authors stress that the many "patterns for bringing religion into the curriculum developed out of the local conditions and the differing points of view of scholars and administrators on those campuses." Milton D. McLean and Harry H. Kimber, *Teaching of Religion in State Universities* (Ann Arbor: University of Michigan, Office of Religious Affairs, 1960), p. iii. A brief historical account of "Religion in Colleges and Universities" by Franklin H. Littell is available in *The Encyclopedia of Education*, vol. 7 (New York: Macmillan Co. & Free Press, 1971), pp. 461-464.

"post-secondary" education. These developments will be discussed in the volume on Education.

Departments in the Liberal Arts

Colleges and graduate schools of liberal arts and sciences appear in the catalogues of research universities as coordinate or coequal, as administrative units, with the various colleges and schools for professional and vocational study.[65] But this should not mislead us into equating the functions of "professional" schools and schools of "liberal arts." In most research universities, the colleges and schools of liberal arts are not only the historical "core" of the institution, but they remain the largest divisions in terms of faculty size and student enrollment and, indeed, form the basis of the institution's public recognition as a university.

Departmentalization of faculties of liberal arts and sciences was not common until the last decade of the nineteenth century, but was so widespread by the first decade of the twentieth century that a university's reputation came to depend on the excellence of its departments in various disciplines, and the "legitimacy" of new fields of study came to depend on their representation—as departments—in the major universities. Departmental structures of faculties of liberal arts and sciences have thus served, at least since the turn of the century, as the principal form in which universities have recognized the autonomy of disciplines as separate branches of learning.

The classifications of higher learning have changed over the years, in institutions of higher education as well as in academies of sciences and in academic libraries. The processes were, of course, different in the three types of institution, but the direction of change has been the same. Departments in the universities, like sections in the academies and like classes in the librarians' classifications, have tended to increase the number. Although a time series of catalogues from a single university will occasionally show "merging" of previously separate departments, splitting, and thus an increase in number, has been far more common.

The increase in the numbers of departments within the divisions of liberal arts may be explained as the result of at least five partly

---

[65] Of 45 research universities for which adequate information was readily available, 32 have grouped all liberal arts and sciences into a single college or school. Of the remaining 13, 8 have two administrative units (one for natural sciences, the other for the humanities and social sciences); 3 universities have three units (separating the social sciences from the humanities); and 2 universities have four units (separating the biological from the physical sciences). Separate schools for the fine arts, performing arts, and/or music, outside the college of liberal arts, exist at 19 of the 45 universities.

independent, partly interconnected reasons: (1) increased specialization—specialties of a subject gaining recognition as new subjects;
(2) desire for greater visibility—assuring that the availability of an
academic program becomes better known to outside observers and
rating agencies; (3) administrative convenience—departments be-
coming too large to be manageable; (4) personality clashes—splitting
of departments because of rivalries among professors; and (5) university politics—adding departments because of ideological pressures (for example, from students seeking recognition of particular
topics as academic fields of learning).

To illustrate these reasons for increasing the number of departments, one may mention biochemistry as an instance of a specialty
developing into an autonomous field. Sociology, anthropology, linguistics, and particularly languages and literatures may have been
instances of greater visibility being sought for existing programs of
study, though administrative convenience may have been equally or
even more important in establishing independent departments for
these fields. Instances of splitting departments because of personal
incompatibilities among some of their members are well known to
insiders but not in need of a public record. Finally, the establishment
of departments such as Afro-American studies may have been decided upon in deference to strongly felt ideological commitments.

It would, in this discussion of university departments, be tempting
to adhere to the customary division of the liberal arts into natural
sciences (or physical sciences and life sciences), social sciences, and
humanities. I avoid this for reasons amply demonstrated in Chapter
3 of Volume I, where I showed that such partitions are not sup-
portable on philosophical grounds and have in fact not been carried
through with any consistency. History is in some institutions counted
among the social sciences but in others among the humanities; psychology appears in different institutions as a natural (or life) science,
as a social science, or as one of the humanities; anthropology and
geography are considered natural sciences at some places, social
sciences at others; linguistics can be found among the social sciences
or among the humanities; and so forth. Thus, if one were to adhere
to the classifications adopted by the individual institutions, findings
would be incomparable and summaries inconsistent.

The philosophical objections to the assignments of subjects to subject divisions are no less persuasive. That mathematics is attached
to the natural sciences has its historical explanation but makes little
sense from a philosophical point of view. As a formal science it
should, together with formal logic, be distinguished from empirical
sciences. Among the best-known philosophers and classifiers of sci-

ence (reviewed in preceding chapters), Francis Bacon, Comte, Cournot, Spencer, Pearson, Carnap, and the *Britannica* propaedists rejected the placing of mathematics with the natural, physical, or any empirical sciences, and gave it a place of its own or one shared with formal logic. Yet, logic is usually in the department of philosophy in the division of the humanities. Moreover, applied mathematics is an auxiliary science to those disciplines to which it is applied, which may be economics and other social sciences no less than the various natural sciences. Indeed, there is more mathematics used in economics than in either chemistry, biology, or geology; and certain fields of mathematics, for example, game theory, apply predominantly to social sciences and have few, if any applications in the natural sciences.

Placing philosophy among the humanities made sense as long as the chief task of the teacher of philosophy was to present and interpret the history of philosophy with special emphasis on the classics. This placement makes little sense, however, when epistemology and mathematical logic are major concerns of the philosophy department.

As a matter of fact, what I called the "customary" division of subject groups within the arts was not at all customary before the twentieth century; and even now the catalogues of many colleges and universities list the departments and interdepartmental programs in alphabetic order, not separated into three or four groups. Such grouping is ordinarily used only for purposes such as specifying distribution requirements in the course selections by undergraduates or voting regulations for the composition of faculty committees. in older catalogues one can find listings of departments that are in some order corresponding to a philosophical scheme but that nevertheless eschew a grouping of the subjects into the questionable three or four divisions. Thus, in the catalogue of Harvard University for 1919-1920, the following sequence of fifteen departments (with some subdivisions) can be found: I. Semitic Languages and History; II. Ancient Languages: A. Indic Philology, B. The Classics (Greek and Latin); III. Modern Languages: A. English, B. German Language and Literature, C. French and other Romance Languages and Literature, D. Comparative Literature; IV. History, Government, and Economics: A. History, B. Government, C. Economics; V. Philosophy: A. Philosophy and Psychology, B. Social Ethics; VI. Education; VII. Fine Arts; VIII. Music; IX. Mathematics; X. Physical Sciences: A. Physics, B. Engineering Sciences; XI. Chemistry; XII. Biology: A. Botany, B. Zoology; XIII. Geology: A. Geology and Geography, B. Mineralogy and Petrography; XIV. Anthropology; XV. Medical Sciences.

This organization is interesting in several respects. (1) It contains a few professional or vocational subjects, which in later reorganizations would be assigned to special schools or divisions, for example, education, engineering sciences, and medical sciences; indeed, ten years earlier, in the catalogue of 1909-1910, even more vocational subjects had been listed: architecture, landscape architecture, engineering (as a department separate from engineering sciences), and forestry. (2) The list of 1919 includes psychology, if only linked with philosophy; but this was progress compared with 1909, when it was conspicuous by its absence. (3) The list of 1919 includes economics, which in 1909 had still been called by its old designation, "Political Economy."

The number of departments in the Faculty of Arts and Sciences at Harvard increased from fifteen in 1919 to twenty-eight in 1949 and to thirty-one in 1976. The small increase, by only three departments, between 1949 and 1976, is somewhat misleading in that three professional and vocational departments of the 1949 roster were eliminated through reassignment to schools or divisions (Architectural Sciences, Engineering, and Engineering Sciences and Applied Physics). Departments are no longer listed in a systematic sequence, but in alphabetic order. Instead of reproducing these lists for several years, which would allow us to see the process of change through consecutive reorganizations, I confine myself to comparing the departmental arrangement of 1976 with that of 1919. Of the fifteen departments in 1919, two were eliminated through reassignment to other divisions or schools (Education and Medical Sciences), three were merely renamed, five were retained without change, and five were split into thirteen independent departments. Of the thirty-one departments in 1976, eight had existed in 1919 (five under the same name and three under a different name), thirteen emerged as a result of splits of old departments, and 10 were newly created.

The five "unchanged" departments are Fine Arts, Music, Mathematics, Chemistry, and Anthropology. The three renamed departments are Near Eastern Languages and Civilizations (for "Semitic Languages and History"), Physics (for "Physical Sciences"), and Geological Sciences (for "Geology"). The thirteen departments resulting from the splitting of five departments existing in 1919 are Sanskrit and Indian Studies, and The Classics (split from Ancient Languages), English and American Literature, Germanic Languages and Literatures, Romance Languages and Literatures, and Comparative Literature (from Modern Languages), History, Government, and Economics (from a combined department of History, Government, and Economics), Philosophy, and Psychology and Social Relations (from Philosophy), and Biochemistry and Molecular Biology, and Biology (from Biology).[66] The ten new departments created between 1919 and 1976 are Afro-American Studies, Celtic Languages and Literatures, East Asian Languages and Literatures, Slavic Languages and Literatures, Linguistics, Visual and Environmental Studies, History of Science, Sociology, Statistics, and Astronomy.

After this lengthy story of the development of departments in the arts and sciences at Harvard, most readers' demand for information of this kind is probably satisfied, and few will want to go through similar accounts for other institutions.[67] Readers will readily accept the affirmation that the numbers of departments and their rates of increase have been very different at different institutions. One example may suffice: The number of departments in arts and sciences increased at Berkeley from thirty-nine in 1919 to forty-three in 1976; and at Princeton from fourteen in 1919 to twenty-six in 1976. The numbers are much higher at Berkeley, but the rate of increase is higher at Princeton.

Up to this point, we have been talking only about the largest fifty research universities in the country. A glance at another category of institution of higher education would seem interesting. I selected five of the best-known private liberal-arts colleges and tabulated the changes in the numbers of their departments betweeen 1950 and 1978; Mount Holyoke, down from twenty-five to twenty-three; Oberlin, down from twenty-two to nineteen; Occidental, up from eighteen to nineteen; Reed, up from twenty-four to twenty-six; and Swarthmore, unchanged, nineteen. The composition of the roster of departments changed over the period, but their total number in the five colleges together remained virtually unchanged: down from 108 to 106.[68]

Public colleges did not show such restraint. I may illustrate this

[66] The processes of departmental splits would look different if we had compared the consecutive reorganizations. By skipping several reorganizations between 1919 and 1976, we obtain a somewhat distorted picture.

[67] More comprehensive and more detailed analysis of the processes of departmental fission and fusion at different institutions will be offered in the volume on Education.

[68] I should take this opportunity to emphasize that the "departments" of one kind of institution are not necessarily the same as "departments" in others. At Reed, for example, divisions of literature and language; history and social science; mathematics and natural sciences; and philosophy, psychology, and education were instituted in 1923. These *divisions*, according to one analyst, served as "the units of administration of instruction [and thus] kept down the tendency to departmentalize," Burton R. Clark, *The Distinctive College: Antioch, Reed & Swarthmore* (Chicago: Aldine Publishing Co., 1970), p. 117. Nonetheless, Reed College recognizes departments within its (now, five) divisions, and as my concern is primarily in the classification of knowledge—not in the administration of the curriculum—the numbers of departments are relevant, even if they serve a less distinctive role than at other types of colleges and universities.

by singling out two colleges operated by the City of New York: the number of departments in the liberal arts increased between 1950 and 1978 at Hunter College from twenty-one to twenty-seven, and at Queens College from twenty to thirty-three.

Special Programs, Departmental and Interdepartmental

Besides increases in the number of separate schools in given institutions and in the number of departments in given schools or colleges, there has been a third dimension of internal academic expansion: increases in the number of special programs. Such programs of research and/or instruction may be departmental or interdepartmental. Departmental programs are offered by members of one department (sometimes with associate members from other departments) in particular areas of specialization, frequently administered by a center or institute supported by restricted funds or outside sources.[69] Interdepartmental programs in areas of interdisciplinary character are usually administered by committees made up of professors from different departments.

Special programs within a department are often a way of cultivating a specialty before it splits off and becomes the concern of a new department. Since this process of fission goes on over time and at different speeds at different institutions, one finds that what is still a special program at one place is elsewhere already a separate department. In some instances, however, loyalty and allegiance to the discipline of which the specialty has been a part will outweigh the separatist ambitions of the specialists and restrain their drive for autonomy. To give examples for both cases, there are special programs in astrophysics and in plasma physics within departments of physics, but at some universities these programs have developed into autonomous departments. On the other hand, special programs in econometric research, international finance, and industrial relations, have ordinarily remained within economics departments, though a few universities have created separate departments of industrial relations.

Interdepartmental programs have mushroomed in the last twenty-five years. Some of them are only half-way stations on the way to autonomous departments; as long as they remain programs, they are

---

[69] One might, with some justification, regard the establishment of centers and institutes for study and research in special fields or topics as a fourth dimension in university expansion. To the extent that such institutes and centers bear on departmentalization in colleges and universities, they will be discussed in the volume on Education. Their function as research institutes will be treated in the part "Research and Development" in Volume VI.

administered by interdepartmental committees. After they have grown into independent departments, they are often staffed with professors holding joint appointments in two departments. Examples are programs in linguistics, operated sometimes by scholars from as many as nine or ten departments, for example, anthropology, psychology, sociology, classics, English, Germanic languages, Romance languages, Slavic languages, and Oriental studies; in demography, operated by scholars from at least three or four departments, to wit, economics, sociology, statistics, and sometimes biology or biostatistics; and in environmental studies, operated by representatives from nine or ten departments, such as geology, geophysics, physics, chemistry, biochemistry, biology, engineering, economics, and political science.[70] Programs in African studies, or in Oriental studies, Latin American studies, European studies, and so forth, would draw support from departments of history, political science, geography, economics, sociology, anthropology, art, and various language departments. A program in oceanography would be carried by representatives from the departments of physics, geophysics, biology, biochemistry, and perhaps some others.

Universities differ in their regulations regarding degrees awarded to students who have successfully completed these programs. At some places or in some cases, the degrees are given in the special field served by the program, at other places or in other cases, the degrees are awarded on certification of one of the participating departments. The students, as a rule, do not care much whether they get their degree in a department or in a program; there are exceptions, however, especially when the program does not provide sufficient depth in the discipline in which the student expects to make an academic career. There is also the danger that students in an interdisciplinary or multidisciplinary program find themselves unable to cope with the problems of identity and regret the loss of security provided by the more structured program in a unidisciplinary department.[71]

[70] For an enlightening account of the experiences from the multidisciplinary program in geography and environmental engineering at Johns Hopkins University, see M. Gordon Wolman, "Interdisciplinary Education: A Continuing Experiment," *Science*, vol. 198 (25 November 1977), pp. 800-804. Wolman explains that "three specialized areas were considered important to the solution of environmental problems: (i) natural processes at the surface of the earth, (ii) social processes and mechanisms of decision-making in society, and (iii) the application of engineering design to mitigating the impact of human activity on environmental systems" (p. 800).

[71] Ibid., p. 803.

Growing Apart and Bringing Together

I have characterized the proliferation of special programs of instruction and research as a third dimension in the internal academic expansion of institutions of higher education. Yet, there is something of a paradox involved here: both the increase in the number of professional-vocational schools and colleges and the increase in the number of departments within schools and colleges are symptomatic of a trend towards more specialization and fragmentation of scholarly-scientific knowledge, whereas the increase in the number of interdisciplinary programs seems to reflect the opposite tendency, namely, to achieve cooperation among those professing different disciplines. We first split the *universitas litterarum* into ever more separate pieces and create for the professors increasing numbers of quasi-autonomous sanctuaries; then we try to reverse the academic diaspora by devising new techniques of "ingathering" the scattered brains to collaborate as a team of multidisciplinary teachers and researchers. First we make them form disjointed clubs, setting up separate housekeeping, then we bring them together for joint undertakings. First we segregate, then we integrate.

The three vectors of expansion of, and within, universities all involve administrative growth. The schools and colleges have their deans; the departments have their heads or chairmen; and the programs have chairmen or directors. All these functionaries have their secretaries, and the members of all these administrative entities meet in plenary sessions or committees to discuss, not ongoing research or the state of their art, but the everyday business of their particular groups. To call attention to this malign growth is not to denounce it. There is sense to it all. There is nothing wrong with specialization when the content of a discipline becomes too rich and too varied to remain a unified body of knowledge; nor is there anything wrong with multidisciplinary collaboration when problems and problem areas demand joint efforts from masters of different disciplines. Thus, the paradox of "segregation cum integration" is not just the result of academic whim, fashion, or empire-building; it is a natural outgrowth of intellectual development: formation of new disciplines and emergence of new problems. Since the solution of problems presupposes mastery of several disciplines, the gap between problems and disciplines can be bridged only by means of multidisciplinary programs.

Perhaps I have rationalized the process of academic expansion a little too volubly. To be honest, one has to admit that large elements of growthmanship, politics, empire-building, and self-advancement do play a role in the development.

Some of the observers of the academic scene have attached different meanings to multidisciplinary and interdisciplinary programs, but their semantic interpretations have not always been consistent. Without trying to impose my own preference on others, I would propose that we speak of *interdisciplinary* research where the problems under investigation require recourse to knowledge of different fields, but of *multidisciplinary* programs of instruction where students are supposed to acquire familiarity with two or more fields in order to be equipped to deal with a broad area of problems (rather than a concretely specified problem).

In a program of Latin American studies, for example, students will be asked to learn some geography, history, economics, political science, anthropology, sociology, and Spanish (or Portuguese). In other words, they should acquire both the languages of the special areas and the languages of the relevant fields; they will be enrolled in a *multidisciplinary* program of instruction. On the other hand, if researchers inquire into the monetary institutions and policies of one or more Latin American countries, economists, political scientists, and sociologists may band together in *interdisciplinary* research; if the research project relates to the stability or instability of democratic institutions, to the influence of the church, the ethnic composition of the population, the systems of criminal law, the rate of industrialization, the educational system and the degree of literacy, and so on and so forth, representatives of different fields of study will benefit from collaborating in *interdisciplinary* research. Needless to say, if a student (of extraordinary capabilities) has industriously studied several disciplines in a multidisciplinary program of instruction and has mastered these disciplines sufficiently to apply them to concrete problems, he can engage in interdisciplinary research all by himself, dispensing with collaborators from various disciplines. He need not bring together a team of different specialists, because he can bring together his successful learning of the various subjects impinging on the problem he investigates. It will be a one-man show, a solo performance of interdisciplinary research.

The Growth of Interdepartmental Programs

It would be exceedingly dull to examine here the time series of statistical averages for groups of universities in order to get a picture of the growth of interdepartmental programs. It is more interesting to look into the catalogues of a few particular institutions. Having selected Harvard for a case study of departmentalization, I choose Princeton and the University of California at Los Angeles (UCLA) as illustrations of the expansion of multidisciplinary studies on the undergraduate level. Both universities offer also wide ranges of programs to graduate students, but the development is probably more significant at the college level, because interdisciplinary study *before* any one discipline has been studied in depth seems to be largely an exercise in superficiality.

If we go back to 1956-1957, a year safely before the 1960s with their "student movement," we find that Princeton offered several options for "interdepartmental concentration." Students could major in one department and work for a minor in another. Thus, an undergraduate in the Department of Art and Architecture had, apart from sole concentration on courses offered in his department, five other choices, one in the Department of Classics, one in the Department of Religion, and three in the Department of History. Students in the Department of Philosophy could choose among four "bridge plans," connecting philosophy with the natural sciences, the social sciences, art, or religion, Besides these possibilities, there were three interdisciplinary programs administered by interdepartmental committees: (1) Special Program in the Humanities, (2) Special Program in American Civilization, and (3) Special Program in Near Eastern Studies. Finally, some alternative combinations were available in the School of Architecture and in the School of Public and International Affairs.

Twenty years later, after the student movement had come and gone, the opportunities for "concentration on dispersion" are far greater. According to the catalogue of 1978-1979, no fewer than thirteen interdepartmental programs are available at Princeton: African Studies, Afro-American Studies, American Studies, Creative Writing, East-Asian Studies, European Cultural Studies, History and Philosophy of Science, Latin American Studies, Near Eastern Studies, Russian Studies, Science in Human Affairs, Theater and Dance, and Visual Arts. In addition, several committees are charged with the task of coordinating programs tailored for and partly self-selected by individual students: in Environmental Studies, Humanistic Studies, International and Regional Studies, Medieval Studies, Renaissance Studies, Urban Studies, and Women's Studies.[72] There are, finally, several interdepartmental programs in the three professional-vocational schools.

If this looks big, it is still smaller than what UCLA offers to its

---

[72] Women's Studies has since been promoted to an interdepartmental program.

undergraduates. The abundance of special programs at UCLA is to be expected in view of its being a public university with an undergraduate enrollment almost five times that of Princeton. A statement on page two of its *General Catalog 1978-79* clarifies the policy of the University of California with respect to its programs:

> Recognizing the value of an interdisciplinary approach to the search for knowledge, the University of California has also developed research programs and curricula outside the usual departmental structure. Today along with libraries, UCLA's interdisciplinary research facilities include institutes, centers, projects, bureaus, nondepartmental laboratories, stations, and museums, and a wide range of interdisciplinary programs of study are available.

The catalogue description of facilities and programs for research distinguishes university-wide and campus-wide institutes and centers from those operated within particular colleges and schools; it lists altogether thirteen institutes and 12 centers (some of the centers as parts of institutes).[73] The description of interdisciplinary programs of instruction lists thirteen that offer B.A. or B.S. degrees, six that are available in conjunction with a departmental major, and another six "preprofessional" curricula. The interdepartmental degree programs are Afro-American Studies, Chicano Studies, Communication Studies, Cybernetics, East Asian Studies, Economics-System Science, Ethnic Arts, Indo-European Studies, Latin American Studies, Mathematics-Computer Science, Mathematics-System Science, Near Eastern Studies, and Study of Religion. The special programs conjoined with a departmental major are African Studies, Asian-American Studies, Diversified Liberal Arts, International Relations, Urban or Organizational Studies, and Women's Studies.

I have sarcastically spoken of "concentration on dispersion" and have expressed that the emphasis on multidisciplinary instruction may be an "exercise in superficiality." I ought to defend the position underlying these remarks. The idea of a major field of concentration in undergraduate studies is based on a sound philosophy of higher

[73] The proliferation of specialized institutes is a phenomenon present in most of the industrialized countries. To give just one example, I reproduce the name of an institute at one of the German universities: Institut für Unterrichtstechnologie, Mediendidaktik und Ingenieurpädagogik (Institute for the Technology of Teaching, the Didactics of Media, and the Pedagogy of Engineering. Note the common semantic element of the three terms, "teaching," "didactics," and "pedagogy," and the common objective, namely, dissemination of knowledge).

education. Its main tenet is that higher education requires both breadth and depth, both distribution of the student's effort over a variety of disciplines and his concentration on one discipline, his major field, or on two at most. Without such concentration, without studying *any* discipline in depth, genuine higher education does not exist. An accumulation of "credits" for nothing but introductory or first-year courses is merely "continuing secondary education." The danger of multidisciplinary programs is that they provide no knowledge in depth, only a smattering in a variety of subjects.[74]

The HEGIS Taxonomy of Academic Teaching

In the historical survey of American colleges and universities, we have seen that, prior to the institution of vocational schools and prior to the establishment of departments in schools of liberal arts and sciences, the classification of academic knowledge was embedded in class schedules and reading lists, not visible either in catalogues or in organization charts. For more recent times, we have both these sources available; they tell a story of substantial variations in the arrangements of subjects taught at different institutions. Often, the same subjects are offered by different departments, and many subjects offered at some colleges and universities are not taught at others. Thus, the names of schools and departments within schools can serve as only a rough guide to the scope of the teaching programs. The growing number of special and interdisciplinary programs conducted outside "traditional" academic boundaries further complicates the task of comparing the course offerings of American colleges and universities.

To facilitate comparisons, the U.S. Office of Education prepared a list of academic subject fields and specialties for a survey in 1968-1969. It was soon found necessary to revise the list in order to accommodate subjects and subsubjects that could not easily be fitted into the slots it had provided. The new publication[75] is usually re-

---

[74] I shall elaborate this position in the volume on Education, but I may report here on a personal experience with a multidisciplinary program. As chairman of a committee on international relations, a program linking political science, economics, sociology, and history, I found not a single student in the program, even on the graduate level, who acquired a mastery in any one of the four subjects. As far as their knowledge of economics is concerned, to call it a smattering would understate the degree of their ignorance.

[75] Robert A. Huff and Marjorie O. Chandler, *A Taxonomy of Instructional Programs in Higher Education* (Washington, D.C.: U.S. Department of Health, Education, and Welfare, Office of Education, 1970).

ferred to as the New HEGIS Taxonomy (for the initial letters of the Higher Education General Information Survey).[76]

The New HEGIS Taxonomy is designed, according to the foreword, to bring the "lists of higher education instructional programs [read: the instructional programs in institutions of higher education] . . . in line with the best current practice." The taxonomy supposedly describes (although the text mistakenly says "prescribes") "how the majority of institutions of higher education actually do organize and record data on instructional programs."[77]

A four-digit code is used for the classification; the first two digits identify the "discipline division," the second two digits, the "discipline specialty." The enumeration of the "conventional academic subdivisions of knowledge and training" contains 24 discipline divisions, each subdivided into (between 2 and 44) specialties denoted by altogether 315 code numbers. A separate section for "technological and occupational curriculums leading to associate degrees and other awards below the baccalaureate" lists another six divisions with together 76 specialties. The two lists together contain 391 coded specialties. An alphabetical index is supplied, which includes some 440 subject titles. There are more index entries than code numbers because several subjects have more than one title, for example, biometrics and biostatistics, or music history and musicology.

The twenty-four academic discipline divisions are here reproduced, with the number of named discipline specialties added between parentheses:

0100	Agriculture and Natural Resources	(with 17 named specialties)
0200	Architecture and Environmental Design	(with 6 named specialties)
0300	Area Studies	(with 14 named specialties)
0400	Biological Sciences	(with 27 named specialties)
0500	Business and Management	(with 17 named specialties)
0600	Communications	(with 5 named specialties)
0700	Computer and Information Sciences	(with 5 named specialties)

[76] The linguistic link-sausage "Higher Education General Information Survey," presumably is intended to mean either "General Survey of Information on Higher Education" or "Survey of General Information on Higher Education." The rules of English grammar, however, want the first adjective to modify the last noun and would thus suggest a different reading, perhaps "Higher Survey of Education in General Information." Should we prescribe a course in remedial English for the creative writers in the Office of Education?

[77] Huff and Chandler, Taxonomy, p. iii.

0800	Education	(with 39 named specialties)
0900	Engineering	(with 25 named specialties)
1000	Fine and Applied Arts	(with 11 named specialties)
1100	Foreign Languages	(with 16 named specialties)
1200	Health Professions	(with 25 named specialties)
1300	Home Economics	(with 7 named specialties)
1400	Law	(with 1 named specialty)
1500	Letters	(with 10 named specialties)
1600	Library Sciences	(with 1 named specialty)
1700	Mathematics	(with 3 named specialties)
1800	Military Sciences	(with 3 named specialties)
1900	Physical Sciences	(with 20 named specialties)
2000	Psychology	(with 10 named specialties)
2100	Public Affairs and Services	(with 6 named specialties)
2200	Social Sciences	(with 15 named specialties)
2300	Theology	(with 4 named specialties)
4900	Interdisciplinary Studies	(with 4 named specialties)

In each of the twenty-four divisions provision is made for an "other" specialty to be specified by institutions offering instruction in a subject that does not fit into one of the designated slots.

The Taxonomers' Vocational Bent

The New HEGIS Taxonomy is a useful guide to instructional programs in American institutions. It reflects the vocational bent in (supposedly) higher education so crassly that it may give a shudder to any serious scholar. For example, the list contains "weaving," "jewelry," and "metalsmithing," all as subspecialties of "applied design," a discipline specialty in the discipline division "Fine and Applied Arts"; and "home decoration and home equipment" as a specialty in the division "Home Economics."

In contrast to this extraordinary specialization in vocational "academic subjects," several of the fundamental subjects of really academic learning are not subdivided at all. For example, sociology is just one specialty in the discipline division "Social Sciences." The same is true of history and of economics; they are mere "specialties" of Social Sciences, and none of their various fields or areas are considered worthy of mention. Ancient, medieval, modern, European, American, Far Eastern history—they all are lumped together as a single specialty of Social Sciences, evidently less important than weaving or fashion design. Macroeconomics, price and allocation theory, income distribution, monetary theory, international economics, industrial organization, and all the rest, are unnamed elementary particles of the specialty "economics" in the discipline division "Social Sciences." Several fields of economics, such as "banking and finance" or "labor and industrial relations," are given the rank of specialties of Business and Management. Thus, if a field has some vocational aspect, it may be promoted to a specialty in a vocational "discipline division." As a subject of the liberal arts it remains unlisted, excluded from the New HEGIS Taxonomy.

Logic, Philosophy, and Letters

The most amazing shocker in the New HEGIS Taxonomy is the absence of "Logic" from the list. Believe it or not, there is no entry for this basic subject of academic learning, not as a division, not as a specialty, not as a subspecialty. And what of "Philosophy"? It ranks as a specialty of "Letters." No subspecialties of philosophy are listed. If someone charitably assumes that logic is meant to be a self-evident subspecialty of philosophy and therefore need not be given an explicit place in the taxonomy, he will be discouraged from this benevolent interpretation by the definition that the HEGIS taxonomists supply for "Letters." This division is defined as consisting of the "subject fields . . . having to do with English language and literature and value systems related to ancient and modern cultures."[78] Or should we accept logic as a "value system" related to our culture?

As a specialty of "Letters," philosophy is in rather strange company: "1507 Creative writing; 1508 Teaching of English as a foreign language; 1509 Philosophy." One can only hope that this complete disregard of logic and low regard for philosophy as academic subjects need not be taken as symptomatic of the actual situation in what are called "institutions of higher education" in the United States. This hope is doused if one takes seriously the introductory declaration of the compilers that their list is "to reflect as accurately as possible the instructional programs and curriculums now in existence or likely to appear in the future."[79]

Attempts to find out to what extent this has been achieved—and, hence, whether the sad impression conveyed by the HEGIS Taxonomy is borne out by the facts or whether most of the institutions are still dedicated to offering education on a higher than secondary level— have been frustrated by a conspicuous absence of statistical information. We do not have any nationwide surveys of course enrollments in colleges and universities. We have mutually inconsistent data on "major fields of concentration" chosen by students in their

[78] Ibid., p. 9.
[79] Ibid., p. 1.

junior year and on the fields in which they received their bachelor degrees. But we have no data on how many students have taken courses in what subjects.

The lack of such fact-gathering is hard to understand, for the data are available in the offices of the registrars of most institutions. I have collected a few samples of such statistics in the form of time series and intend to report my findings for various types of colleges and universities in the volume on Education. In my sample study I will disobey the HEGIS format and will not treat philosophy (Code 1509) as coequal with "poultry science" (Code 0106), "hotel and restaurant management" (Code 0508), "photography" (Code 1011), or "clothing and textiles" (Code 1303). Instead, I will rank philosophy with discipline divisions such as "Biological Sciences," "Physics Sciences," "Mathematics," and "History."

It is perhaps appropriate to close this discourse on the classification of academic teaching and learning with an explanatory note on the term "Letters," which the HEGIS taxonomy took to be one of twenty-four subcategories of higher education. The classifiers may have been unaware of the fact that "Letters" originally stood for academic knowledge, or learning in general, and that the term "university" was, at many institutions of higher education, an abbreviation of *universitas litterarum*—the totality of learning. Later, in the organization of faculties at universities in France, the division between "sciences" and "letters" evolved, though it was much criticized and often rejected by philosophers: "The absurd and deplorable separation of *letters* from *sciences* not only compromises the future of philosophy but also falsifies its history and renders its past unintelligible in setting it apart from scientific speculations in which it always had been rooted."[80]

The quoted protest against the separation of "letters" from "sciences" makes sense only for the cosmopolitan—not the Anglo-American—meaning of science as "any field of systematic knowledge based on research."(This is also revealed by the reference to "scientific speculations," a phrase that some American scientists would reject as a contradiction in terms.) Nonetheless, the inclusion of "Letters" as one of twenty-four academic "discipline divisions" is in accord neither with the wide sense in which some classifiers wanted to contrast "letters" with "sciences" nor with the narrow sense in which other classifiers use the term as encompassing the study of literatures.

[80] Louis Couturat, *La Logique de Leibniz* (Paris: Alcan, 1901), Preface, p. viii. (The English translation is my own.)

Pragmatic and Philosophic Soundness

Perhaps I have not done justice to the HEGIS taxonomy of academic programs. It may be less than fair to demand from a pragmatic scheme, designed to serve statistical surveys, that it also be in harmony with the classification systems of philosophers and encyclopaedists. Indeed, a scheme that harmonized with one such system might be in serious conflict with other systems devised by equally respected philosophers. Yet, despite these concessions to the pragmatic taxonomers, most of the criticisms I have leveled against their attempt remain valid, and I submit that the worst offenses against academic respectability be remedied or removed.

One way to avoid conflicts between pragmatic usefulness and philosophic soundness is to disregard some of the subcategories that some superclassifiers have devised. When I undertake a survey of changes in enrollments in specified subjects or subject classes, my task will to some extent be circumscribed by the classifications used by department chairmen, deans, faculties, registrars, and official recording agencies. If, however, the data are sufficiently detailed, I am free to depart from the grouping chosen by the compiler. For example, if I obtain data on enrollments in history courses, I need not side either with those who regard history as a social science or with those who claim it as a humanistic discipline; instead, I may treat it as a field of its own. Likewise, I need not accept mathematics as a natural or physical science, no matter how many traditionalists may go on doing so; instead, I may enter it as a separate discipline, no matter where, that is, no matter in which field of learning, the techniques it has developed are employed. Again, I need not join the controversy about the "correct" place of psychology, either as a life science or as a social science (or with some of its special ties assigned to one group and some to the other); instead, I may regard it as a discipline that straddles the dividing lines drawn by conventional classifiers and, hence, I can refrain from forcing it into any prefabricated box.

I am aware of the fact that in rejecting the conventional classifications I am flouting a venerable tradition; and such nonconformance may annoy some of my readers. Yet, as knowledge in all fields expands and new fields develop, no grouping of learned disciplines can long remain valid. Every one of the many attempts at classification of learning that have been made over the centuries was sooner or later superseded by another that presumably took account of new developments. To be conservative in classifying the expanding universe of learning would be quite unreasonable.

Postscript 1981

Although the last paragraph of the preceding section was a quite satisfactory ending to the book—I wrote it three or four years ago—I feel obliged to add a postscript to comment on a new classification issued by the National Center for Education Statistics (NCES) in 1978. I do not know why I have learned so late of its existence, but when I did I thought that my strictures against the HEGIS taxonomy of academic subjects may perhaps have become obsolete. To some small extent this is true, but in many other respects my critical comments still apply. In any case, I cannot in good conscience disregard the new official effort: *A Classification of Educational Subject Matter* by W. Dale Chismore and Quentin M. Hill.[81]

Classification of Educational Subject Matter

In a sense, the new classification may not belong in a chapter on universities, because the authors insist that their scheme is valid for all levels of instruction, elementary, secondary, and postsecondary. Yet, the fact that some "introductory subject matter" may fit "instructional levels" below college is hardly visible to those who examine the "coded classification" or the "definitions of educational subject matter"—or even the index. Virtually all entries fit higher education, and most of them fit only higher education.

The new classification is emphatically "differentiated" from the HEGIS taxonomy on the ground that the latter was designed for "instructional programs," whereas the new classification was for "educational subject matter." What is the distinction? "Subject matter represents the substance, manifestation, and countenance of knowledge. Instructional programs, which can and should be differentiated from subject matter, represent the form and style by which knowledge, or subject matter, is transmitted and received." The authors admit that the distinction was "particularly troublesome to those who helped develop this Classification."[82] I sympathize with them. The HEGIS taxonomy classified "conventional academic subdivisions of knowledge and training" by "discipline divisions" and "specialties," and so does the new classification, even if it designates the divisions as "orders" with a coding structure of two digits for

---

[81] Washington, D.C.: U.S. Department of Health, Education, and Welfare, Office of Education, 1978, vi and 223 pp. — Since "over two hundred individuals actively participated in the development of this Classification of Educational Subject Matter," the two authors' or compilers' shares of responsibility may possibly be small.

[82] Ibid., p. 3.

"subject-matter areas" and "each subsequent two digits" representing "another descending order of subject matter."[83]

The classification scheme is based on twenty-two subject-matter
areas, each divided into between five and twenty-seven four-digit
classes.

01	Agriculture and Renewable Natural Resources	(with 14 named four-digit classes)
02	Architecture and Environ- mental Design	(with 9 named four-digit classes)
03	Arts, Visual and Performing	(with 7 named four-digit classes)
04	Business	(with 13 named four-digit classes)
05	Communication	(with 13 named four-digit classes)
06	Computer Science and Data Processing	(with 11 named four-digit classes)
07	Education	(with 12 named four-digit classes)
08	Engineering and Engineering Technology	(with 26 named four-digit classes)
09	Health Care and Health Sciences	(with 9 named four-digit classes)
10	Home Economics	(with 7 named four-digit classes)
11	Industrial Arts, Trades, and Technology	(with 7 named four-digit classes)
12	Language, Linguistics, and Literature	(with 27 named four-digit classes)
13	Law	(with 19 named four-digit classes)
14	Libraries and Museum	(with 9 named four-digit classes)
15	Life Sciences and Physical Sciences	(with 9 named four-digit classes)
16	Mathematical Sciences	(with 12 named four-digit classes)
17	Military Sciences	(with 15 named four-digit classes)
18	Philosophy, Religion, and Theology	(with 16 named four-digit classes)
19	Physical Education, Health Education, and Leisure	(with 7 named four-digit classes)
20	Psychology	(with 9 named four-digit classes)
21	Public Administration and Social Services	(with 5 named four-digit classes)
22	Social Sciences and Social Studies	(with 6 named four-digit classes)

[83] Ibid., p. 4. In Appendix D an attempt is made to explain the distinction between
instructional program and subject matter by illustrations. It is characteristic that all
examples are of vocational programs. Even so, the distinction is not worth bothering
about.

One cannot help being impressed with the vocational obsession of the classifiers and of the educational institutions of the United States. Even if the institutions are so much oriented towards vocational instruction, the classifiers exaggerate this bias by insufficient separation of the subject areas in the liberal arts and excessive separation of the subject groups in the vocational areas. Is it necessary to merge astronomy, biology, chemistry, geology, physics, and three other fields into one subject area, "Life Sciences and Physical Sciences"? Why should philosophy be tied to theology? Could the classifiers not be sufficiently liberal to make history a subject area by itself instead of joining it with anthropology, economics, sociology, and other subjects in "Social Sciences and Social Studies"? Contrast this stingy bunching with the lavish disaggregation of vocational areas, giving first-order subject ranks to "Communication," "Computer Science and Data Processing," "Engineering and Engineering Technology," and "Industrial Arts, Trades, and Technology," that is, five separate subject-matter areas in addition to "Business" and "Home Economics." The result of this procedure is that we are faced with a scheme that gives 16 basic subject-matter areas with, together, 183 four-digit subject classes to vocational instruction and only 6 basic subject-matter areas with, together, 79 four-digit subject classes to academic or liberal education.

The extraordinary proliferation of vocational elements in the classification can be illustrated by the fact that the word "communication" appears 35 times in the scheme, once as the designation of a first-order subject area, 11 times in the names of four-digit classes, 20 times in the names of six-digit classes, and another 3 times in the names of eight-digit subjects.[84] Clearly, the compilers were overly

[84] The wide spread of "communication" may seem so unbelievable that I should furnish some evidence for my statements. "Communication" is one of the twenty-two first-order subject areas, but appears also within six others, namely, Architecture and Experimental Design (e.g., Graphic Communication), Business (e.g., Business Communication; Information Communication Systems), Computer Science and Data Processing (e.g., Communication Control Devices), Education (e.g., Communication and Dissemination), Health Care and Health Sciences (e.g., Emergency Medical Communications), Mathematical Sciences (e.g., Communication Theory), and Military Sciences (e.g., Military Communications). In the first-order area, 05 Communication, eight second-order (or four-digit) areas are distinguished: Communication Technology, Film as Communication, Innovative Communication, International Communication, Professional Practices in Communication, Speech Communication, Special Communication, and Other Communication. Speech Communication is subdivided into various six-digit subjects (e.g., Intercultural Communication, Interpersonal Communication, Organizational Communication, Pragmatic Communication, Rhetorical and Communication Theory, and Speech Communication Education). There are three eight-digit entries under Speech Communication Education: Communication Development, Oral Communication Skill, Instructional Communication. See pp. 8-29.

hospitable in accepting different names of courses offered at two-year colleges, vocational schools, and professional schools as separate "subject matter." (They probably avoided a similar show of combinatoric capacities exercised by instructors in the conventional academic fields, such as physics, geology, economics, literature, and so forth, and thus came up with substantially fewer entries. It would not take more than a few minutes to double or triple the number of entries in economics.)

Great Improvements

Instead of criticizing the new classification for excessive subdivision in *vocational* subject areas and insufficient subdivision in *academic* subject areas, I should perhaps praise it for having taken a big step in the right direction away from the scheme used in the HEGIS taxonomy. Remember my strong complaint about the complete absence of subdivision in the nonvocational "discipline divisions" of the HEGIS scheme, where economics, sociology, and history were shown as "specialties" of "Social Sciences," each without any clue to the many special fields into which the discipline had been divided. Now, the new separation of subject-matter classes represents a great improvement over the amorphous shapes of the "specialties" of the HEGIS age. Economics is shown with 17 named six-digit fields, and Sociology with 15. History has now 9 thematic subdivisions, 14 by geographic areas, 4 by periods, and 3 by groups of persons (minority groups; native American; and women).[85]

The reassignment of philosophy to another first-order area is commendable in that philosophy now figures in the designation of the area, whereas in the HEGIS taxonomy it had only the rank of a specialty under "Letters." On the other hand, the wedding of philosophy to theology may not lead to a happy bond. The greatest advance of the new classification over the old is that it discovered and recognized the existence of Logic. It was given the rank of a four-digit area, named "Logic and Philosophical Methodology," within the two-digit area "Philosophy, Religion, and Theology." To be allowed a place in this household is far better than to be, as before, a nonspecialty in a nondiscipline.

---

[85] I suspect that the authors may explain the absence of subdivision from the HEGIS taxonomy and the presence of subdivision in the new classification by the difference between "instructional programs" and "educational subject matters," a difference I have found too arcane to make sense of. Why, for example, should "metalsmithing" be an instructional program, but "millwrighting" an educational subject matter? Why should "home decoration and home equipment" be an instructional program, but "home furnishing" an educational subject matter?

INDEX

AAAH denotes American Association for the Advancement of the Humanities, 109

AAAS denotes American Association for the Advancement of Science, 108

ABASS denotes Assembly for Behavioral and Social Sciences, 106

Abelard, Peter (1079-1142), 23n, 124n

absolute mind, 61

abstract, mathematics, 71; physics, 38; physiology, 71; sciences, 71, 73; versus concrete, 66, 71; versus general, 71

abstract-concrete, partly abstract, partly concrete, 71

abstract-deductive system, 72

academic diaspora, 158

academic empire building, 158

academies of sciences, 13, 87, 89-109, autonomy of, 90; chronology of founding, 91; government control of, 90; in Austria, 99-100; in Belgium, 98; in England, 93-95; in Europe, 91-100; in France, 92-93; in Germany, 95-96; in Italy, 91-92; in Russia and the Soviet Union, 96-97; in Sweden, 97-98; in the Netherlands, 98-99; in the United States, 100-109; interested in natural history only, 101n; members paid or paying, 90; multidisciplinary and honorary, 89; not aiding Leibniz, 55; private and local versus official and national, 100; private or national, 91; research centers and staff in, 90, 96, 97, 100; specialized, 90, 95n

academy, as name for teaching institution, 89; origin of name, 89n

Academy of Fine Arts, in Berlin, 96; in France, 93

Academy of Inscriptions and Literature, in France, 93

Academy of Medicine, in France, 93

Academy of Moral and Political Sciences, in France, 93

Accademia Nazionale dei Lincei, 13, 91

ACLS denotes American Council of Learned Societies, 106

acoustics, in Comte, 67; in French *Encyclopédie*, 58; in Pearson, 74; in the Royal Society, 94; its place in the systematic table, 59

acquired abilities, versus genetic, 3

action versus speculation, 66

Adam and Eve, 34n

Adam's skill in taxonomy, 34n

Adler, Mortimer J. (b. 1902), 21, 82, 83, 119

administration, in Am. Phil. Soc., 102

administrative growth of universities, 158

Advancement of Learning, 6, 17, 35n, 42-43

aenigmatographia, 51

aeromechanics, 74

Aesop's *Fables*, 129

aesthetics, in Peirce, 77; in Volume VI, 3

aetherial substance, 44n

aetiology, 75

affections and remedies, 40

affirmation, negation, and reunification, 61

African studies, 160, 161

Afro-American studies, 152, 155, 160, 161

Agassiz, Louis (1807-1873), 76

agricultural and mechanical arts, 136

agriculture, at California, 147; in Alsted, 51; in Ampère, 64; in HEGIS taxonomy, 163; in Roger Bacon, 28; in 1978 taxonomy, 169; schools of, 149, 150

agronomy, in French Academy, 93; possibly in Hobbes, 44n

air, water, and fire, 45

Albertus Magnus (1193/1206-1280), 20, 21n, 25-26, 28

Albigensianism, 124

alchemy, in Alsted, 51; in Bacon, 38; in

LIBRARY OF CONGRESS CATALOGING IN PUBLICATION DATA

Machlup, Fritz, 1902-
  The branches of learning.

  (Knowledge, its creation, distribution, and economic
significance; v. 2)
  Includes index.
  1. Learning and scholarship—United States. 2. Learning and scholarship—
Europe. 3. Classification of sciences. 4. Classification. 5. United States—Learned
institutions and societies. 6. Europe—Learned institutions and societies.
I. Title. II. Series: Machlup, Fritz, 1902- . Knowledge, its creation, distribution,
and economic significance; v. 2.
AZ505.M28 vol. 2   001s [001.2]   82-3695
ISBN 0-691-04230-6   AACR2

FRITZ MACHLUP was Walker Professor of Economics and International Finance at
Princeton University until his retirement in 1971. He is at present Professor of Economics at New York University.

DATE DUE

GAYLORD   PRINTED IN U.S A